THE CULTURE GAP

An Experience of Government and the Arts

Hugh Jenkins

MINISTER FOR THE ARTS 1974–1976

LONDON
MARION BOYARS
BOSTON

Published in Great Britain and the United States in 1979
by Marion Boyars Publishers Ltd.
18 Brewer Street, London W1R 4AS.
and
Marion Boyars Publishers Inc.
99 Main Street, Salem, New Hampshire 03079

Australian distribution by Thomas C. Lothian
4-12 Tattersalls Lane, Melbourne, Victoria 3000

Canadian Distribution by Burns & MacEachern Ltd.
Suite 3, 62 Railside Road, Don Mills, Ontario

ISBN 0 7145 2643 6 cased edition

Filmset in Monophoto Baskerville 169
by A. Brown & Sons Ltd., Hull, England

Printed in Great Britain by
Robert MacLehose & Co. Ltd.
Printers to the University of Glasgow

To the women in my life, and *especially to Marie* in whose life I have lived happily.

Contents

Illustrative Section: Facing Part III

Acknowledgements

That part of this book which deals with my period of Ministerial office was submitted to the Cabinet Secretary for his advice, in accordance with the Radcliffe Report on Ministerial Memoirs. To Sir John Hunt, therefore, I express my regret that I have not found it possible, for the most part, to accept the views he was bound to express.

The Report provides, among other things, that 'A former Minister should not reveal the opinions or attitudes of colleagues as to the Government business with which they were concerned' and 'A former Minister should not reveal the advice given to him in confidence by individuals, nor attribute individual attitudes to identifiable persons . . .'

The Cabinet Secretary pointed out that this book does, in fact, reveal opinions and attribute individual attitudes to identifiable persons.

The problem is that our system of Government is less efficient and less democratic than it could be precisely *because* all exchanges between Ministers and civil servants are regarded as confidential when, in the majority of cases, it would be beneficial, both from the point of view of policy and from that of public confidence, that they should be revealed.

As I said to Sir John in our correspondence, 'If one wishes to suggest changes in relationships, this cannot be done without revealing something of what it is one wishes to change.'

Again, the Report says, 'A former Minister should not make public assessments or criticisms of those who have served under him . . .' The Cabinet Secretary pointed out that the book 'contains descriptions of and judgments on' leading civil servants in the Arts and Libraries Branch of the Department of Education and Science, over which I presided for two years.

These 'judgments' are often admiring and my criticism is of the system under which civil servants have to work rather than of individuals. Nevertheless, I tried referring to leading officials by their titles. It was absurd, for in a small Branch they were easily identifiable; I then tried initials but this was even more ridiculous in a book about the arts.

I wrote to Sir John: 'One of the objects of the book is to show how decisions are made and this cannot be done without demonstrating how advice is given by civil servants and quoting opinions expressed by Ministers. Nevertheless I am very ready to go along with the recommendations of the Committee of Privy Counsellors whenever I can do so without damage to the public interest. I regard such damage as being done whenever information is concealed without good reason.'

There are sections of this book which are *about* my fellow Ministers and their views and actions and others which are *about* the civil servants who worked with me and what they said and did. What happened cannot be described without reference to them, and to refer to them other than by name would be to cast a false cloak of mystery over the scene. It would suggest quite wrongly that names were being suppressed because those concerned were engaged in some secret activity. The activity was sometimes in support of my endeavours and sometimes it sought to frustrate them, but nothing occurred which ought not to be known.

Furthermore, any attempt to conceal names would fail, for everyone closely concerned would know who occupied the post, held the first name or was ineffectually concealed behind an initial. And so, far from shielding the individuals concerned, the effort to do so would imply that they had something to hide.

Sir John Hunt seemed to think that the moment this book is published or serialised, the press will descend on those named in it. I fear he flatters our importance, but if I wanted to be sure that something of the sort would occur I could think of no better way than to seek to conceal the names of people with whom I worked on friendly terms, if not always in agreement, for two fascinating years.

The recommendations of the Radcliffe Committee were not adopted by the Government until January 1976 and I suppose I could therefore argue that I accepted office in 1974 without being subject to these restraints; I could also urge that Ministerial memoirs already published have driven coach and horses through the rules. My main argument, however, is that the rules are too restrictive; that it is desirable that they should be relaxed and that a junior Minister in an area remote from national security is well placed to advance the reality of open Government. Furthermore, I would suggest that unnecessary secrecy debases the currency of security and weakens the respect in which the preservation of vital confidentiality is held. Finally, I consider it wrong to deprive the electorate of information about the processes of Government, for where they are bad they remain unchanged in the dark: the people are entitled to know and I hope that other ex-Ministers will contribute to the general fund of knowledge.

Nevertheless, I recognise that I can only reveal my own version of reality; that it may differ from the reality of others and may be hurtful to a few. To them I can only say that it is not my purpose to harm anyone and, if it is any consolation, I have myself been injured intentionally and by experts and feel none the worse for it now.

Nevertheless, in case it does not become clear in the following pages, may I say here that I seldom felt any personal dislike for those who opposed my Ministerial policies. Furthermore, I was rarely conscious of such hostility in others. No sense of animus normally clouded my day-to-day relations with senior civil servants such as Deputy Secretary Willy Wright and Under Secretary John Spence. Sometimes they believed me to be mistaken and rather less often they were right; occasionally they sought to frustrate what I was trying to do but I saw that as inherent in the system and in their upbringing and training. Their opposition could be persistent, and was often adroit, but I never thought it malicious. On the contrary, more than once they saved me from making a fool of myself.

As will be seen, from time to time I was angry with people and had one or two transferred elsewhere, but the atmosphere was happy and I understand that my time was generally regarded as one of cheerful hard work.

Many times I was at odds or out of touch with the Prime Minister, Harold Wilson, with the Chancellor of the Duchy of Lancaster, Harold Lever or with the Secretary of State in whose Department I served, first Reg Prentice and then Fred Mulley. I also had occasional brushes with Treasury Ministers. These differences did not, so far as I am aware, stem from, or result in, personal hostility. This equally applied to Lord Gibson and other arts establishment figures. I have frequently worked among non-socialists and naturally expect them to oppose me. My concern is to beat them; I see no reason why I should also hate them for they are frequently much more pleasant than their views would seem to permit. Those who knew me appeared to feel the same in reverse; real hostility came from persons I had never met.

To turn to personal acknowledgements:

The suggestion that I should write a book came from my first American Secretary, Sharon Genasci, who is married to an American and lives in England. My second American secretary, Ruth Kaplan, helped me with that book but it was not finished when I abandoned it on becoming Minister for the Arts in 1974. Alison Greene came when Ruth left to join the Royal Shakespeare Company as their Press Representative. She suggested that I should keep a diary during my Ministerial period but returned to the United States to marry and was replaced by my present American Secretary, Lois Blasenheim, who has worked both on the diaries and on this book and has typed most of it. To all of them I owe a debt of gratitude not only for their work but for the friendship my wife and I have enjoyed with them and their families.

This is equally true of Mary Giles who was my Ministerial Private Secretary at the Arts and Libraries Branch of the Department of Education and Science.

I should like to express my appreciation to my successor, Lord Donaldson, who made the files of my period available to me without hesitation, and to the staff of the House of Commons Library for their unfailing, ready and cheerful help at all times.

To all those who appear in this book and to the many more who have influenced the course of events in which I have played a part I extend my thanks where they are due and commiserate where they are not.

Finally, my gratitude to Marie who either read the typescript or had it read to her and by her trenchant comments made this book better, or, perhaps, less bad. Whichever it is, I alone am responsible.

September 1978

PART I

CHAPTER ONE

End and Beginning

My original intention was to revise for publication the diaries I kept during the last part of my period as Minister for the Arts. I soon realised that this would not do – not only would they need to be completely re-written to avoid repetition and to clarify obscurities, but they began in the middle of a much longer story. It was that story which needed to be told.

When I began to write this book I recalled what I tell constituents who come to see me at my surgery.

'To begin at the beginning . . .' they say.

'No.' I reply. 'Begin at the end. Tell me what caused you to come and see me. We'll go back to the beginning later.'

So to begin at the end. Not at the end of the story, it is endless, but at the end of a couple of the best years of my life.

This was my last Ministerial day: April 20th, 1976:

'Number 10 would like you to be available to call on the Prime Minister at any time today.'

'Christ,' I thought. 'This is it.'

'Who was that?' asked my wife.

'I am about to receive the chopper,' I replied.

'Nonsense,' said Marie, He's going to make you a Minister of State and long overdue too.'

I was finishing my overnight box at home. The letter I had just signed was one I had dictated myself (civil servants hate Ministers doing this) and I had been well pleased with it. I looked at it again. It was to the new Chairman of the Association for

Business Sponsorship of the Arts, Lord Goodman, and it summarised, I thought succinctly, the changes which needed to be made so that the Association could become the recognised medium for the encouragement of commercial patronage of the arts. I decided to send it (copy to Campbell Adamson,[1] I wrote). The next letter was to Brigid Brophy and Maureen Duffy of the Writers' Action Group. This was a reply to a letter from them complaining, reasonably enough, about the failure of the new Public Lending Rights Bill to go as far as everyone would have wished.

I put the letter back in the box without signing it.

Downstairs Tony Howell, the driver of my official car, was waiting.

'This may be the last time you will be driving me up.' I said.

'Hope not,' said Tony.

At Belgrave Square, Cathy Maher, the messenger, was wearing a long face. 'Never mind, eh?' I said. 'Let's have some tea.'

Private Secretary, Mary Giles, came in.

'This is it, don't you think?' I said.

'Hope not,' she replied.

Back to the car and to the GLC at County Hall, where I had arranged to visit the Archives. I found it difficult to concentrate but remember, nevertheless, telling them about the Marx Memorial Library at Clerkenwell Green, hoping they might take an interest in order to prevent further deterioration there. The staff unearthed a copy of the motion I had moved as a member of the old LCC on 9th February 1960 demanding that the building of the National Theatre be started. It was carried and building did start. Should I now be Minister at the official opening? I had rather looked forward to that.

Upstairs at lunch with the Vice-Chairman of the Council, Marie was with us. She had tipped him off and there was a sense of tension round the table.

Mary Giles was called away and came back to whisper in my ear that I was expected at Downing Street at 2.45 pm. We left, going first to the House of Commons. On my desk was a copy of my Weekly Progress chart showing all the things I expected to

[1] Then Secretary of the Confederation of British Industries.

bring to fruition in the next few months. I banged it with my fist and for a wild moment felt that Marie might be right. On the walls Lois Blasenheim, my Parliamentary Secretary, had pinned newspaper cuttings which had announced my dismissal many times over the last two years. This time there was no such forecast.

Mary sat with Tony in the car outside No. 10. 'Good Luck,' they said, without conviction.

In a small room, like a dentist's waiting room, were three of my younger Parliamentary colleagues – Norman Atkinson,[2] Leslie Huckfield,[3] and Michael Meacher,[4] whose appointments turned out to be for 2.25, 2.30, and 2.40. In spite of this, no sooner had I sat down than I was called.

'I go to prepare a place for you,' I said.

'Good luck,' they said.

In the Cabinet Room alone, Jim Callaghan stood near the middle of the long and narrow oval rosewood table.

'I'm sorry, Hugh,' he said. 'This is the unpleasant part of my job. I know how well you've done, but I need another Minister in the Lords. Your job can be done from there and I have someone who can do it from there. It's part of the pattern, so there it is. There's nothing political about it.'

'Well,' I said. 'I was, in fact, expecting to return to the back benches later this year, but there are some things I was hoping to finish. Still, I suppose one must make way for younger people.'

'Oh, I'm not putting it on that basis,' said Jim. 'In fact, your successor, Lord Donaldson, is in our age bracket.'

I felt suddenly angry but pushed it down. What was the point? He was going on and getting less convincing. There was nothing to be done but escape decently.

'If it hadn't been for you I might not have been here,' I said. This was a reference to a unique incident years ago when, as a member of the National Executive Committee, Jim's was the unexpected vote which had rejected the recommendation of Ray

[2] Refused job offered.
[3] Appointed Under-Secretary of State, Department of Industry.
[4] Transferred from Department of Health and Social Security to Department of Trade.

Gunter's Organisation Sub-Committee that my selection as candidate for Putney be not endorsed.

'Yes,' he said. 'We are old friends in spite of policy differences. she said.

I went straight out. Back to the House, from where I phoned Marie at County Hall. She was shocked and angry. 'Who the hell is Lord Donaldson,' she asked. Good question. I looked him up in Who's Who and there he was. Retired farmer, born 1907. I was born in 1908.

Lois came in and I told her. I sent Mary over to Belgrave Square to prepare for my departure and discussed some constituency correspondence with Lois. Then we picked up Marie, and Tony drove us to Belgrave Square for the last time.

We took down to the car some personal things which Mary had gathered together. A portrait of me by Joan La Dell, the original of a Daily Mirror cartoon and one of Mark Boyle's fascinating constructions.

Mary put the Writers' Action Group letter on my desk. 'You didn't sign this one,'

'Premonition,' I replied and signed it, adding a note at the end.

We all had a drink. Tony and Cathy came up and sat around with the others. An Assistant-Secretary came in, hesitantly, looking distressed. 'Come and join the wake Colin,' I said. They said they were sorry and I thanked them for all their work. The day before I had done one of my periodical tours of the offices. Those I saw had all talked so much that I did not get down to the basement which I had intended to visit the following week.

'Pity,' said Mary. 'One of the ladies down there in records bought a new dress for the occasion and now you'll not see it.'

We went home, Tony's face wearing uneasy mourning as we said good-bye. Marie prepared some food and we looked at television. I remember seeing my face briefly on the screen and Alex Lyon[5] smiling bitterly. To bed and into a deep sleep at once. The indigestion which had been troubling me lately seemed to have cleared up.

Next morning I saw the official announcement that Donaldson was to be Minister of State.

[5] Under Secretary at the Home Office, dismissed at the same time.

CHAPTER TWO

First Person Singular

This book is about the arts and government and about my own experiences in the job of Minister for the Arts. But how did I get there? Certainly not by design.

My father, Joseph Walter Jenkins, would never have met my mother but for my grandmother dying of typhoid in London about a hundred years ago. Tired of starving in Welsh Wales, grandfather, with his wife and family of four teenage girls and five young boys, was on his way to a new life in America, when the sudden death of his wife took the heart out of him and he decided to settle in the Holloway Road and sell milk. He could speak no English so the family nearly starved in London. Trying to make a living, grandad watered the milk and, weeping and incoherent, had to be bailed out of prison by his own children. He later remarried, having left his first family to father another eight children. It was said that no woman could see grandad without wanting to love him. Clearly he was no mean hand at it himself. Grandfather's first progeny were vigorous and intelligent youngsters and one way or another they managed to stay out of the workhouse. However, three of the boys, Dan, Jenkin, and William Rees succumbed to consumption, drink and adventure and did not last long in manhood. It was said that Jenkin had the finest voice of them all.

Joseph, the youngest, ran the streets of London barefoot until his legs had to be put in irons because of ricketts, but at the age of fourteen he got a job, an office job with the Dunlop Rubber Company. He had always been good at figures. One of the girls, Annie, joined the Civil Service and kept the family for a while.

She was an early socialist influence in my life. Another sister, Jenny, married Richard Morris who had a good job with Debenham and Freebody, the outfitters, and became Coalition Liberal MP for North Battersea in the post-war Lloyd George administration. Elizabeth and Margaret also married Welshmen and returned to Aberaeron where they ran a hotel and a public house.

My father was doing well with the Dunlop Company when he was invited by his surviving brother to join him in the Blenheim Dairy which Johnnie had set up in Lancaster Road, Enfield, then a small town to the north of London where the horse trams had their terminus. He married the daughter of the local butcher, Florence Gater, and they were a handsome couple. I was born over the dairy on the 27th July 1908 and christened Hugh Gater Jenkins. Mother would not have the Welsh Huw. I had only one sister who was not born for another seven years.

Mother did not like living over the shop and as Dad prospered we moved to 80 Gordon Hill. I went to the Board School where the Headmaster, Mr Vincent, and his wife taught me to read music. From there I went to the Grammar School where I sang Phyllis in Iolanthe. The local paper said I was the success of the evening and Mother kept the cutting until she died a few years ago aged 91. Mother had the gift of curiosity. She always wanted to know everything; what I had done with my pocket money; and 50 years later, what were the Americans doing in Vietnam?

I was solo boy in the choir at Christchurch (Congregational) Enfield and won medals in singing competitions. I strongly disliked the jealousy and backbiting which accompanied these contests and decided that as soon as I was free to make my own decisions I would not compete with anybody for anything. I enjoyed singing in the chorus at the annual concert of the Church Choir. The choirmaster, Vincent Evans, was a sort of genius who wrote the words and composed the music and produced the entire show. In one chorus we were supposed to have arrived from the Far East and sang 'Ah Wah Tah Nah Siam – Ah Nah Siam.' Dr Harold Watts (Mus Doc. Oxon) taught me to play the piano but, as I was without manual dexterity, I did not get very far. Soon I found the Church was cheating on my extra solo payments (five shillings, 'Hear my Prayer' seven shillings and six pence 'I know that my redeemer liveth'). I tried to bring the boys out on strike but they wouldn't back me so I pretended my voice had broken and sang no more. Father suspected I was lying and hit me, but when he forced me to sing the following Christmas at a party at home, my voice had really broken and the noises that came out embarrassed everyone and left me in tears.

My father wanted me to know what life was about, so he used to wake me at four in the morning and take me out with him pushing the milk cart and filling the cold iron cans in the slummy streets of Enfield. On Saturdays I had to do a stint as lather boy in Mr Tucker's Barber shop along Chase Side. I did not mind using the brush but hated rubbing frothy soap into stubbly chins. On the other hand, Dad wanted me to enjoy the things he had missed, so I had a bicycle and sometimes we used to go out for a spin in the T-Model Ford on Sunday instead of going to the PSA (Pleasant Sunday Afternoon) concert in the school hall. There was much singing in our house, mainly the popular ballads of the day. We could all strum a few notes on the piano.

On Saturday afternoons my father would take me to see Charlie Chaplin, Pearl White or William S. Hart at the Queen's Hall Cinema, so I knew all about America.

My parents insisted on paying the quarterly fee of £3. 17s 6d at the Grammar School, although I had passed the examination, because Dad said he did not want me held in contempt as a scholarship boy but wanted me to get the same treatment as the sons of gentlemen, little aware that in the post-great-war period, good masters were scarce and schooling quite appalling. The Headmaster was a sadist and the walls of his study were lined with whips ranging from a huge cat o'nine tails to a tiny swagger cane. He would march up and down fingering them and, taking down one or another, would thrash the air with a shuddering whistle.

In those years I had a mental thirst which I could not slake. I read four books a day and on Saturdays would take them back to the Carnegie Library in the evening so as to renew my ration for Sunday. Some week-ends I would cycle the 17 miles over to Uncle Johnnie and Auntie Sally who by then had a large house at Sudbury. There I would play tennis and other games with my cousins and listen to the gramophone, returning to regale my parents with imitations of everything I had heard from Galli-Curci to Louis Armstrong and back to Caruso.

When I was fourteen Mother persuaded Dad to sell the milk business and to buy a house in Margate which she planned to run as a boarding house for summer holiday-makers. The plan was a failure but my father had great success as conductor of a local church choir. My parents felt I ought to stay at the Grammar School in Enfield until I had matriculated, so it was arranged that I would live with old Mrs Ebben next door. 'Grandma' Ebben was not related but people made close friends in those days. Grandpa Ebben suffered from senile dementia and was always defecating about the house and having to be cleaned up by Grandma or her daughter, Helen. It was an intensely religious household. A son, Harry, played hymns on the harmonium and there was grace before every meal. Downstairs there were oil lamps but you went to bed with a candle and, in winter, a stone hot water bottle. Putting out the candle you crept into a high deep feather bed cowering with unmanly fear in the doom-laden dark.

I had never been able to let X equal anything for I could see no reason why it should. Clearly I would not pass the Matric so why sit for it? I left for school each morning, but put my grammar school cap in my pocket and went up to London looking for work. There was none and soon I was in the dole queue. When my parents found out I was taken to their new home in Margate where I got a typing job with a firm of publishers called Arthur H. Stockwell Ltd., who specialised in publishing songs and poems at the expense of gullible writers. The fortunes of the firm took a dive when one of the national newspapers exposed the fact that they sold almost nothing, hiding most of their stock in the basement and living on the surplus between what the authors paid and what it actually cost to publish.

Back to London, in and out of work. Office boy, telephone switchboard operator. I read voraciously all the time; at the British Museum and everywhere. I read Marx's Capital while standing in the dole queue. It seemed convincing. Once I told my Aunt Annie I did not think much of George Bernard Shaw. 'That, Hughie,' she said, 'tells us more about you than it does about Mr Shaw.'

Uncle Dick, who was himself out of work following the fall of the Lloyd George Government, told me that if I bought a Lincoln Bennett bowler hat I would get a job without difficulty. I spent every penny I had on the hat but it did not impress the publisher Victor Gollancz. Nor did I. In those days people out of the army and with degrees were begging to work for peanuts. So it was back to the dole queue but I had to walk there as I had no money left for the bus. All the same, I liked Uncle Dick who was cheerful and had time for you. He left me his Encyclopaedia Britannica.

When I was in work I bought a second-hand motor-cycle and toured Britain. I visited France and Belgium and went to the theatre, high in the gods. I bought a tail suit on the never-never and once won a prize as a ball-room dancer. Most of the time I laughed and sang, accompanying myself on my banjulele, and I read and read. I was always very high-spirited and have never been down-hearted for long. Girls liked me and I liked them.

Then I fell in love with Marie and in those days that meant marriage. Return to Margate and a job as an agent with the Prudential Assurance Company; then to Canterbury, promotion and wedding bells. A house and settling down to be a successful insurance man, but hating it; it was then, in the early thirties, that I began to think politically in a serious way. I joined the Labour Party and the Left Book Club and wrote articles in the Union journal advocating insurance nationalisation. Then more promotion and to Maidstone, but soon the war, the Royal Observer Corps, the Battle of Britain, the Royal Air Force, a commission, fighter-controlling by VHF and then to night fighters and Radar. Posted to the Far East I spent my embarkation leave on a speaking tour for Labour candidates in the 1945 General Election having rejected a chance to become a candidate myself. I spoke for George Brown, Geoffrey de Freitas and others and as I did so in uniform, I was a success wherever I went and whatever I said. I found I could speak as well as sing on a platform.

The day I arrived in India they dropped the Bomb on Hiroshima. I was horrified and perhaps it was in expiation that I marched to Aldermaston and back many times in later years. I had time to think and in the Grand Hotel, Chowringhee,

Calcutta, in the monsoon season, patting toilet powder into a fine paste with sweat, I decided that if I got back I would sell no more insurance. With time on my hands I wrote a story and sold it to the Calcutta Statesman and, as a result, was invited to broadcast from All-India Radio. When I was posted to Rangoon the war had ended. Not fond of idleness, I went up to Rangoon Radio which was being converted from a Psychological Warfare Broadcasting Unit into a Forces Radio Station. The man in charge was taken ill so I got myself seconded to the Government of Burma and became English Programme Director at Rangoon Radio.

Tests in the RAF had revealed that I had an exceptionally high IQ, and with this knowledge at the age of 33 I was suddenly filled with new confidence. I became convinced that, within reason, I could do almost anything I wanted to do. I might do it inexpertly but I could do it.

Charged with this self-assurance I worked feverishly and happily for a year in Rangoon, doing everything. I wrote most of the programmes and broadcast them myself. I set up the first Forces Brains Trust and acted as Question Master. I drove around in a jeep with an early wire recorder which broke down when I tried to record Hamlet which John Gielgud was performing in the local theatre with an ENSA company. Instead, I took him up to the studio where he read poetry. I did all the gramophone broadcasts, inventing one called 'Breath of Britain' with its Halitosis spot, a satire on the famous, or infamous, 'Voice of America'. There was a shortage of gramophone records so I had a prógramme called 'Same Tune from Rangoon' which contrasted different orchestras playing the same piece. For this broadcast I affected a deep American voice, 'Same toon' I would say, 'from' (deep down) 'Rangoon' (almost a shout). It was pretty dreadful, but it went down tremendously well.

I made friends with General Aung San, Head of the Anti-Fascist Peoples' Freedom League who was thought by the old Burma hands at that time to be a Communist Dacoit or Bandit Chief. In fact, he was the undisputed leader of his country and I invited him up to the Radio Station to broadcast in English. There was a hell of a row and the Governer General himself, Sir Reginald Dorman-Smith, came up to the studio to broadcast a message, undoing the damage. Not long after, I was on the boat home.

All the same I was able to convince Aung San that the new Labour Government was not the same as the dug-outs who had come back to Burma with the Army and perhaps helped to pave the way for the Attlee-Aung San agreement. In 1946, it was touch and go whether a new war would break out between the Burmese and the British. In the following year, soon after the agreement was signed, Aung San, together with six of his front bench colleagues, was murdered by fascists in the Parliament building in Rangoon. It was tragic, for he was a lovely man and I admired him as much as I did Nye Bevan, not only with my mind but in my heart.

Demobbed, I tried to join the BBC, was twice accepted but twice a curtain came down after forms had been filled in. I tried to get a passport to go abroad for a holiday but there was great difficulty and eventually after Marie and I had performed what was perhaps the first sit-in – at the Passport Office – I got one which allowed me to go anywhere in the world *except within the British Empire.*

What was it all about? I can only guess but, in retrospect, there are a number of possibilities.

On the way home from Rangoon two Army Officers whom I had persuaded to join the Forces Brains Trust, told me that they were both members of the Communist Party. Add to that Aung San; consider how my own left-wing Labour views got into the Rangoon Radio transmissions, and the scandal of how the King's Christmas Day 1945 Broadcast relayed by Rangoon had been followed by Noel Coward singing 'Mad Dogs and Englishmen'; consider that I had shed my uniform in favour of a longyi and was known by my Burmese colleagues on the station as U Yan Kin. It was clear that I must be a subversive, especially as it had to be pointed out to me that King's Regulations demanded that the chin must be shaved. Most damning of all, the Burmans actually regretted my departure and 'Rangoon Calling' published a little poem ending 'U Yan Kin is gone.' The rest was a straight crib from Dryden but I was nonetheless moved.

Later I raised hell with Chris Mayhew, whom I had met at a Fabian School during the war and who was the responsible

Under Secretary at the Foreign Office at the time. Eventually I received an unconditional passport and something near to an apology,but the incident came sharply back to me nearly 30 years later when I was subject to a Security check on becoming Minister for the Arts. Security is a system under which the suspect cannot be told why he is under suspicion; there is no appeal against an Executive decision; errors can never be rectified unless, by chance, you happen to know the right Minister. Such a system is despicable and poisonous.

Soon after the passport incident I was offered an appointment to continue broadcasting either in Hong Kong or Rhodesia. I rejected the idea as by that time I had decided to be a trade union official and joined the National Union of Bank Employees, later transferring to Actor's Equity.

That was the crucial step. I found the NUBE job in the columns of the 'New Statesman' and, starting as Greater London Organiser, soon became Research and Publicity Officer and Editor of the 'Bank Officer'. I also acted as Secretary of the Barclay's Bank Negotiating Committee. But, with few exceptions, I had little in common with bank employees and in 1950 I applied for the vacancy of Assistant Secretary of Equity, again advertised in the 'New Statesman'. I got the job out of 300 applicants mainly because Gordon Sandison, the General Secretary, was determined that the post should be filled by a trades unionist rather than an actor and Sybil Thorndike, who was on the Selection Committee, agreed with him. I remember that Laurence Olivier, Edith Evans and John Clements were among those who chose me.

In the same year I fought my birthplace, Enfield West, a safe Tory seat, for Labour against Ian Macleod, and Harold Laski rose from his sick bed to speak for me. For some years I had been active in the Fabian Society, directing Summer Schools and lecturing, but as the Society moved to the right politically, I moved left and although I have always remained a member I found my political home in 'Victory for Socialism' which I chaired; in the Campaign for Nuclear Disarmament, which I helped to found; and later in the Tribune Group. I have always been a left-wing Parliamentary socialist, Marxian like Laski rather than Marxist. Neither communism nor the Communist

Party have ever attracted me, but I despise the profit motive and always see my enemies on the right rather than on the left. After my aunt's well deserved rebuke I studied Shaw, Wells and Cole but always regarded G. B. S. and the Webbs, brilliant and industrious though they were as politically unreliable and essentially élitist and undemocratic.

In all this my wife, Marie, has worked with me and at the same time carved out a local government career of her own. We have much in common, are often together, quarrel most days but never go to bed in disharmony.

In 1955 I fought Mitcham unsuccessfully. I had thought I should win and we had moved to Pimlico to be near the House of Commons, but the Boundary Commission decided otherwise. Disappointed, I abandoned Parliamentary ambitions and settled for membership of the London County Council. We moved out to Putney to get a flat overlooking the river where we still live. In 1962 Putney found itself without a candidate as Anne Kerr who was expected to fight the seat had been chosen for Rochester. I was asked to stand and refused, but eventually decided that the unwinnable Putney, a safe Tory seat even in 1945, could be won for Labour and so it proved.

During these years close knowledge of actors enhanced rather than diminished my admiration for their skill. By this time I understood that I had little creative ability and determined to devote the rest of my life to the protection and advancement of those who possessed such gifts, for it seemed to me that here was the true salt of the earth.

Equity, and my own predilections, brought me into close contact with all the arts. From these years stem a number of convictions tested by experience. For example, there is no line to be drawn between the arts and entertainment; high skill can be wasted on trash: and trash can be transmuted by skill into something like art; all art has an economic base; the sources of finance for art and entertainment must be various; in the arts there must be many employers and consumers; artists can easily be corrupted by money and even more easily lost for ever because of lack of money; that to produce an apex of high art it is necessary to have a wide based pyramid of competence; that geniuses do not spring out of nowhere; art reflects the society that begets it but also influences that society; art can as easily be killed by Government neglect as by Government suppression; it is the duty of Government to provide all those art forms which cannot be sustained by other sources of finance and to provide means for all its people to have access to them; that developments in the arts and communications frequently foreshadow the general trend and the direction in which society is moving. As Oscar Wilde said, life imitates art.

I also learned that the arts are interdependent upon each other, and should be seen with entertainment, the media of communication and with all the means of mechanical and electronic reproduction of performance as a single area of Government concern; that together the whole area is economically viable but separately must decline. I saw that there must be universality of concern but multiplicity of control; that we must aim towards self-administration of art by artists and their organisations, but that the State has a vital role to play in fostering art and artists and in bringing them to the people.

Finally, I became convinced that once men and women were mated and were housed and fed, art was the thing that mattered and many of the other preoccupations of mankind were but chaff in the wind.

CHAPTER THREE

The Culture Gap

We live in a divided world. What is more we are obsessed by division. It is what our communicators, themselves divided into populars and heavies, drum into us all the time. The nations are grouped into the East and the West, there are the goodies and the baddies; blacks and whites; Protestants and Catholics; the young and the old; workers and shirkers, and so on, *ad infinitum*. Confrontation and competition is the name of the game; it is the motivation of the acquisitive society and those who prosper in it seek to widen the incentive differentials on which it depends.

This is often unconscious. Disraeli was genuinely horrified by the two nations he recognised as existing in economic terms. A hundred years later the gap is smaller, but although Labour Governments are committed to increasing equality, we have done little to narrow the vast property gap. We are bedevilled by the generation gap, the power gap, the sex gap and what this book is partly about, the culture gap.

In her book, Dr Janet Minihan[1] argues that until the end of the last century a common or shared culture existed even within the great divide of enormous wealth and appalling poverty of the Victorian era. This premise was so much taken for granted that the main reason for state investment in culture was the universal belief that art was morally uplifting and that the contemplation of great works would implant the virtues of the rich into the hearts and minds of the poor. The effect of the Elgin Marbles, said Tory MP J. W. Croker[2] advocating acquisition at public

1. *The Nationalisation of Culture*, Hamish Hamilton, 1977.
2. *Hansard*, 1816 Col. 10344.7.6.

expense, would be 'to create, stimulate, to guide the exertions of the artist, the mechanic and even the labourer.' The first Select Committee on the Arts and Manufactures (the conjunction is significant) was told that local arts schools would improve the morale of the lower orders 'in a very short period of time', while the great Lord Shaftesbury believed that once the National Gallery was built the 'Industrious classes'[3] would desert the ale-houses in favour of spending their time in rapt contemplation of Titian and Reynolds.

Today, the acquisitive society is so firmly established that, a short time ago, the Sunday Times asked people which great painting they would like to *own*. At their invitation, I wrote an article for them expressing my deep love for Monet's 'Water Lilies' but insisting that I did not want to own it. I preferred it to stay where it is: in the National Gallery. Perhaps it is not altogether surprising that the article was never printed.

Always more an illusion than a reality, the notion of the common culture began to collapse by the end of the 1860's. A decade later Whistler was proclaiming art's independence from morality, from social responsibility and almost from humanity itself, and by the time of the First World War, the artist had explicitly divorced himself from the general public. His appeal became elitist and often incomprehensible to the masses.

The arrival of the popular press and later of the cinema, the gramophone, radio and finally television might have healed the breach and, indeed, there were times when we were touched by the joy of shared appreciation: by a great music hall performer at the turn of the century; by a Chaplin silent movie in the First World War and by BBC Radio in the second one. What is more, [3]. during World War II, conscious and strenuous efforts were made by the Churchill/Attlee Government to create a sense of national unity. The knowledge of being, for a time, alone; the rationing, the blackout and the blitz, all these helped to form a nation which felt itself to be united in a struggle for survival.

Artists of all kinds were engaged by the Government to bring home to people that they were the inheritors of a great culture which was threatened by the barbarous might of fascism. Henry Moore drew people asleep in the London Underground stations

[3]. *Hansard*, 13.4.1832 Col. 69.

during the blitz, and they saw themselves through new eyes, some perceiving, perhaps for the first time, that there was a reality beyond that of the photographer.

Sadly, as is recorded in more detail in the next part of this book, the attempt to assert a common culture did not long outlast the end of the war, but at the time it was widely believed, certainly by those who had fought, that victory would usher in a new world in which we should remain, as we had become, one people.

In his 'British Achievement in Arts and Music' the writer, historian and critic, Jack Lindsay said: 'It would be easy, no doubt, to exaggerate the extent to which the developments have created a settled demand or stirred an enduring activity among the people. Culture, like freedom, is never something which once gained can be taken for granted; it is a matter of ceaseless effort. What is certain is that under the extremely difficult conditions of war with all its rigours and rationings we have been able to do much more than maintain cultural standards. We have made an incalculable leap ahead, creating for the first time in England since folk-days a genuine mass-audience for drama, song, music.'[4]

That was true, but the optimistic Marxist Lindsay under-estimated the strength of the capitalist system. He did not foresee, indeed no one did, the development of a huge transatlantic anti-culture; an overwhelming torrent of technically competent but often mindless and anti-social pap, aimed at the most easily stirred instincts of consumers and producing enormous monetary rewards in the process. In the search for maximum profit capitalism has exploited and appropriated the world of entertainment and has asserted command of the main and ever more powerful media of communication.

In our time the opium of the people is not religion, it is palatable misinformation: synthetic sex and violence on the television screen and bogus indignation in the popular newspapers. There is a conspiracy, in which politicians must take their large share of the blame, to conceal from the public the realities of their situation in the nuclear age and to engage them in passionate debate about the absorbingly unimportant and the

[4]. *Pilot Press*, 1945.

salaciously trivial. That conspiracy has re-opened, deepened and widened the culture gap which today separates the book reader from the Sun glancer; the concert-goer from the football fan; the serial viewer from the Open University student, the phoner-in from the Radio 3 listener.

Social historians like Tawney, Leavis, Raymond Williams and Richard Hoggart[5], though arguing from different points of view, are united in telling us that the world in which we live is essentially divided and divisive. Merchandisers 'identify' their 'markets' and serve them with 'products' which must be easily assimilable, widely acceptable and highly profitable. While the production and distribution of consumer goods through multiples and supermarkets has been of undoubted benefit, in the cultural sphere the search for the mass audience and the identification of minorities has been gravely damaging.

The culture gap has grown into an abyss, accepted, unremarked and unbridged. Indeed, the very progenitors of culture divide the population into recognisable market categories based on income, education, age and sex. They determine their target and aim for it: the popular dailies go for the mass market; the heavies are up-market; the theatre is for the salariat, pop concerts for the young, symphonies for graduates, opera for the well-heeled, while the visual arts are for the wealthy. Books are bought and borrowed by the middle-classes who are purported not to frequent football grounds or racecourses, except in special boxes and on special occasions. The Royal Family makes token appearances at many points to demonstrate the universality of its own tastes, but it really prefers horses.

Although the battle to sustain a common culture was lost in the theatre with the disappearance of the Music Hall, the struggle has not altogether been abandoned. The Working Men's Club is essentially separatist as is the West End commercial theatre, but in the supported theatre conscious efforts are made to appeal to the alienated wage-earner.

In broadcasting, the BBC with its four national radio transmissions and its two television channels, all divided on

[5]. *Mass Civilization and Minority Culture*, F. R. Leavis. *The Acquisitive Society*, R. H. Tawney. *Culture and Society*, Raymond Williams. *The Uses of Literacy*, Richard Hoggart.

cultural lines, has caved in completely. ITV would like to follow suit but cannot make the division effective in television without the coveted fourth channel for which it yearns. Commercial radio is in the popular market and makes little attempt to cover the wide potential range of the medium or even to fulfil its franchise promises.

In addition to the divisions within the various arts communications and entertainment forms, there are the divisions between them. Where they should sustain each other they are not permitted to do so. Government responsibility institutionalises the divisions. The Arts Minister looks after the visual arts, music, ballet and opera, libraries, museums, galleries and the art cinema. The Department of Trade, on the other hand, has responsibility for commercial film which it discharges most indifferently; furthermore, when what should be an organic whole is separated, both parts languish. In so far as anyone is responsible for broadcasting it is, of all people, the Home Secretary, who is also supposed to take an occasional interest in the press. In addition, together with local authorities and the Treasury he shares responsibility for the apparatus of censorship. Publishing and the press, however, through their organisations, look to the Department of Trade in certain respects.

Finally, the Arts Minister, through the Arts Council, is responsible, not only for theatrical companies but for theatrical buildings; yet in the case of the national museums and galleries, he is concerned only with their contents while the buildings fall on the vote of the Department of the Environment.

The whole ludicrous set-up happened by accident but could not have been better designed if the object was to ensure that cultural unity is avoided at all costs. It is a tribute to the strength of British culture that its separate manifestations manage to survive as well as they do.

At the same time the Establishment exists and is very ready to speak with a single voice whenever the preservation of the acquisitive society calls for unison. An example was the referendum on the Common Market when the public were offered the opportunity of buying the pro-EEC newspaper of their own free choice. The style was different, the culture served was not the same, but, with the inconsiderable exception of the Morning Star, the message was identical.

This book shows how strong is the market economy even in an area which should be remote from its mercenary heart; the story must raise once again the question of whether Parliament is capable of making more than cosmetic improvements upon the ugly face of capitalism.

When I became Minister for the Arts in 1974 I saw it as my duty to try to do something about the culture gap. This book (inter alia) tells how I set about the task, where I succeeded, how I failed and was fired. Should I have left well alone? I think not, for if, as I believe, a divided society is a sick society, I could only have left ill alone. But let me be clear about one thing. I value low comedy and high art. I like brass bands, jazz and Grand Opera. My own culture is catholic yet patchy, but I revere all artists with undying passion: music and literature were my first loves, but the theatre took hold of me artistically as well as professionally during my years as an officer of Equity.

As Arts Minister I was always looking for the man outside and wanted to bring him in to enjoy the great treats he was missing. I was not one of the boys seeking to preserve my little bit of expertise, to swank about my own cultivated tastes within a charmed circle. I was never in that circle, and what I wanted to do more than anything else was to break it open and let the world in.

CHAPTER FOUR

The Arts and Politics

It follows from what I have said already that I believe that the promotion of the arts should be a major concern of Government. Furthermore I believe it to be the case that the cultural disenfranchisement of the majority of the people is a necessary consequence of the acquisitive society. In none of the advanced Western states have the mass of the people been encouraged to form and develop their full artistic potential and the common taste is brutalised by sales messages which grow more strident and sillier every year.

A generation taught at school to acquire the rudiments of artistic performance and appreciation is, with a few gifted exceptions, then thrust into a world which despises art and regards those who cherish it as affected ninnies. So the mural is 'Chelsea Rules – OK' and punk gets punkier as protest becomes inarticulate, and the creative urge is chanelled into noise and destruction. We have become an aimless society so why should we be surprised if those given a hard materialist stone instead of the bread of vision, throw it at us in rage and frustration and seek release in alcoholic rampage.

Marxists would argue that the culture of a country is economically determined. So it is, but Parliament can profoundly influence both economic and cultural development for good or ill. The future of the arts in this country, and in any other, is therefore a *political* issue.

To take an example, the treatment of visual art as a form of investment is a phenomenon of our own time, and one of the objectives of social policy should be to break the idea of art as the

B

bingo of the cultivated rich. The association of fine art with great wealth must be reduced if the masses are to be culturally enfranchised. As Minister I aimed at a vigorous, vital and general enjoyment of the arts and a more universal production of art and craftwork throughout the community. I have nothing but contempt for the international art market. It is a racket none the better for being operated by cultivated smoothies. The object in this area should be to stimulate new patterns of patronage better adapted to a more egalitarian society, for the relatively restricted role of the arts in our present economic mix is not only unsocialist but actively anti-social. A spread of patronage among a wider section of the community would not restrict but enlarge the freedom of the artist, for art and private property have not been indelibly linked in the past, and there is no reason why they should be so linked in future.

I do not, therefore, agree that the office of the Arts Minister should be an apolitical portfolio and, perhaps, some of my own problems stemmed from the fact that the Labour Government of which I was a member had no coherent view on the point. Although the first Arts Minister, Jennie Lee, argued that *subsidy* of the arts was not a partisan issue, I thought that this was for the purpose of establishing the arts as a normal and natural recipient of Government aid.

I was happy that throughout her period of office Jennie Lee used to call me her 'unofficial parliamentary private secretary' and was generous in her acknowledgement of such help and advice as I was able to give. As the result of Jennie Lee's work there was never at any time any question in Parliament about the size of my monetary demands, although they doubled in my two years of office. The struggle for cash took place within the Government, not in the House of Commons. I could have rested on Jennie Lee's laurels, kept a low profile and stayed out of controversy. Instead I chose to try to move forward.

My experience leads me to the conclusion that fundamental change is necessary but that it will not be made without a complete re-fashioning, not only of the organisational structure of the Arts Council but also of wider relationships between Party and Government.

The Labour Party has a clear understanding of the need to

make the arts 'more democratic and representative of those working in arts and entertainment' as the 1974 Manifesto said but the 1974 Labour Government had no such understanding and I fell, partly, because my determination to try to implement Party policy in this and in other ways, made me a nuisance. It was felt that my unpopularity with the Establishment would rub off on the Government as a whole. Furthermore, I advocated the Wealth Tax at a time when the Government had decided to shelve it and this was distinctly embarrassing to the Treasury.

The need to move away from 'Lady Bountiful' methods of arts patronage; from dollops of money handed down from the representatives of authority to the grateful peasants below, is well understood outside this country.

The British tend to see their political and economic set-up as a half-way house between Russian communism and American capitalism. Similarly, the introduction to an American symposium on culture sees the pluralistic US patronage scene as an attempt to find a 'middle way – difficult, perhaps to maintain – between the all-embracing, respectful and enlightened control over cultural activity that is assumed in France and the disinterested, even detached – if also concerned and thoughtful – approach of the British.'[1]

Stripped of its elaborate politeness, what this means is that the French are *dirigiste* in their arts patronage, (which they are or have tended to be) while we are so in love with our 'arms-length' principle that our Arts Ministers all understudy Pontius Pilate.

Wherever one travels in the world of arts patronage, the British are seen as the exponents of a rather wild scattering of limited seed as against the more generous, yet selective, husbandry practised elsewhere. That some of the British seed falls on stony ground there can be no doubt, but many lovely flowers have also bloomed.

In the symposium to which I have referred, the British point of view is put by Lord Goodman who contributes the most urbane of all the essays and finishes with the bold assertion that 'the artist's contribution to society exceeds in its purpose and value that of any other.'[2]

[1] *A Symposium on Culture and Society*, Encyclopedia Britannica, 1977.
[2]. Ibid.

The American writer and arts administrator Waldemar A. Nielson shows a greater awareness of the realities of the world in which we live:

> 'This is a time when the boundaries between art, recreation, and social therapy are blurring. It is a time when the standards of judgment appropriate to art are in violent dispute. "High and low are really separate cultures." writes sociologist Herbert Gans. "Each has its own artistic standards, its own concept of good taste, its preferred arts and artists. Which culture people prefer depends on their income, occupation, and cultural education at home and at school."
>
> However radical such a view may seem to traditionalists, it is a mild reflection of the spreading revolt against what is seen as the "colonial approach", by which is meant the endeavour to transmit cultural values downward from a cultivated élite to the masses. There is a rapidly growing public, involved in everything from square dancing to wood carving, which is unwilling to allow its activities to be characterised as mere expressions of uneducated taste. It is insistent that the primary aim of cultural policy should be to encourage active participation in the arts, not passive exposure to the art object or performance. At the outer fringe there is a militant minority, small but influential, which rejects all traditional culture in favour of discordant, politically motivated art forms.'[3]

This view is underlined by the Frenchman, Jacques Rigaud, who is Assistant Director General of UNESCO.

> 'In former times the masses were excluded *de facto* if not *de jure* from the culture of the élite, in which they could participate only after social advancement. Today universal education, the demand for equality, and the growth of mass media oblige us to recognise the right to culture of the vast majority of people, even if the people do not place this right at the top of their list of priorities.'[4]

Rigaud goes on to argue that if the state fails to evolve a policy to meet this 'right to culture' it will inevitably support and establish élitism in the arts. I believe this to be profoundly true and plainly so in our own country.

3. Ibid.
4. Ibid.

Jacques Rigaud shows, at least to his own satisfaction, how a national cultural policy can be reconciled with artistic freedom. He says:

> 'Culture must have a place in the debate and policymaking by which a democratic society defines its own future. If it does not, the natural tendencies of cultural life will be to widen the gap between the elaborate, sophisticated culture of the élite and the increasingly limited culture of the masses.'[5]

In 1964, Harold Wilson, the then Prime Minister, understood that it was necessary for the prestige of Government to make a gesture towards the arts; to establish a Ministry and to allocate more money than hitherto. He did not realise that the appointment of Jennie Lee was but the beginning of a long struggle. He was not alone in believing that anyone who enjoyed the arts was a 'cultural snob' and did not open his mind to my passion to bring the world of art to the people as a whole. I think he *did* grasp the point when I once said that the powers needed to appreciate a performance of ballet were the same as those required to enjoy football, except that football was rather more difficult. But in his political decisions. Wilson was a sucker for the arts establishment and fell a ready victim to Cabinet colleagues with greater artistic pretensions. When Roy Jenkins advocated my replacement by Lord Donaldson, he resisted because I was protected by the substantial shadow of Lord Goodman and by Jennie Lee, who in turn invoked the ghost of Aneurin Bevan, but Wilson gave me little support once he had appointed me and kept me in a junior ministerial rank. Only when I was on ground he knew something about – the cinema – did he trust my judgment. In all other areas of the arts he preferred to listen to Lord Gibson, to Harold Lever and others rather than to the Minister he had himself appointed. He listened to them because they were not seeking change and were not urging socialism or democracy, for by then Harold Wilson had long passed the point at which he still retained a desire to refashion the world. Jim Callaghan never at any time showed much interest in or appreciation of the arts and it was entirely natural that he should replace me with someone who would give no trouble and do no more than keep things ticking over.

5. Ibid.

What then can we do to be saved? A vital proposal in the Labour Party Arts document[6] is the adoption of the idea of a Cabinet Minister with responsibility for the Arts, Communications and Entertainment. I would add Sport. Not only ACE but ACES. Such a Minister would control a department not only of size but one which extends from the élite to the popular. This is important. In none of the Governments that I have examined is this essential bridge between high art and popular entertainment spanned at the level of political decision.

I would emphasise the importance of the recommendation that such a Ministry should embrace the media of communication. There is nothing in British society so bad as the appalling manner in which we present it to ourselves and to others.

But how are these changes to be brought about? My own experience, as will be seen, is not encouraging. Only a fundamental structural change in the relationships between Party and Government will trigger off similar changes in relationships throughout society.

The questions that really count are these. In what direction does the river of power flow? Is the Prime Minister the servant or the master of his Party? At present the river of power is reversed at the Parliamentary lock. The leader of the Party is chosen at Parliamentary level and he then chooses his own Government, thereby halting in his person the flow of power up from the electorate through the Party, containing it in his authority and becoming from that moment the sole fount of all decisions. The direction is reversed and democracy becomes oligarchic; every member of the Government depends upon the Prime Minister for his office and one fallible man with all his inevitable areas of ignorance is erected into a position of power enjoyed by few other leaders. The British Prime Minister is not under control or influence, he is paramount.

If, instead of electing only the Prime Minister, the Parliamentary Party chose the entire Cabinet (leaving the PM to allot and, if necessary, re-shuffle, the portfolios) and the Cabinet then chose the rest of the Government collectively, the fate of individual Ministers would no longer rest in the hands of a single man. The strength of all Ministers would be increased and the

6. *Arts and the People: The Labour Party*

authority of the Prime Minister would be diminished. That is as it should be. In such a community there would be no danger of élitism being confused with excellence. A community which not only pretends to democracy but practices it at all points will be one which enjoys the arts and crafts at every level. It is this that concerns me here.

The involvement of all backbenchers in the process of Ministerial selection would enable discussion to take place on such questions as the sensible distribution of responsibilities. Although the PM would continue to allocate Portfolios among the Cabinet presented to him, it would become entirely proper to require him to appoint a Cabinet Minister responsible for all the areas of art, communication and sport with detailed duties divided among a couple of juniors. This proposal, already Party Policy, would, for the first time, introduce an element of coherence into the scene. The effects would be profound. Members of an elected Cabinet would become much more eager to fulfil the Party programme if only as a means of staying in office. With such a system we should have had a wealth tax and by now the fears of the arts plutes would have been shown to be groundless.

Party policy to make the Arts Council more democratic would have been carried out and the resentment and suspicion which is fouling up arts patronage would have been reduced. The Regional Arts Associations would probably be funded directly from the Ministry rather than through the Arts Council, providing a greater diversity of patronage and, with full Cabinet backing, Public Lending Right would now be on the Statute Book. It is likely that an elected; or partly elected, Arts Council, would by now have evolved a points system by which it would seek to show that its decision-making processes in the distribution of the state's bounty are based on more than custom, convenience and pull. The voice of the regions would be strengthened and expenditure on the arts would not merely be a power enjoyed by local authorities, but a mandatory obligation exercised in the same way as local authority educational and library obligations are already fulfilled – that is to say, with central Government broad guidance and financial support, but with detailed local control. The Labour

Party arts document has some interesting ideas on how artists and their organisations might be involved in the decision-making process at local level.[7]

If such a system had operated during my own period of office, not only would Public Lending Right be augmenting the incomes of authors by now, but we should probably be contemplating extending the idea to the public lending of paintings and other works.

The purpose of this book is not to justify my period of office as Minister for the Arts nor is it to write the last part of my autobiography. My concern is to describe the post-war development of Government policy towards the arts in this country and to indicate the way it should progress.

The purpose of Government is to provide a full life for the governed. This means that government must be self-government: that peace shall prevail within and without our borders; that from each according to his ability and to each according to his needs shall be the aim.

I believe that it is the duty of Government to enable all its people to flourish individually and collectively; to encourage beauty and creativity, to seek to leave the world a better place. Politicians do not ask themselves every day, 'is this a contribution to making things better', and thus they spend much of their time operating at well below their best.

In the arts the effort must be made to increase availability, understanding and participation, to loosen the grip of the wealthy, and to strengthen the influence of artists themselves. These things I tried to do but regrettably found little interest among my colleagues in Government.

So it is right to pose the question now: What should be the relation between politics and the arts and can my experience of Government contribute to an answer?

I have been in politics in one way or another most of my adult life. I have a high concept of my calling. I believe as profoundly as ever I did in Parliamentary Socialism and I am not at all cynical. Sometimes I despair, but that is not the same thing, for when I do I have only to think of the people we politicians are

7. Ibid.

there to serve, and especially the rank and file members of my own party, to have my convictions renewed.

Now that we have lost our religious faith and have no universal belief in a world hereafter, surely it is more important than ever that we should spend our time making the only world we have and know more wonderful than it is. Should not our first priority be to see that every human being develops the great qualities within him to the full?

Is such an aim beyond the purposes of Government? I think it ought not to be and that our priorities must be re-examined.

Democracy is precarious and imperfect, but if we trace post-war developments in the Government's attitude to the arts we may reach the conclusion that the time is ripe for further progress; that, indeed, it is overdue.

PART II

CHAPTER FIVE

Before Jennie Lee

A brief summary to 1964

Throughout history the attitude of rulers towards the arts has been ambiguous: they have been loved and hated, admired and feared. In earlier times, especially in Europe, the Church was a major patron, so too was private patronage, but the principal reliance has been on the state. Greece and Rome, Germany and France, Monarch and Count, city and state, all have both suppressed and supported the arts, the latter often from motives of self-aggrandisement and display. Nevertheless, the colossal development of the arts in France under Louis Quatorze, for example, reaffirmed and enriched Western civilisation. On the Continent, and especially in Germany, the tradition of patronage by the state was maintained by the separate principalities and dukedoms, but the centralisation of Government in London and the early arrival of the industrial revolution in Britain combined to reduce the status of the municipality. These developments, coming before the invention of the cinema, gramophone and broadcasting, produced the Music Hall for the new urban proletariat and with it, the notion of a profit-seeking rather than a subsidised theatre. Show Business was born.

Support from Victorian Governments was limited to grudging sums paid toward the construction of a few buildings to house the vast treasures which had been privately, and often nefariously, acquired by British travellers who had explored the world. The gift of paintings and antiques and other works to the state was often made conditional upon the construction by the government of buildings to house them. It was expected that a bonus in the shape of a refined and other-worldly working-class would emerge as the result of this relatively trifling expenditure. Perhaps the art-lovers of the day recognised that their more philistine masters, brought up on the *laissez-faire* doctrines of Adam Smith, could only be sold the proposition of even minimal investment in the arts on the basis that enlightenment would dawn even on those living in squalor. The pervasive legacy of the Puritans prevented any public investment in the theatre and helped to hold back the construction of the National Theatre until our own time.

From the beginning the Labour Party has placed the arts high on its list of priorities and in its 1918 major statement of policy, 'Labour and the New Social Order' called for increased provision 'for the promotion of music, literature and fine art, which have been under capitalism so greatly neglected, and upon which, so the Labour Party holds, any real development of civilisation fundamentally depends. Society, like the individual, does not live by bread alone – does not exist only for perpetual wealth production.'

It was a wonderful start and the first Labour Government, Ramsay Macdonald's minority administration of 1924, proposed to give powers to local authorities to spend the product of a penny rate on the provision of entertainment facilities, but the Lords, as reactionary as ever, amended the bill to deprive authorities of power to aid the arts, confining them to sport and recreation. The commercial theatre managements were an active lobby in this, for in those days there was still big money to be made in the provincial theatre; commerce, of course, has always sought to confine public enterprise to loss-making activities. It was sad that this pioneer Government fell before it could implement its other plans to build the National Theatre and abolish the entertainment tax introduced during the 1914/18 War.

About this time progressive local authorities began to take an interest in museums and galleries, Liverpool, Leeds and Lincoln prominent among them. By the outbreak of the Second World War there were no less than 400 museums financed by local authorities, but money was too meagre in many cases to provide for significant acquisitions or adequate housing. The great national collections depended on private donors, for the

Treasury did little more than provide minimum maintenance.

These were the great days of the British Drama League which, privately founded and financed, established amateur acting as the British indoor sport and thus helped to sow the seed for the flowering of the theatre in our own time. In 1920 the Academy of Dramatic Arts received its Royal Charter, but no money, and in 1937 the first site (in South Kensington) for a national theatre was purchased by the Memorial National Theatre Committee entirely without aid from public funds. The Old Vic and even the Vic-Wells Ballet were equally unaided in their early days. Opera, however, has rarely survived without public funds and, in the twenties, first Sir Thomas Beecham's company and then the British National Opera Company went bankrupt.

The Second Labour Government in 1930 with Philip Snowdon as Chancellor took the amazing step of supporting Covent Garden Opera through the BBC to the tune of £40,000. When the Conservatives entered Macdonald's National Government, they soon put an end to such socialist capers.

Immediately prior to the Second World War the total government expenditure on the arts was less than one million pounds, almost all of which was spent on the national museums and galleries.[1]

Even before the First World War the cinema was well on the way to replacing the theatre as the regular form of popular entertainment. Audiences rose rapidly during the war but the nascent British production industry could not be sustained and by the early 1920's Hollywood had conquered. Belatedly discovering that other countries had legislatively protected themselves from the American influx, the Baldwin Government produced the first Cinematograph Films Act in 1927. The cinema was placed under the control of the Board of Trade; regulations and quotas were introduced which were intended to ensure that at least one fifth of the films exhibited were made in Britain. This simply encouraged the production of the cheap

---

[1] Government Expenditures on the Arts, 1938–39. Arts museums and galleries £483,031, (a) Direct expenditure £333,188, (b) Allied services £36,070. Other arts bodies receiving Exchequer aid £36,070, Royal commissions, etc. £14,119. Historic buildings and their contents, and ancient monuments, by Minister of Works £54,529. Total £920,937. HM Treasury, *Governments and the Arts in Britain* (HMSO, 1958), p. 22.

'quota quickie'. In 1937 the Chamberlain Government introduced the second Cinematograph Films Bill extending the
quota and establishing the Cinematograph Film Council as a
watchdog which had no concern for the *quality* of the British
film. Fortunately, however, Parliament had established the
British Film Institute in 1933. It was financed out of a levy on the
proceeds of Sunday showings of films, an average of about £9,000
a year, on which minimal budget the Institute set about the task
of establishing film as an art form. Generally the Tory attitude to
the cinema between wars was as niggardly and as uninspired as
their stance on the arts as a whole.

It can be argued that the Government-granted BBC monopoly
of radio or 'wireless' as it was called, was the basis for the great
contribution which radio made to the culture of this country. For
a time the gap seemed to be closing. The BBC was originally
the British Broadcasting Company controlled by the larger radio
manufacturing companies and granted a monopoly license by
the Postmaster-General in 1923. The Lloyd George Government
imposed a total ban on the import of foreign radio receivers and
paid to the BBC half the proceeds of a compulsory license paid by
each listener. The single transmission was not only a technical
and economic inevitability, it was culturally orientated. John
Reith, the Managing Director, rightly saw the BBC as a great
educational force. He believed that as those listening to news and
popular programmes would inadvertently listen to other
broadcasts. religious, moral and artistic enlightenment would
brush off on them. Indeed the Charter of the Corporation which
succeeded the Company in 1927 referred to broadcasting as a
means of 'disseminating information, education and
entertainment.'

The BBC monopoly was firmly defended during this time, not
least by the Director-General who said 'It is God's doing.' The
BBC may have been the instrument of the Almighty but it was
also that of the Government. In those early days the Company
did not attempt to take up even the establishment-type
impartiality of later years. During the 1926 General Strike for
instance, although the BBC never degenerated to the level of the
official newspaper, the British Gazette, the trade union case was
never stated on the air and no supporter of the strike, no Labour

MP even, was allowed near the microphone. Some reports of TUC statements were broadcast, but as Asa Briggs says in his monumental 'History of Broadcasting in the United Kingdom'. 'There is little doubt that BBC News assisted the Government against the strikers.'[2]

In the years that followed, the independence of the BBC from Government control and from the influence of Parliament was gradually established. It was not until the war years that a much greater national emergency gave the Government the right and the duty to interpret the national interest to the Corporation and to require conformity. By then the BBC itself was a part of the establishment, and those who ran it knew their place in the scheme of things as well as the leaders of the Church or the directors of the Bank of England. Their role was to be independent inside the avaiary, to fly about freely but not to question the shape of the cage and, preferably, not to be aware of its existence.

While there can be little doubt that the Corporation would do the Government's work in a future emergency as well as it did in 1926 and throughout World War II, the BBC has nevertheless demonstrated that it is no mere creature of its paymaster. No Government has made any attempt to control programmes and this experience was valuable as a precedent when the Arts Council came to be established after the war.

An unexpected consequence of World War II was the serious entry of the British Government into patronage of the arts. The story of ENSA and CEMA is well known, but whereas the Entertainments National Service Association, founded in 1938, was and remained a body doing the very necessary job of bringing entertainment to the Armed Services, the Council for the Encouragement of Music and the Arts, formed in 1939, had wider responsibilities. Although Government-supported from the beginning, CEMA was also financed from American sources by the Pilgrim Trust. W. E. Williams, later to become Secretary General of the Arts Council, was on its governing body. CEMA's first Chairman. Lord Macmillan, was succeeded by J. M. Keynes who later described its role as being 'to carry music, drama and pictures to places which otherwise would be cut off

2. Vol. 1 p. 95.

from all contact with the masterpieces of happier days and times; to air-raid shelters, to war-time hostels, to factories, to mining villages . . .'3

The Pilgrim Trust withdrew in 1942 and CEMA began to receive a grant-in-aid on the Government's education vote, rising to nearly a quarter of a million pounds in 1945/6. With CEMA aid, the great London Orchestras and the main provincial ones such as the Liverpool Philharmonic and the Hallé, not only remained in being during the war but toured the country and were heard by new and wildly enthusiastic audiences of thousands in factories, churches, cinemas and other halls. I recall hearing the London Philharmonic in Peterborough Cathedral in 1943 when I was in the Royal Air Force, but the real audience for these concerts was the hard-pressed civilian population.

Sadlers Wells Ballet also toured throughout the war and performed in London parks to crowded audiences. CEMA gave additional support to drama companies and organised its own tours to all parts of the country. In addition to the famous visits of the Old Vic with Dame Sybil Thorndike to Welsh mining villages, CEMA went into theatre ownership and subsidy and in 1942 alone organised over 300 art exhibitions of all kinds throughout the land. As Keynes said on BBC radio in 1945, 'At the start our aim was to replace what war had taken away, but we soon found that we were providing what had never existed, even in peace-time.' Indeed it was estimated that of the factory and hostel audiences, only about two percent had ever seen a play before.

In 1942 CEMA set up Regional Offices and was engaged in a good deal of direct provision. In 1943/44 more than half CEMA's total income was spent on music which, during the blitz was not only well received but passionately demanded by a large public. Just over 16% of the then total expenditure of £135,000 was spent on drama, 10% on visual art, and 21% on administration.

When the Pilgrim Trust bowed out in 1942, their Annual Report, referring to the first two years of CEMA, said: 'The demand has, in fact, presented a continual problem of supply and has dissipated scepticism about the public response to un-

3. *The Listener* 12.7.45.

accustomed forms of beauty in sound, thought and design. In two years its art exhibitions have attracted more than half a million visitors; the plays given under its auspices, a million and a half; the number of its concerts in all parts of England, Wales and Scotland almost reached eight thousand.'

CEMA was the foetus which became the Arts Council. The organisational structures of the Council to-day and the benevolent autocracy of its ethos are essentially those created for CEMA by Maynard Keynes. The advisory panels which still exist were originally set up in 1942 and the decision to seek a Royal Charter was taken in 1945. In June of that year, Sir John Anderson, Chancellor of the Exchequer in Winston Churchill's Caretaker Government, said that CEMA was to continue after the war 'to encourage knowledge, understanding and practice of the arts . . . with the name of The Arts Council of Great Britain.'[4]

When the Arts Council replaced CEMA it was decided, unwisely, to transfer responsibility for the new body from the Department of Education to the Treasury; control was not returned to the Department of Education until 1964, after the appointment of Jennie Lee by Harold Wilson as first Minister for the Arts. The Arts Council's grant in 1946/7 was £350,000. In 1977/8 it was over £50 millions.

Nevertheless, as we have seen, the importance of the arts was widely recognised during World War II. Perhaps nations as well as individuals are subject to that wonderful concentration of the mind which Dr Johnson suggested comes to those about to be hanged.

In its first Annual Report the Arts Council quoted Keynes as saying that 'The day is not far off when the Economic Problem will take a back seat where it belongs and the arena of the heart and head will be occupied, or re-occupied, by our real problems, the problems of life and human relations, of creation and behaviour and religion.'

He could not have been more wrong. The needs of the Arts Council increased at a much greater rate than its grant and the more money it received the hungrier it became for still greater resources. So far from economic problems receding in import-ance, the Arts Council grew increasingly preoccupied with

4. *Hansard* 12.6.45 Col 1482.

money. As Rabelais said, 'Appetite comes with eating,'[5]

However, the Council's early role was peripheral, and it was only with the collapse of the commercial theatre in the provinces around the late fifties that it was seen that the burden of maintaining the performance arts outside London now rested upon the Arts Council. As the money increased the demands grew still faster. As it moved into the millions the Council lost its earlier content and began to feel querulous and deprived. As in the case of individuals, needs grow so as to exceed the money available. In the entertainment arts, the expectations both of performers and of audiences grew faster than inflation which, in itself, jumped in the arts at a rate much higher than the general increase, for reasons detailed by Baumel and Bowen in their book, 'The Performing Arts – The Economic Dilemma.'[6]

But these difficulties of the future were the ambitions of the immediate post-war years and in 1949, advocating the National Theatre Bill in the House of Lords, Lord Esher said that this country was 'about to enjoy an Athenian summer of great interest and charm.'[7] The Arts Council agreed and saw its main task as being to bring that summer about; to make it bright and warm and, if possible, eternal.

The Arts Council became less and less involved in the direct provision of entertainment and touring as commercial managements reaped the benefit of a post-war boom. Unhappily, the Council decided to close down the regional offices established originally by CEMA. The charge against the Council of being a London-based élitist body stems from that decision and from the Council's consistent refusal to change its organisational structure to admit of any nominated or representative element among its membership or on its advisory panels. Even its Scottish and Welsh Committees are centrally appointed by appointees. In practice this came to mean that the senior staff of the Arts Council made recommendations which were invariably accepted. Thus the feeling developed that the Arts Council was a self-perpetuating oligarchy of ingrown Londoners. This was never wholly true, but the damage was done, the image was set and it

5. *Gargantua*, Ch. 5.
6. *1966 Twentieth Century Fund*, New York.
7. *Lords Hansard.* 17.2.44. Col. 998.

has remained.

Keynes did not live to become the first Chairman of the Arts Council. Shortly before he died he gave a famous broadcast talk which has often been quoted. In it he looked forward to *'regular* (my italics) attendance at the theatre and concerts as a part of organised education.' He laid it down that the task of the Arts Council was 'not to teach or to censor, but to give courage, confidence and opportunity.' He rejoiced that 'at last the public exchequer has recognised the support and encouragement of the arts of life as part of its duty' and he ended: 'The purpose of the Arts Council of Great Britain is to create an environment, to breed a spirit, to cultivate an opinion. To offer a stimulus to such purpose that the artist and the public can each sustain and live on the other in that union which has occasionally existed in the past at the great ages of a communal civilised life.'[8]

I doubt whether anyone believes that we have achieved that. Nevertheless, the groundwork was laid for an unprecedented involvement of government in the arts. At the same time, the tradition that the Arts Council was free to make its own decisions without Government interference was firmly established. In its Annual Report for 1956 the Council said that 'successive Chancellors have invariably said that they will not interfere with the Arts Council's discretion' and added that there had been 'no single instance' of the Government 'requiring or directing or even advising the Arts Council to do this or not to do that.'[9]

The first Charter of the Arts Council charged it with the duties of developing 'greater knowledge, understanding and practice' of the arts and to increase their accessibility to the public, 'to improve the standard of execution of the fine arts and to advise and cooperate with our Government Departments, local authorities and other bodies on any matters concerned directly or indirectly with those objects.'

In those early years such phrases as 'few but roses' emphasised the élitist nature of the Council's approach. In the dual task laid down in their Charter of raising standards and spreading appreciation, the emphasis in all annual reports was on quality. In reality, of course, quality comes, or does not come, from the

8. *The Listener* 12.7.1945. p. 31.
9. *The First Ten Years*, Arts Council. p. 12.

artist – the state merely provides the means for the artist to be good or bad.

In his report for 1953/4 Secretary General W. E. Williams said, 'If half a million pounds of public money now invested annually by the Arts Council and Local Authorities in opera, ballet, music and drama in this country were withdrawn, nearly all the national institutions of music and drama in this country would have to close down.' This was a novel concept of government dependence and perhaps the Arts Council was aiming to establish the *idea* of public finance for the arts and thus preparing the way for the relatively massive injections of public money in later years. Note, however, that it was the *national* institutions which had become dependent. Outside London, theatres generally still managed without subsidy or with very little, and early fringe and experimental activities received almost nothing. Thus, while London's established arts institutions were maintained, support elsewhere was abysmal. When the roses were few their perfume was rarely experienced outside London.

In spite of increasing consciousness of shortage of money and a gradual awakening to the true nature of the problems it had to face, an air of self-satisfaction pervaded all the Council's early reports. Even as late as 1962, the Council nearly fell over itself when it received an additional £445,000 over the previous year from Selwyn Lloyd, then Tory Chancellor of the Exchequer. This caused the Secretary General, the delightful Bill Emrys Williams, to call his Annual Report for that year 'A Brighter Prospect'. Of course, as a Tory Government had actually cut the grant a few years before, Selwyn Lloyd must have seemed a king compared with some of his predecessors.

Government support of the arts increased much more rapidly in the area of museums and galleries than did the grant of the Arts Council and, for example, in 1958/59 it was more than five times as large. It was not until after the appointment of Jennie Lee that the Arts Council moved into the big money and became a spender to match the cost of the great national institutions. It is, perhaps, as well to bear in mind that even today the annual cost of the British Museum exceeds that of the National Theatre and the new British Library will cost ten times as much to build as the

National Theatre.

The annual grant to the Arts Council crept up very gradually during the Labour Government of 1945 by around £100,000 a year to £875,000. With the arrival of the Tories on the scene in 1951 it suffered a heavy cut which was not fully restored until 1957. However, by the time Labour returned to office in 1964 the figure was just over £3 millions.

This country, as J. K. Galbraith has reminded us, is now more economically obsessed than most others and certainly more than it has ever been in the past, but the Arts Council sought to uphold an aspect of the non-material. In doing so, however, the Council itself has become more and more enmeshed in the economic obsession until today, although the Council receives much more money than it did in the past, it spends much more time discussing its own economic problems and those of its clients than it ever did in earlier days. Keynes did not foresee, nor for that matter did most other people, that the desire for material wealth can never be satisfied and that greed would soon replace the survival motivations of wartime as the major preoccupation of the Western world.

Gerald Croasdell, who became General Secretary of Equity, was deeply engaged in television negotiations in the early sixties, and this meant that theatrical matters fell to my lot. I interpreted my function in Equity as not only to seek to improve the conditions of work for my members but to try to make sure that there was work for them to do and places for them to work in.

With this in view I took a leading part in the formation of the Theatres Advisory Council which was and is a sort of Parliament of the theatre, bringing together all the representative bodies, managerial, trade union, and other societies representing the theatre as a whole whenever there was a need for a united voice. I acted as Joint Secretary of the TAC with William Kendall, a civil servant who was and is as maniacal about the theatre as I am myself. Together we set out to defend our charge against all comers. At its first inception in 1962 the commercial Managers were very wary of the TAC and the cost of running the new body fell almost entirely on the trade union side. This meant that TAC work had to be voluntary spare-time endeavour by people for the most part associated with one or other of the sixteen theatrical bodies who made up the Council. The Arts Council was in from the beginning and the Drama Director, then Jo Hodgkinson, helped to draft the constitution. Sir Bronson Albery committed the West End Theatre Managers in principle and the other bodies followed suit with varying degrees of enthusiasm.

As joint-secretary of the TAC I found myself on the same side as the Arts Council and its officials. I persuaded the present Lord Esher's father to become the Chairman of the new body. With the old Viscount I had the same sort of relationship as I later developed with Lord Goodman: a shared passion for the arts and personal liking to set against total political hostility. On one occasion way back in 1950 I helped the old boy on with his magnificent winter overcoat and complimented him on it. 'Ah,' he said, 'with you socialists in power I wear the fur on the inside of me coat.' And he did.

From its early days the TAC included the following:—

Member Organisations
Association of British Theatres Technicians
Association of Touring and Producing Managers
British Actor's Equity Association
British Theatre Association
Council of Regional Theatre
Institute of Municipal Entertainment
League of Dramatists
Musicians Union
National Association of Theatrical and Kine Employees
National Operatic and Dramatic Association
Society for Theatre Research
Society of Theatre Consultants
Society of West End Theatre Managers
Stage Management Association
Theatre Management Association

Associated Organisations
Arts Council of Great Britain
Arts Council of Northern Ireland

British Centre of the International Theatre Institute
Theatre's National Committee

Representatives were persuaded to attend the inaugural meeting by holding it at the Arts Council, in the old building in St. James Square, and sending out the invitation in the magic name of Lord Esher. After his death I felt it essential to maintain the establishment image of the TAC and persuaded the third Lord Faringdon to succeed to the Chair. Gavin Faringdon was a. gentle, unassuming person and few people realised that his convictions were well to the left of centre. Norman Marshall, a tower of strength, remained Vice-Chairman and Bill Kendall and I remained joint secretaries. Harry Francis of the Musicians Union was, and is, Treasurer. From the early days most of the drudgery fell upon Ethel Langstreth of the British Drama League and I was delighted that her great services to the theatre were recognised in an Honours list during my period of Ministerial office.

In 1958 I had been elected for Stoke Newington and Hackney North on to the London County Council. At the Selection Conference I had said that one of my main purposes would be to get the National Theatre built and I insisted on this going into the Election Address, together with opposition to the pretence of civil defence against nuclear war. Once on the LCC I had moved a motion to build the Theatre which had been accepted by the Leader, Ike Hayward[10] and by 1962 things were beginning to move.

My first period of service on the Arts Council was as a member of the Drama Panel from 1962 to 1966.[11] When I began, I was

10. Sir Isaac Hayward, Labour leader of the LCC.
11. The following were among those who served on the Drama Panel in the early sixties:
The Drama Panel – Hugh Willatt* – Chairman.
Elizabeth Barber, Michael Barry, Wynyar Browne, Stewart Burge, Nancy Burman,* John Bury, Andrew Cruickshank, Bonamy Dobrée, Jane Edgeworth, Michael Elliott, Martin Esslin, Robin Fox,* Val Gielgud, Wyn Griffiths, Peter Hall, Margaret Harris, Frank Hauser, Jocelyn Herbert, Hugh Hunt,* Barbara Jefford, Hugh Jenkins,* John Kennedy,* J. W. Lambert, A. H. Marshall, Val May, Leo McKern, Bernard Miles, Yvonne Mitchell, John Mortimer, John Neville, Laurence Olivier, Harold Pinter, Joan Plowright, Patrick Robertson, Reginald Salberg, Elizabeth Sweeting, Dorothy Tutin, T. C. Worsley.
*Members of the policy sub-committee.

Assistant General Secretary of Actor's Equity and great care was taken to make it clear· to me that I was there in a personal capacity and not as Equity's man. The Arts Council panels are appointed by the Council on the recommendation of the Chairman of each panel who is advised by the Director of the relevant department.

I think it was now widely known that I was obsessed with the theatre. Hugh Willatt, who was then Chairman of the Drama Panel probably agreed with Drama Director, Jo Hodgkinson, that my personal dedication was such that I would not be seen as that dangerous animal, a delegate. In fact, I *did* report back to the Equity Council any Drama Panel decisions which I felt to be important or when I needed to know where Equity would be likely to stand. There was never any complaint about this; perhaps I was discreet. If so, as Jennie Lee once told me, it would hardly be in character.

The Panel met quarterly and its meetings were always useful as they brought together a great body of expertise on the theatrical problems which filled their agendas. The real work however, fell upon the Policy Committee which met monthly. This was a sub-committee of the Drama Panel and like the Panel itself it was chaired by Hugh Willatt whose tremendous contribution to the Arts Council is always underestimated, concealed by his modest and quiet demeanour.

This policy committee was responsible for two theatre reports, in 1964 and 1967. Neither of them was made public but they led up to the major survey of the English Theatre which was published in 1970.[12] The curious thing about these earlier reports, which attempted a first assessment of the needs of the theatre in England, is that they were accepted by the Arts Council and largely implemented. The contribution made by the Arts Council Drama Officers in providing the Committee with accurate information was vital. In the reports we categorised all the theatres in the country and proposed vastly increased grants for 1965 and 1966. As a result of these developments the theatre moved further out of the field of commerce into that of public service.

12. *The Theatre Today in England and Wales:* Arts Council, 1970.

As Joint Secretary of the Theatres Advisory Council I had appeared in a Planning Enquiry at Wimbledon when the Theatre was saved. The occasion exposed a weakness in the planning legislation in that theatres were lumped in with other 'places of assembly' and one of the first things I did as a new MP in 1964 was to get them pulled out into a separate category of 'theatres, cinemas and music-halls.' Unhappily, I could not get theatres separated from cinemas but it did mean that from that time on Bingo could not be introduced without permission for 'change of use' being applied for and granted.

The majority Labour Government of 1945 accepted the responsibility of maintaining in peace-time a larger involvement in the arts than had been thought appropriate by any previous British Government. It was no more than that, but it was significant for two reasons. First, a pattern of support was set in which, uniquely throughout the world, successive British Governments agreed to pay the piper without making any attempt to call the tune. Secondly, it was just before the communications revolution, when mechanical and electronic reproduction of performance created new forms of entertainment and separated the performer from his audience. The older forms, plays and concerts, which fed the media found that they were nurturing cuckoos which were turning them out of the nest. The state and municipalities had to choose between allowing the theatre to die outside London or accepting much greater responsibility for its survival. As is customary in Britain, a compromise was reached. It was decided to keep the arts half alive.

CHAPTER SIX

1964–74. Decade of Decision

A view from the Back Benches

More artists and theatre people took part in the 1964 General Election Campaign in Putney than has ever been the case anywhere in this country before or since. Clive Dunn, a gifted artist as well as the funniest young-old man, drew a flattering portrait of me which we used for our posters instead of the traditional photograph. John Chaloner, a publisher, took innumerable newsworthy photographs, Edna O'Brien, the novelist, took the chair at an election meeting and gave a big party when we won, Harry Corbett took part, complete with the Steptoe horse and dray, and we had an enormous fund-raising function at which Putney people were almost outnumbered by stars of stage, screen and radio, as they used to be called.

On the election day, another tremendous surge came over from all parts of London and we had the Z-Cars team knocking up reluctant voters.

MP for Putney

The outcome was that, to my surprise and delight, we won Putney, hitherto a solid Tory constituency even in 1945, for the first time ever and on an uncompromisingly socialist platform. We have held it at every election since.

In my maiden speech, I said, among other things:[1]

> I have been talking about housing and I turn to another housing problem, that of housing the arts, and make reference in particular to the theatre.
>
> In this sphere, too, we find that private enterprise is making no serious contribution. The theatre of the future will be publicly

[1] *Hansard* 10.11.64. Cols. 914/5.

owned. publicly built by public authorities from public funds or it will not be built at all. I am very sorry to find that there was no mention of the arts in the Gracious Speech. I only hope that the words:

'other measures will be laid before you'

will be allowed to embrace a number of urgent steps to be taken in this field. For example, for reasons which will not stand a moment's examination, the late Government excluded theatres from the protection of the Offices, Shops and Railway Premises Act, in spite of the recommendation of the Gowers Committee that they should be included. On another occasion I should like to dilate on the extraordinary consequences of this decision. The auditorium and the manager's office are now under regulation and supervision, but the backstage area, where most of the work is done, is not. This could and should be put right quickly.

There is another anomaly which urgently needs correction. In 1950 the Use Classes Order was tidied up and the then existing classification of theatres, cinemas and music halls was lumped together into a rag-bag of uses called 'Places of Assembly', which included Turkish baths and places where indoor games are played. No serious damage was done by this change for many years, but then came bingo. A number of owners of cinemas and theatres found themselves able to change the use of their buildings within the class without asking anyone for permission, and the results have been quite catastrophic. They need not have been.

The Order could have been changed back to its original form without difficulty, but it took years to convince the over-esteemed Minister who was in charge of these matters at the time, and when, after long argument, he was finally convinced, he said:

'We would not be justified in amending the Order solely for the purpose you have in mind. If, however, it later becomes necessary to amend the Order for other purposes, I will see that your case for an amendment in relation to theatres is considered afresh.'

Meanwhile, all over the country theatre after theatre and cinema after cinema was pulled down or went over to bingo. Whether or not in any particular case the change was or was not justified was never examined because no change of use was theoretically involved. On another occasion I should like to take the House – if that is permissible – through the scarcely credible correspondence with the ex-Minister, but I must not be controversial on this occasion, and in any event I must come to a close.

What are the ends that we seek? Do we want scientific progress,

material security and comfort for their own sakes? Let us admit it
– yes, we do. But over and above these needs stands the need of the
individual to fulfil and to be fulfilled, to experience, to contribute,
to acquire abilities and tastes, to exercise his skill and powers of
appreciation. Money spent to this end is the best public expenditure that there is. I hope that there will be more of it and I
welcome the appointments which have been made in this field
and in particular that of the hon. Member for Cannock (Miss
Lee), whose late husband, Aneurin Bevan, with that foresight
which in some quarters is only now beginning to be understood
and appreciated, was largely instrumental in providing the 6d.
rate which local authorities can use to develop artistic and
cultural activities. It is now for us to see that these powers are
augmented and used so that the lives of our people may be
enriched.

Not being used to the customs of the House, I was startled by
the flattering terms in which this speech was received. I soon
caught on.

Jennie Lee's White Paper

Jennie Lee had been made first Minister for the Arts in the new
government under Harold Wilson's premiership, but there was
some confusion about her role. Her office was first located in the
Ministry of Public Buildings and Works and her first answer to
Parliamentary Questions related to the Palace of Westminster. In
her next one she revealed that her job had not been defined and
she was to carry out an examination of what her functions should
be. Meanwhile, responsibility for Government financial support
for the arts would remain with the Treasury.

However, the next time she was up for questioning Miss Lee
described the previous Government's expenditure on the arts as
trivial' and early in 1965 the famous White Paper 'A Policy for
the Arts – the First Steps'[2] was published and Miss Lee was
transferred to the Department of Education and Science. In
great confidence Jennie had shown me the White Paper in draft
and in association with Ted Willis[3], I had put forward a number
of suggestions, some of which were adopted.

Although the White Paper was Jennie Lee's, it was issued to

[2] *Cmnd.* 2601. HMSO.
[3] Lord Willis, the writer

Parliament under the name of the Prime Minister, for two reasons. First, it gave the document greater standing, and second, it went far beyond the range of Miss Lee's authority and touched on such matters as education, films, television, historic houses and ancient monuments, all of which were the responsibility of other Ministers. Here was a chance, alas missed, to locate responsibility for all these matters in the hands of a single Minister of Cabinet rank.

The White Paper is a revolutionary document; the second sentence a resounding declaration which should be pinned to the wall of anyone responsible for the disbursement of public monies to the arts and artists:

> 'No one would wish State patronage to dictate taste or in any way restrict the liberty of even the most unorthodox and experimental of artists.'

The paper ranged widely and declared war on the culture gap.

> 'No democratic government would seek to impose controls on all the things that contribute to our environment and affect our senses. But abuses can be spotted and tackled, high standards encouraged, and opportunities given for wider enjoyment. It is partly a question of bridging the gap between what have come to be called the 'higher' forms of entertainment and the traditional sources – the brass band, the amateur concert party, the entertainer, the music hall and pop group – and to challenge the fact that a gap exists. In the world of jazz the process has already happened; highbrow and lowbrow have met.
>
> Radio and television have much to contribute to the encouragement of artistic activity and appreciation. If little is said about them in this White Paper it is largely because in this field the Government have no direct responsibility. These media are managed by public corporations whose relationship with the Government is defined by statute. How the corporations use broadcasting time and deploy their resources is for them to decide.
>
> But it is clear that radio and television have enormous opportunities in the sphere of the arts, and their responsibilities to the nation are correspondingly great. Radio has done much for drama, music and poetry. The use of television for similar purposes is still at a relatively early stage, but it is to be hoped that the introduction of additional channels for television will

encourage further experiment and development. If in time a
greater number of local stations is set up, these will have an
important part to play in the encouragement of local artistic
activity and the enrichment and diversification of regional
cultures.'

Jennie Lee's testament was the most farseeing and significant
statement of Government policy on the arts ever issued in this
country. I am not aware that it has been surpassed elsewhere. It
called for a more 'coherent, generous and imaginative' approach
to the arts. There has been some generosity, perhaps a little
imagination, but even now, thirteen years later, there is still
nothing coherent about the relationship of Government to the
arts.

It has to be said that while Jennie Lee rose to her opportunity
magnificently, Harold Wilson failed in 1964 as he did ten years
later, to give the Minister he had appointed the powers needed to
break through establishment inertia to the new world which was
attainable given full Prime Ministerial and Cabinet authority. A
Minister has to administer what exists as well as to strive to
change it. Both Jennie Lee and I received good support in the
first of these tasks but in the second the backing fell far short of
what was needed and, in my own case, eventually vanished
altogether.

All the same, a number of valuable immediate decisions were
announced in the White Paper: to put the new Minister in the
Department of Education and Science; to increase the Arts
Council's grant substantially; to press on with the regional arts
associations; to find additional funds for the London orchestras;
to increase the purchase grants for the national museums and
galleries and to aid individual artists and writers. On Page 18:

'By far the most valuable help that can be given to the living artist
is to provide him with a larger and more appreciative public.
Everything possible must be done to enlarge the area of
appreciation of the arts while at the same time guarding against
any lowering of standards.'

This recognition was not followed by specific proposals and I
believe it to be true that all Ministers and Government agencies
have been more successful in generating the practice of the arts

and crafts than they have in widening and deepening the understanding, purchase, borrowing and visiting among the public as a whole. This task is not only for Government; it is also necessary for artists to reject cultural apartheid.

A reference to the monopoly of film distribution in the White Paper was followed by nothing more than a feeble report from the Monopolies Commission and no important changes. The educational possibilities of television were explored and the Open University, in the development of which Jennie Lee was to play a key role, was forecast. In 1965 everyone believed that the age of leisure was about to break out. To-day we have it but it is unequally distributed and is called by the old-fashioned name of unemployment.

The White Paper called upon local authorities to spend money on the arts but ten years later a Labour Government was doing its best to restrict public expenditure on everything including the arts, while the Tories had repeated their old trick of cutting the Arts Council's grant.

Nevertheless, in 1965, the White Paper's rousing optimism inspired many to open their minds to new possibilities. To quote again:

> 'Today a searching reappraisal of the whole situation in relation to cultural standards and opportunities is in progress. More and more people begin to appreciate that the exclusion of so many for so long from the best of our cultural heritage can become as damaging to the privileged minority as to the under-privileged majority. We walk the same street, breathe the same air, are exposed to the same sights and sounds.
>
> Nor can we ignore the growing revolt, especially among the young, against the drabness, uniformity and joylessness of much of the social furniture we have inherited from the industrial revolution. This can be directed, if we so wish, into making Britain a gayer and more cultivated country.
>
> It is fitting that the present Government should seek to encourage all who are furthering these aims. The proposals outlined in this White Paper, though no more than the first steps in the direction of a fully comprehensive policy for the arts, demonstrate the Government's concern that immediate progress should be made.'

Only those first steps which Jennie Lee could take herself as

c

Minister for the Arts were essayed and it would be easy to be
cynical about the Government's failure even to attempt to walk
the higher ground it surveyed. However, it would also be churlish
to underestimate the magnitude of the achievement so far and
easy to fail to appreciate to the full the fundamentally better
climate within which the discussion now takes place.

On 27th April 1965, Arthur Blenkinsop, the Labour member
for South Shields, having been successful in the ballot, initiated a
debate on the White Paper, giving broad and general support.
The fact that the Government itself had not provided time for the
debate was significant. It is, perhaps, unfair to regard Nicholas
Ridley as representing Conservative opinion on the arts, but
there was no complaint from his fellow Tories when he advocated
that the Arts Council should be brought under Parliamentary
control, nor when he went on to propose an increase in seat prices
and a reduction of subsidy for the Royal Opera House and for the
supported theatre generally.

In the debate I said I doubted whether any weekly-wage
earner ever entered the Arts Council's building except for the
purpose of cleaning it and went on to put forward suggestions for
making the Council more democratic. I proposed that Jennie
Lee be given overall responsibility including that for television
and films and went on to praise the White Paper, saying:

> 'It says that the State exists so that people may collectively
> expand their spirits.'[4]

Replying to the debate, Jennie Lee immediately attacked the
Tories for their parsimony over the previous thirteen years and
went on to quote from her White Paper as follows:

> 'In any civilised community the arts and associated amenities,
> serious or comic, light or demanding, must occupy a central
> place. Their enjoyment should not be regarded as something
> remote from everyday life. The promotion and appreciation of
> high standards in architecture, in industrial design, in town
> planning and the preservation of the beauty of the countryside are
> all part of it. Beginning in the schools and reaching out into every
> corner of the nation's life, in city and village, at home, at work at

---

[4] *Hansard*, 27.4.65. Col. 268.

play, there is an immense amount that could be done to improve the quality of contemporary life.'[5]

And she concluded:

'There is a great longing for us to be more of a community. Before we arrogantly say that any group of our citizens are not capable of appreciating the best in the arts, let us make absolutely certain that we have put the best within their reach.[6]

It was not until February 1966 that the first vote for the arts was announced for which the new Minister was responsible. A jump in the total vote to over £6 millions was received with great enthusiasm and from then on the rate of increase each year was of the order of a million pounds or more against the £100,000 of earlier years.

The importance of Jennie Lee was not, however, only or even mainly, a matter of money. The arts need a Government spokesman with authority and charisma. They were fortunate in their first Minister.

The Protection of Performers

In my early days in Parliament I was busy trying to get more adequate control over the employment of children in entertainment. I had been horrified by the gross exploitation of children on the stage – for example, the use of girls of twelve as the second line of the chorus in pantomime. They had been paid a few shillings a week and the conditions of employment were frightful.

The employment of children under 12 was illegal on the stage but in films and television the law was not enforced, with the result that even babies were employed under hot lights to sell all kinds of merchandise. I had originally been concerned in my Equity capacity because of the undercutting of actors which the practice encouraged, but I became increasingly anxious about the children themselves, for they had no one to look after them, their parents being often the most eager of exploiters.

I raised the matter in the House on 23rd July 1965[7] and received a promise that regulations would be introduced to bring matters under control. I did not want this, for I suspected that the regulations would have the effect of legalising what was then

[5] *Hansard*, 27.4.65. Col. 294.
[6] Ibid.
[7] *Hansard*, 23.7.65. Col. 223 et seq.

illegal. This proved to be the case and in spite of all I could do, the net result of my efforts was to give statutory blessing to the employment of children of school age and below school age which is legal in no other developed country.

Sadly, I gave up a hopeless struggle against ill-informed public sentiment. Parliament will pass without protest a bill to provide non-existent protection against rare pornographers, but it will not protect the young from earning when they should be learning.

I was returned with an increased majority at the 1966 General Election. Lucky in the ballot, I chose to introduce a bill to regulate employment agencies. In this I was originally moved by the gross exploitation of performers by some entertainment agents who were also employers and used their agency licenses as a means of deducting 10% from the wages of actors they engaged. Anyone who refused did not get the job.

It was suggested to me that I should widen the bill to regulate the conduct of *all* private employment agents so as to enable the Government to ratify the Convention of the International Labour Organisation on the subject. In return, the Government would support my bill. Unwisely, I agreed. Unwisely, for the outcome was that the Bill incurred the hostility not merely of the entertainment agents, but of the powerful Employment Agents Association who included not only the office employment people but the head-hunters whose expertise consisted of persuading top people to move from one job to another and taking vast and undisclosed fees in the process. Often they would take money for shifting leading scientists and technologists to America and more money to bring them back again after a disillusioning year or so. All this is conducted in great secrecy and they rightly saw my bill as threatening that secrecy. Their lobby gained the support of such formidable debaters as Michael Heseltine and Nicholas Ridley,[8] and with some other Tory help these two delayed the Committee stage until the bill needed Government time to complete its passage through the House. That support and time had been promised, yet when I went to see Ray Gunter, the Minister of Labour who was responsible, I found him curiously evasive.

[8] Conservative Members of Parliament.

In despair I eventually went to see Dick Crossman who was Leader of the House at this time.

'Your Bill is dead,' he said.

'But why?' I asked. 'It received Government support on Second Reading, from the Minister himself.'[9]

'Of course, but he's against you privately. Not so much against your bill but against you personally. He will do nothing to help you.'

'Why not?'

'He doesn't think you should be here at all. Remember you took your Party banner on the Aldermaston March and as a result his Organisation sub-committee recommended the National Executive not to endorse your canditure? Remember that the recommendation was lost because, for once, Jim voted Left rather than Right? Well, then, now Gunter has a chance to do you an injury and he has done it. Your Bill is dead.'

And it was. Whether all this was true or partly Dick's romanticism, I never found out for it seemed pointless to go up to the ghastly Gunter and ask him whether he killed my Bill out of personal political spite or out of right-wing hostility. The trouble with left-wingers is that we are not good haters. We do not operate in that way and are always taken by surprise when the right translate political enmity into personal vendettas.

In 1972 Kenneth Lewis, the Tory Member for Rutland, was lucky in the ballot and introduced an Employment Agencies Bill. It left to regulations, to be issued subsequently, many things I had included in my earlier failed Bill but Lewis and I, who were poles apart on most issues, worked closely together on this Bill and he was generous in his acknowledgement. The measure eventually mitigated many of the evils I sought to tackle when in my early Parliamentary inexperience I agreed to bite off much more than any backbencher could chew without full Government support.

Films

In the autumn of 1966 the Government introduced a Bill to extend the life of the existing film legislation. The Monopolies Commission had already examined the distribution and exhibition side of the industry and had reported in favour of

[9] *Hansard*, 24.6.1966. Col. 1155.

leaving ill alone, but the report had not been published and this legislation was simply to give the Government time to come up with some fresh proposals.

This they did more than three years later when Gwyneth Dunwoody who was then at the Board of Trade introduced a bill which, while it did nothing revolutionary or permanent, at least prolonged the life of the industry by maintaining Government support.

In the Second Reading debate, I spoke at excessive length but unmemorably. Mrs. Dunwoody knew her stuff having worked for the Film Producers Association and the Bill did the essential things of funding the National Film Finance Corporation and providing a basis for the National Film School to come into being. At that time the production industry was doing well and Gwyneth Dunwoody's confident forecasts did not seem outlandish. The Bill prolonged the framework of Government support for the industry for a decade; the British quota was retained, as was the levy on exhibitors receipts and there was provision for support for the British Film Institute.

Keith Joseph said the Tories would not oppose the Second Reading but he made some ominous remarks about their intentions when they returned to office which were fully realised when they later reduced Government support and turned the industry into a lame duck.

Theatre Censorship

In 1966 a Joint Committee of both Houses of Parliament was set up to consider the position of theatre censorship. The Arts Council appointed a special committee to make recommendations to the Joint Parliamentary Committee. On it were representatives of its own Drama Panel, of the commercial managers (Society of West End Theatre Managers, Theatrical Managers Association, Theatres National Committee) of the League of Dramatists and of the supported companies, the National and Royal Shakespeare Theatres, the English Stage Company and the Council of Repertory Theatres, as well as some other distinguished individuals. This Committee recommended the abolition of the Lord Chamberlain's pre-censorship, the commercial managers *alone* dissenting. The following quotation

is from the Arts Council's Report which is printed as one of the
appendices to the Joint Parliamentary Committees' Report.[10]

> The attitude of theatre managers to pre-censorship is sharply
> divided. "Commercial" managers would retain it; the others
> would abolish it. The only dissentients on the Committee of
> Enquiry which recommend abolition were the two representing
> commercial managements, though they had some differences
> with each other. Their loyalty to the Lord Chamberlain,
> however, is understandable. For whereas the present system
> deprives dramatists of many rights that all other citizens enjoy, it
> endows managers on the other hand with the unique privilege of
> effective immunity from prosecution by the law; a privilege which
> is in the gift of the Lord Chamberlain. It is no more than human
> that managers should cling tenaciously to such a privilege.'

Mr. Emile Littler was one of the representatives of the
commercial theatre on this Committee, and when he came before
the Joint Parliamentary Committee to give evidence, as a
member of that Committee, I pressed him on the point.[11]

> *Jenkins:* 'How do you explain the situation that it is the managers
> who are apparently most at risk who seem to want to take the risk
> and the managers who, whatever happened, would not expose
> themselves to the risk who seem to want to keep the censorship
> going? 'Is it that you are in fact not wishing to establish a
> censorship for yourselves but a censorship for somebody else?'
> *Littler:* 'It is only the subsidised theatres really that can afford to
> put on dirty plays.'
> *Jenkins:* 'Are you suggesting they cost more?'
> *Littler:* 'No, they can take the risk . . .'
> *Jenkins:* '. . . Are you saying that you wish to protect the taxpayer
> because, if these chaps are allowed to take the risks, the taxpayer
> will have to stand the consequences . . .?'

Mr. Littler was accompanied by another commercial
manager, on this occasion, Mr. Peter Saunders, who intervened
at this point.

> *Saunders:* 'I will not use the word "dirty" but the adventurous
> plays are put on by the aided theatres, the subsidised theatres,
> because commercially, they are a much greater risk . . .'

[10] HC 503 19.6.67 HMSO.
[11] Ibid.

In advocating that he should no longer exercise the function of stage censor, the Lord Chamberlain, then Lord Cobbold, pointed to the absurdity of the situation in that the stage should be subject to a pre-censorship not imposed on films, on broadcasting or on television.

The Joint Committee unanimously recommended in favour of the abolition of the role of the Lord Chamberlain and this, as its membership was as follows, was more than a little surprising.

LORDS	*COMMONS*
Earl of Scarborough (Cons)	Mr. Andrew Faulds (Lab)
Earl of Kilmuir (Cons)	Mr. Michael Foot (Lab)
Viscount Norwich (Lib)	Mr. Emlyn Hooson (Lib)
Lord Tweedsmuir (Cons)	Mr. Hugh Jenkins (Lab)
Baroness Gaitskell (Lab)	Sir David Renton (Cons)
Lord Lloyd of Hampstead (Lab)	Mr. G. Strauss (Lab)
Lord Annan (Ind)	Mr. William Wilson (Lab)
Lord Goodman (Cross-bench)	Mr. St. John-Stevas (Cons)

What is more, the Committee reported in 1967 and the following year the Chairman, George Strauss, successfully moved in the House of Commons a Bill to give effect to the recommendations.

The Bill received a Second Reading without division, and in Committee only one amendment was put to the vote. This was an attempt by Mr. St. John Stevas to forbid representation of any living member of the Royal Family. He was supported only by Mr. Dodds-Parker and the Bill became law without amendment.

It has been pointed out since then that the 'freedom' which the stage has grasped so far has been that of the presentation of sex and nudity and the utterance of words not in such common use as some playwrights would have us believe. The new power to criticise Governments, Heads of State, political systems and persons has been lightly used and until it is effectively wielded our dramatic range must be regarded as limited by self-denial for which producers, dramatists and audiences must share the blame.

The 1968 Theatres Act brought the stage into line with literature in that, in effect, the offence of 'obscenity' may be charged against a production, once mounted and presented. However, this may only be done with the consent of the Attorney

[11] Ibid.

General, so to that extent – and it is a considerable one – the theatre is less vulnerable now than the cinema.

It is worth re-emphasising that but for the fact that no prosecution can now take place without the *fiat* of the Attorney General, which has never yet been granted, this Act, instead of freeing the theatre from unreasonable restraint, would have exposed it to casual prosecution by private individuals of a restrictive turn of mind.

Theatre on Sunday

A Private Member's Bill to legalise Sunday Theatre opening was introduced on Friday, 8th December 1967 by Will Hamling, the late and lamented Member for Woolwich West. I was a teller for the Ayes, with John Parker, the Labour Member for Dagenham, and the Bill secured a Second Reading by 29 to 18. This was most remarkable for, under quorum rules, the opposition could easily have terminated the proceedings prior to the vote by calling for a count and staying out of the Chamber. As less than 40 would have been present the debate would have been adjourned. Alternatively they could have talked the Bill out by continuing to speak at 4 p.m. thereby forcing the supporters of the Bill to seek a closure, which needs a hundred members.

When the Bill returned to the Chamber on the next private Members Bill day (which has to be a Friday) 3rd May 1968, after its Committee stage, this is precisely what they did. This time there were 72 supporters of the Bill and 28 opponents, but closure of the debate was not granted. It was deferred until 24th May and, going to the bottom of the list of Private Members Bill, was disposed of by the simple process of a few members shouting 'Object' at 4 p.m.

It is very difficult for a backbencher to change the law in this country if he is not backed by more than 100 hardcore supporters prepared to place the measure above the strong conflict of spending Friday in their constituencies or at home. The rules are slanted against change and are designed so that a few opponents can prevent it. Things generally stay as they are unless a substantial number of members are determined to change them.

I have been greatly frustrated in my Parliamentary life by this fact. I am a changer and many things which should have been done quickly have been done too late or not at all because I have been unable to rally enough supporters to my causes, which have often not been the day-to-day bread-and-butter issues that occupy the front pages of the papers. We did not get Sunday opening of theatres because people did not care much about it one way or the other; we did not get Public Lending Right for authors later for the same reason and because there were a handful of determined opponents.

And so in each case, as is the intention of Parliamentary tradition, no change was made. It was maddening and it appeared to be an abuse of Parliament, but it was not. Frustration of change by the exploitation of procedure is the name of the game. There are worse games, but it is time to change the rules.

In the case of Sunday Opening I exploited the procedures of the House myself and got it on to the statute book by the following stratagem: early in 1972 Jennie Lee, by then a peer, moved a Sunday Theatre Opening Bill through all its stages in the House of Lords. It came over to the Commons and in the usual way was committed to a Standing Committee. On Friday 21st April, I moved a Motion discharging the Bill from the committee and committing it to the Whole House. So that it should not be noticed, I put the Motion down the day before.

When the Speaker put my motion, there was no objection. The Speaker then said: 'Committee, what day?' I said, 'Now Sir.'

After a slight demurral the Speaker put the Question, 'That this House will immediately resolve itself into the Committee.' Again, there was no objection. And so the House went into Committee, the Mace was taken down and the Speaker replaced by the Chairman of Ways and Means. There were, of course, no amendments to consider. So straightaway, the Chairman reported this to the Speaker, the Sergeant-at-Arms marched up again, back went the Mace, up came the Speaker. I reported that the Committee had considered the Bill and had made no amendments and moved Third Reading. This was agreed without debate and the bill was passed for Royal Assent and became law, all in about two minutes and with no discussion.

There was, of course, some subsequent complaint about this, but those who lack strength must be quick, and the opponents of change received a lesson that the price of stagnation is eternal · vigilance.

In the outcome, the change in the law had little immediate effect, as the trade unions and managerial associations were unable to reach agreement and what had been forbidden by law still did not take place because actors valued their Sundays off at a price the Managers were usually not prepared to pay.

Radio and Television

On the adjournment of the House at 5 a.m. on 22nd June 1966 I raised the subject of pirate radio.[12]

At that time the Government were doing nothing to prevent the proliferation of pirate stations which had met the pop music demand the BBC had failed to recognise. I said that there should be a new radio network, publicly owned, publicly capitalised but financed by advertising. Replying, Tony Benn, who was Postmaster-General at the time, made reassuring noises. The Government intended to act; how and when he did not say, but he was full of hope.

I was rather impatient in those days, and as nothing transpired, on 3rd August I introduced under the ten-minute rule procedure a bill:[13]

> 'To enable the Postmaster-General to establish a Television and Radio Authority for the purpose of running the fourth Television Channel, setting up a National Popular Radio Programme and acting as parent station to local radio stations and to abolish pirate radio whether operating within or without territorial waters.'

Pirate radio had been tolerated by the Tories, some of whom were financially interested in it. I argued that advertising need not control the output, urging that what counted was not the source of the revenue but who owned the network.

The Government did, in fact, move somewhat in the direction advocated in my 'Broadcasting Enabling' Bill and I withdrew it in favour of their 'Marine etc. Broadcasting Offences Bill', plus some assurances about the Government's intentions which were contained in a White Paper published in December, 1966.

[12] *Hansard* 22.6.66 Col. 858 et seq.
[13] *Hansard* 3.8.66 Col. 473.

In June 1967[14] I advocated that the Levy which the Government deducts from the vast profits of the programme companies should be applied *after* and not *before* programme expenditure, that is to say from *net* rather than from *gross* profits. Some years later this procedure was adopted with highly beneficial results on the quality of ITV programmes. A decade later, the Annan Committee made recommendations broadly in line with the positive part of my Broadcasting Enabling Bill of 1966.

Local Authorities and the Theatre

At my suggestion in 1964, the Theatres Advisory Council approached the Association of Municipal Corporations and a big joint conference on Civic Theatres was held at County Hall, London in February 1965. Jennie Lee agreed to open it and 'The Stage' ran a special supplement.[15] I explained that originally the TAC had been formed to save old theatres but was now advising local authorities on building new ones. I suggested that the theatrical pound of the future should be ten shillings from the box office, five shillings from the Treasury and five shillings from the local authority. Then Alderman Waugh of Coventry spoke proudly of the Belgrade Theatre in that city, Alderman Goldstone of Manchester told of their plans, Councillor Mrs. Bray of Leeds complained that no special reference had been made to them, Councillor Dyke of Dunstable spoke of their problems as did Councillor Tierney of Scunthorpe and, before the day was over, the ball of municipal pride and emulation had started to move. We knew that the theatre outside London would survive.

In all this, the work of my Joint-Secretary, Bill Kendall, was invaluable for he possessed the good civil servant's quality of making sure that what was started went on rolling. Together we secured the willing agreement of the Association of Municipal Corporations to the establishment of a joint body. I knew it would have to have a complicated name and, determined that it should at least be pronounceable, secured eventual agreement on SACLAT – the Standing Advisory Committee on Local

[14] *Hansard*, 28.6.67. Col. 461.
[15] *Civic Theatres*, Theatres Advisory Council and *The Stage*, 1965.

Authorities and the Theatre. The very existence of this body gave standing to the TAC and each year a score or more proposals for new municipal theatres or for the reconstruction of older ones was processed by the TAC and/or its affiliate, the Association of British Theatre Technicians.

Conferences were held outside London, addressed for example by John Neville, Stephen Arlen and Councillor Harper of Sunderland and the TAC helped to secure the cushioning of the supported theatre against the impact of Selective Employment Tax – and what a nice tax it was compared with VAT. I became Chairman of SACLAT in 1967 and succeeded Lord Faringdon as Chairman of the TAC in 1970. I resigned when I became Minister in 1974 and was followed by Mrs Renée Short, MP.

Theatre Surveyed

It was in the years 1967 to 1970 that the earlier unpublished Arts Council Reports on the theatre were used as the basis for a full scale examination under the chairmanship of Sir William Emrys Williams who lost his beautifully written report and had to write it all over again.[16] This was the membership of the Committee: Sir William Emrys Williams, Hugh Beaumont, Lord Bernstein, Colin Chandler, Sir John Clements, Patrick Donnell, Michael Elliott, Richard Findlater, Robin Fox, Alfred Francis, Frank Hauser, Hugh Jenkins, J. W. Lambert, Oscar Lewenstein, John Mortimer, Sir Harmar Nicholls, Sir Max Rayne, Derek Salberg, Cecil L. Smith, Wendy Toye, Kenneth Tynan, Hugh Willatt (until August 1968).

As is usually the case, by the time the report was published in 1970, the situation had changed. One of the main recommendations, the establishment of a Theatre Investment Fund, took another six years to bring to fruition and by then the commercial theatre in London was not suffering so acutely from the dire shortage of private cash which had been the cause of the original initiative to establish a state-supported fund to invest in the unsubsidised theatre. In this I had my way on one important issue. Throughout I was insistent that the Fund should be entirely separate from the Arts Council's other funds; that though the supported theatre and the commercial theatre should co-

[16] *The Theatre Today in England and Wales*, Arts Council. 1970.

operate with each other and complement each other, they should not mix. I was boringly repetitive with my argument that public money must never get into private hands, and in the end I won. The relationships between the commercial theatre and the supported theatre today are as they should be. Public money is quite separate from all other investment. If this principle had been adopted as a general practice in industry in the last decade, billions of public money which has been thrown uselessly away would have been saved.

At my suggestion Emrys Williams had asked Peter Lowman, who worked for the Labour Research Department, to carry out a survey of the ownership and control of theatres, producing managements and agencies, taking into consideration links with television and the cinema. Some years earlier, in 1953, 'Theatre Ownership in Britain' had been published by the Federation of Theatre Unions[17] and had revealed the existence of 'The Group', a classic horizontal semi-secret monopoly in theatre ownership and production, embracing Howard and Wyndham, Moss Empires, Associated Theatre Properties and Stoll and presided over by the least talkative of the Littlers, the appropriately named Prince. The Lowman Report showed that this had been replaced by a form of vertical integration and was referred to in the Emrys Williams Report in a Chapter called 'Operation Octopus: Monopoly in the Theatre.' Since the earlier report, the Grades had arrived on the scene and Lew had quickly perceived that while the gravy in the theatre was getting thin and scarce, in television it was rich and plentiful. So Prince had been moved over and Lew's Associated Television Corporation acquired Stoll, Moss and Associated Theatre Properties, while Lew's brother, Bernard Delfont, was on the way to controlling EMI and had a large finger in many another entertainment pie. The Emrys Williams Report thought that there might be a case for setting up a Theatre Ownership Board under Government aegis to acquire theatres. Nothing was done at that time, but in 1973

[17] Written anonymously by Malcolm Dunbar who subsequently became, at the suggestion of Gordon Sandison, a member of the staff of Equity. He had been the youngest Captain in the International Brigade and was an intellectual Communist with a superb mind and a delightful sense of humour. Some time later he left his clothes on the beach and swam out to sea off the South Coast. His body was found not long after.

the Arts Council published a further report by Sir James Richards.[18] This was mainly concerned with West End Theatres and it will be interesting to see whether the Theatres Trust which was set up in 1977 with Lord Goodman as Chairman and myself as Vice-Chairman can ensure that London theatres remain and continue to fill the vital place they hold in the British mosaic.

Back in 1970 the Williams Report was worried about this vertical monopoly or integration both in its links between the various media and between producing managers and theatrical agents, but there were no flies on Lew Grade and, without waiting for legislation, he took action to rid himself of any charge of controlling the whole scene. Nevertheless, the Report was uneasy about the extensive interlocking of the entertainment and mass communications industries:

> 'The effects of one on the other was not examined, but might merit further consideration. For instance, one-fifth of ATV is owned by the International Publishing Corporation (IPC) and IPC own almost 30 per cent of the voting shares of ATV. Two IPC directors sit on the Board of ATV. IPC own the Daily Mirror, Sunday Mirror, People and Reveille, all mass circulation newspapers with considerable influence on public opinion and reviewing plays considerably influences the audience likely to attend those plays. Similarly, ATV and Thames Television (part-owned by EMI) can financially influence plays by televising them in whole or in part. In the broader entertainment field, ATV's control of the Pye Records and recent acquisition of the Beatles' company, Northern Songs, raises questions of ATV's promotion of songs and records on its TV channels. Also IPC controls influential journals in these fields such as New Musical Express, Melody Maker and Disc and Music Echo.
>
> We found the Octopus exercise both interesting and revealing. Whilst no monopoly in the theatre has been found, there are large concentrations of power in the hands of some companies and individuals which could affect the types of theatrical production and the availability of employment for actors. Because of this, as we have stated earlier in this chapter, there is still a need to keep a vigilant watch on a situation which could be radically altered, in such circumstances, for example, as one or two further mergers

---

[18] *Planning and Redevelopment in London's Entertainment Area with Special Reference to the Theatre*, Arts Council, 1973.

among the West End theatres or activities allied to the theatre. It does not at present seem likely that such a situation will develop but so long as it remains a posibility as it does – it would become a matter of public concern and to that extent a case for consideration by the Board of Trade.'[19]

I suggested that the recommendation for further consideration should be referred to the Theatres Advisory Council and got Peter Lowman to submit an outline of possible further investigation. He did so, but when I attempted to get the TAC to pursue the matter, the managerial representatives stuck their toes in. I could see that if I pushed the TAC into sponsoring a survey which would reveal the truth about these matters, I could only do so at the cost of breaking up the Association, for the Managers would have walked out. So I abandoned it.

I referred the project to the Federation of Theatre Unions, but little more was heard and it may be that one of the consequences of the growth of the supported theatre has been to reduce some of the dangers which loomed large only a few years ago. Nevertheless, in the area of the arts, of entertainment and of communications any threat of monopoly, private or public, must be resisted.

Grants for the Arts—A Committee Reports

My good friend Mrs. Renée Short, the energetic Labour Member for Wolverhampton South-East, has a talented and charming daughter who after completing her training was unable to obtain work as an actress. This, unhappily, is quite customary, but Mrs. Short was also Chairman of the Estimates Committee and she decided to look into the causes of such an undesirable state of affairs. The Arts Council had heard of Renée Short's Committee with great alarm and had been prepared for hostility and philistinism. They had therefore been delighted to be received with understanding and courtesy, and when the Report came out, were immensely relieved to be given a fairly clean bill of health.

[19] Ibid. p. 66.

In his introduction to the Arts Council's Report for 1968/69
Lord Goodman was amusing about all this and it may be that in a
He said:

> 'The Report which ultimately emerged would certainly encour-
> ages us in complacency and self-satisfaction if there were the
> remotest possibility of our being exposed to such moral
> shortcomings. Happily immune from them, we can read it with
> an objective eye and note that, although few public institutions
> have emerged so triumphantly from microscopic scrutiny, there
> are nevertheless comments and criticisms which require our
> attention. It is better that we should give our energies to
> correcting even minor defects revealed than sit purring and
> licking our paws at being so agreeably stroked by the nice
> Committee.'

However, Goodman's comment skated over the primary
recommendation of the Estimates Committee that the Council
should carry out a study on how performing artists could be more
'fully and directly' represented on the Arts Council and its
Panels. In fact, this recommendation was badly worded. It
becomes clear from the context that what the committee was
advocating could have been more properly described as
nomination or election rather than representation. As it was, the
Arts Council was able to reply that a very large number of
performing artists of all kinds are appointed to the Council and its
panels and always have been.

At that time I was a member of the Arts Council, having been
appointed by Jennie Lee in 1968. The other members were: Lord
Goodman (Chairman), Sir William Coldstream, (Vice-
Chairman), the Hon. Michael Astor, Frederick R. Cox, Colonel
William Crawshay, Constance Cummings, Cedric Thorpe
Davie, Peter Hall, the Earl of Harewood, Frank Kermode, J.
W. Lambert, Joseph Lockwood, Colin H. Mackenzie, Dr Alun
Oldfield-Davies, John Pope-Hennessy, Sir Leslie Scarman,
George Singleton, Sir John Witt.

At a fully attended meeting of this Council on 30th July 1969, I
had raised the question of introducing a nominated element on to
the Arts Council. I suggested that the Regional Arts Associations
should be represented by people put on by them rather than

chosen by us. This proposal was not received enthusiastically and was buried by asking the Chief Regional Adviser to report on it, which he did in due course, in a negative sense.

The Renée Short Report was a most valuable and comprehensive one published under the title of 'Grants for the Arts'.[20] It was not debated in the House of Commons until February 1970. I made it clear in the debate that I was not a party to the Arts Council Bourbonism. The Council had made it plain that they were opposed in principle to democracy, but I commented that it was a very bad principle and continued:

> 'We are very afraid of democracy in this country. We have to put up with elections which bring a wide range of representatives to this House and it is conceivable that among us are some who might not have been appointed if they had not been elected. I am treading on rather delicate ground here, but we know that, despite this, the system of every member being directly responsible to his own electorate works better than any other and is a protection against the disadvantages of appointment. Yet despite that knowledge, we run away like the plague from elections in all our other activities. We even refuse to elect our own Government, preferring to chose one man and vest in him the absurd responsibility, the wholly undesirable power, of choosing the rest of the Government. The fact that occasionally he has a stroke of brilliance and chooses someone like my Right Hon. Friend the Minister is no justification for the general proposition.
>
> As far as the Arts Council is concerned – and here I speak as an appointee and recognise the occasional wisdom with which such choicés are made – I am persuaded that there is a halfway house and at least one-third of the Arts Council members and one-third of the membership of every panel should be appointed from among nominees proposed by organisations concerned with the work of the Council and its panels.
>
> Every regional association should be entitled to a place on the Arts Council. By this means the availability, the knowledge and the responsibility which has made the Arts Council such a success – and it is a great success and is admired throughout the world – would be preserved. The introduction of a semi-representative or nominated element would remove the danger of the Council

[20] *Cmnd.* 4023. 1969.

becoming ingrowing or getting clique-ish, which is the environmental disease of all appointed bodies. It would also reduce the criticism of and complaints against the Arts Council. Much of this criticism and those complaints arise not from the Council and the panels being very often wrong, although obviously sometimes they must be, but because they are right or thought to be right in a remote and superior sort of way; the impression perhaps is that they know it all and we poor devils out in the sticks have no say. That is the sort of feeling which one knows there is about the Arts Council going around the country.

They should have their say and the organisations should have their representatives on the Arts Council who would return to them and give an assurance that it had been said.'[21]

At the next meeting of the Arts Council I was congratulated on this speech by Sir John Witt, the Vice-Chairman of the Council. I wondered if this was in spite of the section I have just quoted. Elsewhere, I had shown that it is quite impossible in this country to adopt the American practice of private support for the arts by taxation relief. The cost is phenomenal and the benefit ratio about 1%. On this I had said:

'The great virtue of our system, a virtue pinpointed by the examination we are considering, is that public money spent on the arts is under control. We can examine it and know how much it is. We can criticise if we think that it is being spent wrongly. Under the American system no one knows what is happening, the individual charges up his expenditure against tax, and he makes the choice. From his point of view he may make the right choice, but the collective choices of all the individuals may not add up to the sum of the national priority. This is obviously wrong.

I do not wish to deprecate the work done in the United States as a result of the system there. It is a generous system, and it works for a very wealthy economy. Substantial and good artistic work is done as a result, but a close examination of the American scene persuades me that it should not be applied in our country.

But I believe that our source of revenue of patronage is too closely centralised.'[22]

In this for me unusually long speech, I proceeded to spell it out a little more:

[21] *Hansard*, 5.2.70. Col. 689/90.
[22] *Hansard*, 5.2.70. Col. 686.

'I hope that at some stage, although it will obviously not be in the immediate future, we shall have a regional form of Government and regional organisations will then be able to draw on their own local resources. This is the ideal, and we should move towards it as quickly as possible, breaking away from the gross over-centralisation of this country. With the possible exception of France, we are the most centralised country in Europe, and I would not exclude some Communist countries from that statement. We shall not be effectively decentralised until the sources of revenue begin to be local sources. It is not sufficient to redistribute national revenue. We also need to create local sources of revenue.'[23]

I went on to suggest that the arts were, in any event, going to need a great deal more money in future:

'It has been said tonight that the Arts Council's budget has increased to nearly £8 million, and that this is a very large sum. It is large compared with the money available when the Arts Council started after the war – I think that the figure 20 years ago was about £500,000 – but the budget today is not large compared with the calls which will be made upon the Arts Council in the coming years. Some American economists have done some work on this question and have shown that, for reasons I will not go into now, calls upon patronage suffer from a sort of geometrical progression and that once one sets one's feet on this escalator it is no use supposing that one will ever arrive at a plateau.

We have to face the fact without shirking that in future the community will have to carry a larger burden of expenditure upon the arts. In order to encourage the House to face this, I would point out that we are taking £30 million a year out of the entertainment world in ITV levy. Therefore, when we are thinking of the amount of money which ought to go back into the entertainment arts we should remember the £20 million to £30 million which is being taken away, rather than the £8 million, which is the figure my Right Hon. Friend arrived at and for which she deserves every credit. We must tell the Treasury: "You must raise your sights very much higher. To do the job properly, you must think in these sort of terms." '[24]

---

[23] *Hansard*, 5.2.70. Col. 686.
[24] Ibid. Col. 687.

They have since done so but they are still taking the money out of television.

The Arts Council does not cost anything. It is simply handed every year about the same amount of cash that the state has mulcted from commercial television in return for a franchise to advertise goods for sale in every home in the country. And why is the franchise so valuable? Because people look at the advertising. Why do they do so? Because they see actors performing and hear musicians playing in between the commercials. This money stems from performance and it is only right and proper that it shall be handed back so as to maintain the root stage performances without which the standard of electronically-reproduced performances would collapse.

Let not anyone imagine that the taxpayer is finding vast sums of money to sustain the arts in this country. He is doing no such thing. The entertainment business is sustaining itself, as it always has done, by making the pot-boilers pay for the good stuff, only nowadays it is being done in a rather complicated way and with the assistance of the state.

I went on in this speech to say something which must have sounded rather odd to my socialist comrades, but as it represents a basic element in my approach to the arts, and indeed to the whole world of ideas and communications, and as I maintained the position firmly as Minister, I will quote it:

'I think we must guard against the possibility of the Arts Council becoming too strong. I have no doubt that the future is with public patronage, that it will grow and that the commercial element in all the arts is likely to continue to decline. I do not greatly welcome this because I think that the role of the private patron is important in the community. I think that the private patron will long remain, and rightly so, the most important element collectively in the purchase of individual works of art. There is little doubt that generally speaking, the commercial element is in decline. It is very likely that industry itself will follow, perhaps a decade or so later. But just because the future is with public patronage, we must avoid the development of a single source as the sole fountain of public funds, and when regional government comes, and I think it will, regional arts associations will be financed from their own sources.

> Meanwhile, the balance between central and local sources is badly out of true. I do not think that the Arts Council is finding too much, but that local sources are not finding enough. I do not think that the Arts Council spends too much on London but that Manchester does not spend enough on Manchester, Glasgow not enough on Glasgow and so on. The balance needs to come up from local sources, not down from the Arts Council. We need to level the rate of arts spending up, and not spread it more thinly from a single national source.'[25]

I concluded with a tribute to Jennie Lee, 'the person all of us who have anything to do with public patronage know to be the source of our inspiration. Under her guidance this Government has the proud knowledge of having become a great patron of the arts. This is a fine achievement and nothing and no one can take that away from them.[26]

A few months later, however, the electorate took the Government away from them, and the Secretary of State's observations on the Renée' Short Report were made by a new Conservative incumbent, Mrs Margaret Thatcher, who said on the matter of the Arts Council and democracy, 'appointments are made on the basis of personal qualities and experience and it would be contrary to past and present policy to appoint members who were directly representative of particular interests.'[27] In sum, the Estimates Committee was told to get lost and it did, disappearing into a new body called the Expenditure Committee.

Under the Tories

Putney had never been won for Labour before 1964 and no one, certainly not I, believed that it could be held for socialism except in a generally favourable situation. I was therefore even more surprised than when first elected, to find myself a Member of Parliament when colleagues in supposedly safer seats were not and a Tory Government was in office. I had never expected to be an opposition member and I recall sharply even now the great

[25] Ibid. Col. 688.
[26] Ibid. Col. 693.
[27] Observations by the Secretary of State and the Arts Counci. *Cmnd.* 4023.

exhilaration of our unexpected victory draining away as with my
Putney comrades we sat around the television set after the count
at the Town Hall and realised that although we had won, the
Party as a whole had lost. In this General Election as in others
much credit was due to Ian McGarry who was my Election
Agent from the beginning, until to my great pleasure, he became
Assistant General Secretary of Equity in 1976.

Jennie Lee, however, was defeated and in Harold Wilson's
resignation Honours List, became Baroness Lee of Ashridge.
Harold Wilson appointed Andrew Faulds to be Shadow Minister
for the Arts in the Commons and in June 1971 he attacked the
proposal to levy museum charges. He was quite unnecessarily
aggressive, denying to the Minister, Lord Eccles, the title of
connoisseur (which I regard as offensive enough) and calling him
a 'commercial collector and part-time dealer' and using Eccles'
Private-Eye sobriquet of 'Smartie Boots'.

The reply came from Mrs Thatcher, the new Secretary of State
for Education, who made it clear that the Trustees of the
Museums and Galleries would be forced to impose charges by the
Government even if they did not wish to do so. It was a most
blatant example of doctrinaire politics and to their credit, one or
two Tories found themselves unable to support their Government
in the lobbies. They did not include Mr. St. John Stevas who
voted for museum charges, though three years later he
congratulated me on removing them.

In 1970 in the House I was soon engaged in fighting to
preserve the Equity union shop from the threat of the Conserative
Industrial Relations Bill. I put down amendments and supported
others at all stages, and as the Bill ground its way along it became
clear that what was happening was that the Conservatives were
gradually being educated in the realities of trade union practice.
They had drawn up the Bill upon the assumption that the Closed
Shop was a Bad Thing – now they were being forced to face the
consequences of its prohibition. I said:

> 'Equity has a vested interest in the maintenance of contractual
> obligations and is a strict disciplinarian trade union. Equity tells
> actors that they may not break contracts; it collects fines when
> they are imposed. It acts as the disciplinary organisation through-

out the entertainment industry. If we take away from this union the power to exercise 100 per cent union membership we will destroy discipline in an area where, if discipline is destroyed, the whole structure will collapse.'[28]

I was supported in debate by several Tories but none followed his voice with his vote and the Equity shop was held together with difficulty and with the help of the most responsible managers by a series of complicated arrangements until Labour returned and restored to trade unions their liberty to uphold the freedom of the many by restricting the license of the rogue individual.

In January 1971, as a member of the Arts Council, I took part in a discussion about a financial problem which has always bedevilled relationships between the Government and the Council and its clients. It arises from the fact that as prudent business organisations the major theatrical companies try to accumulate reserves and to carry them over to the following year. The Treasury, however, works on a year to year basis; it regards money handed out as a grant-in-aid and anything unspent should be returned. Money granted in respect of one year cannot be held over. If it is, it should be taken into consideration and the grant for the next year reduced accordingly.

The Arts Council stands poised uneasily between these two monetary philosophies. On the one hand, it tells its clients that they must not accumulate reserves; on the other, it tries to do so itself so as to have something in hand against unexpected demands. The Treasury dislikes this intensely. The Arts Council, however, in 1971 had been backed by the Estimates Committee and decided to carry over a reserve of about £350,000. The problem was to recur again and again, and when I became Minister three years later it landed slap on my plate.

The autonomy of the Arts Council in relation to Government is extended by the Council to its beneficiaries. The Government does not tell the Council what to do and equally the Council does not tell the Boards of its dependent theatres how to conduct their affairs and, what is more, the best Boards do not try to tell their Artistic Director what to do. At every level, however, there are understandings about what the money is for and how it may be

[28] *Hansard*, 28.1.71. Col. 863.

spent and at every level it is understood that if trust is forfeited or if there are a series of errors of judgment, the consequences must be a diminution of financial support or a change of personnel or both.

Throughout the years the view had been expressed from time to time, and not without authority, that the Government's involvement had reached a point at which there was a duty to adopt more *dirigiste* methods of patronage. So when the new Minister for the Arts, Lord Eccles, made a most ominous speech in the Lords, I took advantage of a Consolidated Fund debate to put a shot across his bows. Eccles had talked of his disquiet at the use of public money to finance 'works which affront the religious beliefs or outrage the sense of decency of a large body of taxpayers.'[29]

Jennie Lee had already expressed concern in the Lords and at 1.30 a.m. on 15th February 1971 I pointed out that if the Arts Council were asked to exercise a censorship by the purse no commercial manager would risk putting on a production so damned.

'If Lord Eccles and the Arts Council connived together to keep certain plays out of public support, in so doing they would be conniving to keep those plays off the stage altogether. Having, on an all-party basis, got rid of the pre-censorship of the Lord Chamberlain, with the enthusiastic co-operation of the Lord Chamberlain himself, the Government would apparently be seeking to recreate it here in an even less defensible and more hamfisted fashion than occurred before. I hope that on further consideration this will not commend itself to the Minister.

What will the procedure be? What would be the wording of a convention between the Arts Council and the Government and between the Arts Council and its beneficiaries? Who would interpret the convention? How would it be applied? To every play? To each play? If so, who would read the plays? Who would be responsible for carrying the can and saying "yea" or "nay"? Would it apply to the general output of a company, and, if so, what would the yardstick be?

Would it be one dirty or blasphemous play per season, like a dog being allowed one bite? Most companies run for years

[29] *House of Lords Official Report*, 3.2.71. Col. 1210.

without even attempting to breach the conventions. This new procedure, if it were adopted, might possibly be an invitation or encouragement to have a go. At present the relationship between the Government and the Arts Council and the boards of theatrical companies is one of mutual trust. The Government appoint to the Council people who they hope and trust will not bring public patronage into public disrepute by being either stingy or repressive on the one hand or profligate and unbridled on the other.

Times change and the Arts Council must change with them, not too slowly or it will lose the confidence of creative artists, yet not too quickly so that it ceases to be representative of the generality of informed opinion in the arts. The only way to avoid falling from that tightrope occasionally is to refuse to walk it. The Arts Council knows that it is there to walk the tightrope. It has done so in a manner which has brought to this country great international renown. Occasionally the Council falls out with a board of management but it does not attempt to tell the board its job nor to say what plays it shall or shall not present. I thought that Lord Goodman put it well in the evidence he gave to the Estimates Committee on 10th April 1968, on page 46, when he said in reponse to a question from the Chairman:

"We set very much store upon emphasising very strongly that we retain our total independence, secondly that we are not operating under a Ministry of Culture, and thirdly that the organisations we subsidise have as much independence as we have ourselves. Those are the three principles we try to operate."

That is why the relationship between the Government and the Arts Council and the Arts Council and its beneficiaries is important because for once we have it right. This is why in raising this matter I have raised it as a question of the relationship between the Government and arts. It is a delicate balance and if it is upset we shall live to regret it. We have these relationships wrong elsewhere, in business both public and private for instance. We consistently get them wrong under all Governments. We have them wrong with our political parties. The relationships are certainly not always correct between front- and backbenchers. A mutual trust which should be there sometimes seems to escape. We certainly have the relationships all wrong in relation to films and the Press, and this goes for radio and television. However, in the arts we have the relationship right.'[30]

[30] *Hansard*, 5.2.71. Col. 1408 et seq

After going on a bit about the Press I continued:

'I am sure that there is not a serious man or woman connected with the theatre, commercial or supported, who would think it a good idea to add to the existing restrictions on the theatre, and I hope that we will hear no more of it.'

The Arts Council had been criticised for giving an indication to some theatres that it hoped to come to their aid in future years and on this I said:

'Another matter is the Arts Council's indication to, for example, Salisbury, Peterborough, Derby and Bolton that, although the Council had no money to help them with their plans for a future theatre enterprise, it hoped to have some, and to assist in the building of new theatres, all being well, in years to come. The Council has been told pretty clearly that it should not have said any such thing. I believe that that is technically quite right, but how could local fundraising efforts have been maintained if this naughty nod or wink had not been given?

Some way must be found of allowing the Council, perhaps in consultation with the Minister, to enter into future commitments, so that local authorities can have some security in providing for a theatre when they are reconstructing their urban areas. Otherwise, it is impossible for the Council to sit mumchance when local authorities say: "We are contemplating rebuilding our urban area. In two years' time we shall have a theatre. Shall we provide for it in our plans?" If the Council is to sit mum and say: "We must not speak a word about what is to happen in two years' time," it seems to me to present such an impossible situation that it is necessary to find a way out of the dilemma.

One way would be an arrangement between the Arts Council and the Minister that together they might agree, without any formal commitment, that the Council would in future look favourably upon such a project, the details and arrangements for which had been clearly set out before even any moral undertaking was given.

It is not for me to say that the Arts Council is perfect. That would not be true. It can be said, however, that within limits of human fallibility Britain has evolved a way of supporting the arts which some study has persuaded me has considerable advantages over other systems that I have examined in various parts of the world. Its continued success depends upon the preservation of a series of understandings which have been built up and maintained under successive Governments. Whoever undermines those understandings will not be doing the nation a service.'[31]

After a long and stylish speech by Norman St. John Stevas, and a shorter and more effective one by another Tory, Jeffrey Archer, the Government's reply was given by Mr. Van Straubenzee at his most pompous. He not only defended the Government's intention to start charging for entry into the national Museums and Galleries; he even adopted Eccles' views about attachment of strings to public money in the arts asking:

> 'Is the cause of the arts as a whole to be advanced by causing grave affront to the majority of people who at present provide the funds which have helped to make the arts flourish?'[32]

I intervened. He had said that Lord Eccles was going to pose this question to the Arts Council. Was it also Government policy that their will should be imposed? Van Straubenzee waffled for a full column. Then he said:

> 'Ultimately, as my noble Friend said, "the conscience and taste of a well educated public are the only censors worth having in a policy to raise the quality of life." It is reasonable to ask that before that conscience is affronted and that taste repelled those who produce plays and performances which affront and repel should themselves be convinced that the overall experience and impact is one that can be justified on artistic grounds. It is sometimes necessary to shock, but this makes it the more important to ensure that the shock has meaning and purpose and is not just a piece of sensationalism.'
> *Jenkins:* 'Would the Hon. Gentleman give us some examples of those plays which affront and repel?'[33]

Van Straubenzee refused to be drawn and the debate ended at 3.38 a.m. Parliament heard no more of any Government attempt to impose standards on the Arts Council and I think, therefore, that it may not be the case that no good is ever done after midnight.

[31] Ibid.
[32] *Hansard,* 15.2.71. Col. 1437.
[33] Ibid. Col. 1439.

All the same, the complaint by Eccles had already been sent to the Arts Council. In a letter to Lord Goodman the Minister had said that some subsidised companies were putting on productions of an obscene and blasphemous character. The Chairman had drafted a letter to all the Council's beneficiaries reminding them of their responsibilities in this matter. I immediately objected strongly, saying that most beneficiaries needed no such reminder and where they were going over the top, the Council's assessor on the appropriate Board could drop a hint. Lord (C.P.) Snow disagreed with me, but the majority of the Council came over to my side and it was eventually agreed that a statement in that sense should be drafted for the consideration of the Council. As finally agreed and issued, it probably only reminded beneficiaries that they might be rather more adventurous than they had intended.

At this time, as part of the triennial grant system, the Council was engaged in asking its clients to forecast their budgets for the next three years. In the theatre this could be little more than guesswork, but it pleased the civil servants. During 1971 also, the Arts Council was represented on a committee set up by Lord Eccles to examine Public Lending Right but as they were on the wrong lines little progress was made.

My term of office on the Arts Council expired with that of Lord Goodman. I met his successor, Patrick Gibson, at his request and formed a good impression of him. A Tory, I thought, but an honest and capable man. I had enjoyed my period on the Arts Council and after a year I rejoined the Drama Panel and remained a member of it until my appointment as Minister in 1974.

By this time I knew my way round the organisation of all the arts and no wool could be pulled over my eyes, for I had watched the civil servants at work on the Arts Council on which they represented the point of view of the Department of Education and Science, the Treasury, and the Scottish Office. I had crossed swords with them and learned to respect them, and I knew that there was a power in the land quite independent of the Government and that was the power of the bureaucracy. If he had to choose, the civil servant would serve his department rather than his Minister. But in those days I had no idea that I should ever become engaged in that struggle.

When the Tories introduced their Sound Broadcasting Bill to establish Commercial local radio my opposition was not to a second radio network, nor even to its dependence on advertising, but to its inadequacy and to its ownership. In Committee I moved against the involvement of local newspapers, arguing that what was proposed was communications incest. In this I had some Tory support. There was already too much reduction in variety in the media. A different accent did not alter the message. The Government persisted and I had no doubt that Labour was right to oppose the Bill throughout, saying: 'The Bill cannot commend itself to this side of the House. It is not the sort of alternative that we want. It will not contribute anything much in the way of employment. I doubt whether it will contribute anything at all to the cultural life of the country or to the enjoyment of listeners.'[34]

I was wrong on the last point. Commercial radio has contributed a good deal, not only to the enjoyment of listeners but to their information.

Andrew Faulds, Shadow Spokesman for the Arts, opposed the Third Reading of the Tory Bill to introduce Museum charges with the best speech he made in that role. Prime Minister Edward Heath was said himself to be an enthusiast for Museum charging.

In November 1972 St. John Stevas, who had become Tory spokesman for the Arts in the Commons, introduced a Bill to increase the money available to build the National Theatre by Two Million Pounds. In the debate I attempted to amend the Bill to make it open-ended and in advocating this I told how I had put down a motion as a member of the LCC in 1960 as the result of which Sir Isaac Hayward had put a pistol to the head of the then Tory Government and virtually forced them to disgorge their £1 million contribution to the building of the National Theatre. But they had made it a condition that the LCC should bear not only an equivalent million but any sum by which the cost might exceed that total of £2 millions. However, in 1969 when the roles were reversed and the Tories were in power at County Hall, they had ratted on the agreement and refused to exceed the £1 million so that the excess had to fall on the National Government—hence the present Bill. I suggested that

[32] *Hansard*, Col. 1386 – 12.4.72

there woul be further increases in costs and that the Bill should provide for that by removing figures and substituting 'such sums as the Secretary of State may determine'. St. John Stevas disagreed saying that £2 millions was 'generous' which proved to be nonsense and two years later I had to correct, as Minister, the consequences of his failure to accept my amendment. There was no good reason for this Tory kowtowing to the rigidities of the Treasury, for they still maintained complete financial control even without legislative limitations.

This summary shows how in the first three years of the seventies the Conservatives substituted Jennie Lee's splendid brightness, optimism and faith by constriction and restriction.

In November 1973 the Government in the person of the then Home Secretary, Robert Carr, introduced a muddled little measure called the 'Cinematograph and Indecent Displays' Bill which sought to control advertising displays, 'What the Butler Saw' machines and club cinemas in a single Act. It seemed to me that some supporters of the Bill must spend time walking around Soho especially to get themselves disgusted. The Opposition, Alex Lyon leading, reserved its position until the Committee Stage and gave the Bill an unopposed second reading. In Committee an extremely jolly time was had by all. It lasted from the 22nd November 1973 until 22nd January 1974 and that was the end of the Bill for there was then no time for it to return to the Chamber before the House porogued in preparation for the forthcoming General Election. This was just as well, for although the Committee removed some of the undesirable and laughable consequences of the measure, its basic confusion between a desire to protect the public and a determination to restrict personal liberty was unresolved and, indeed proved unresolvable.

It had been known for some time that the Leader of the Parliamentary Labour Party, Harold Wilson, had become dissatisfied with his Shadow Arts Spokesman, and when Andrew Faulds acted as one of the sponsors for Dick Taverne who had returned to the House as an Independent after defeating the official Labour candidate at a by-election, it was expected that Faulds would lose his job there and then. This, however, was not the Wilson way. He waited until Lord Eccles was replaced by St. John Stevas as Arts Minister and one day in the Lobby touched me on the shoulder and asked if it would be convenient for me to join him in his room for a moment. He told me that he had decided it was time for Faulds to go and asked if I would replace him temporarily as Shadow Spokesman.

'I am not offering you the job if we win the next General Election,' he said. 'There is an age problem.'

As I had already passed my 65th birthday. I knew what he meant, but I said I would gladly fill in and, indeed, would enjoy doing so.

I had known Harold Wilson since the days of the Attlee Government. I recalled him coming to speak for me when I lost to Robert Carr in Mitcham in 1955. We talked before the meeting in a dingy café and as I was a nuclear disarmer and he was a firm NATO supporter, we agreed we should lay off foreign affairs. I was, therefore, never under the illusion that he belonged to the Left of the Labour Party. He was, like Attlee, slightly left of centre, but as the available alternative when Wilson was chosen leader of the Party was the regrettable George Brown, neither then nor at any other time and in spite of profound policy disagreements, did I have any doubt that he was the best Leader we had and the best Prime Minister we had. The death of Aneurin Bevan was a disaster, but if Hugh Gaitskell had remained Leader the thirteen years of Tory rule after 1951 would probably have been thirty.

St. John Stevas appeared on the front bench as Arts Minister and I as Shadow on the same day, 11th December 1973. I asked him to increase the Arts Council's grant from £17 millions to £20 millions and received an understandably non-committal answer. However, when I succeeded him a few weeks later I was astonished to find that he appeared to have agreed to a cut in the rate of increase.

Soon after my Shadow appointment I moved a motion[35] in the Chamber proposing a Royal Commission to examine the Cabinet system of Government and claiming that the system was partly responsible for the failure of successive Governments to carry out their electoral undertakings to the full. I suggested that

[35] *Hansard*, 30.11.73 Col. 864

all members of the Governing Party should be involved, as in the case of the local Government committee system. The debate was adjourned, but a couple of years of Government and experience of the consequences of the Cabinet system upon non-cabinet members of the Government and upon backbenchers, has convinced me that my criticism of the system was well-founded.

At the last Question time before the first General Election of that year, on 29th January 1974,[36] I asked St. John Stevas how he was getting on with a scheme to pay authors from central government funds some reward related to the use of their books by borrowers from public libraries. He said he was studying the practical problems, but when I moved into Belgrave Square a few weeks later I found that little progress had been made.

[36]*Hansard* 29.1.74 Col. 224

D

above: **Mr and Mrs Jenkins** on their wedding day, 1903.

top right: Hugh Jenkins age 2½.

bottom: Hugh Jenkins age 15.

1964. Hugh Jenkin
Marie Jenkins, Dan
Sybil Thorndike, Se
Kevin Walsh, Jan
Munn.

1964. Hugh Jenkins
and Harold Wilson.

1966. Harry Corbe
Hugh Jenkins on
Labour bandwage

right: Lord O'Brien, Marie Jenkins, Hugh Jenkins, Jennie Lee greeting H.M. The Queen.

centre: In the Ministry: Michael Herzig, Tony Howell, Ann Simmonds, Hugh Jenkins, John Spence, Colin Graham, Pat Curran, Willy Wright.

bottom: Personal staff: Tony Howell, Marion London, Mary Giles, Hugh Jenkins, Cathy Maher, Chris Kempson.

At home: Marie and Hugh
Jenkins.

PART III

CHAPTER SEVEN

Minister for the Arts

Having held Putney in the Tory win of 1970 we expected to retain the seat in 1974 and did so. Labour had no clear majority, but with 301 seats we were the largest Party and the Queen sent for Harold Wilson. However, when Parliament met on the 6th March 1974, the Government was not complete.

In the days after the February election old and new members of Parliament met casually at the House of Commons. In the tea-room members, including some with whom I had no close political affinity, were kind enough to tell me that they hoped my Shadow appointment would be confirmed by the Prime Minister in office. I expressed doubt, repeating what Harold Wilson had said about my age and they expressed surprise and said how young I looked and how there was no one whom they would rather see as Arts Minister. I felt flattered and very warm towards such disparate people as Fred Willey (whom I once met by chance in the Cathedral at Chartres), Peter Shore, who had been appointed Secretary of State for Trade and who was not only a constituent but an old friend, and many others including fellow-members of the Tribune Group (never much interested in the arts) and new MPs I had never seen before. I had just decided that the House of Commons was really a very kind place when Andrew Faulds passed by looking handsomely evil.

'You will not expect me to congratulate you if you get my job,' he hissed hammily. I looked at him and realised for the first time why my American secretaries always called him Rasputin.

The Arts job is rightly regarded as a plum post. I had never expected to become a Shadow, let alone a Minister and, although it was nice to know I had friends, I spent the few days trying to assure myself that I would not be too disappointed if someone else got the job. I was in good health; I had just won my fourth election in a seat I had never expected to get or hold; I loved being an MP and thought myself a good one, and I was happily married after nearly forty years. So if it came, splendid; if not, well, life was good as it was.

All the same, I knew more about the organisation of the arts than any other MP, and when people said I was the right man for the job I had no difficulty in recognising their perception. I would be in charge. I would run things for the arts and artists and I would not be run by civil servants.

So, when the next afternoon, on Thursday 7th March, a messenger handed me a note with a request that I should call at the PM's Room in the House I went along feeling unusually jittery. In the outer office, Marcia Williams was busy on the telephone. I had always got on well with her, as indeed I do with most women, and if she was as influential with Harold as they said I did not think she would be against me. But was he really going to appoint a man of pensionable age to his first Government job or was this to break the news that a younger man or woman was going to get it?

Inside, the PM was sitting at the middle of a long table and, smiling slightly as he busied himself with his pipe, motioned me to sit beside him and said at once:

'I'm offering you the Arts job, Hugh, in spite of what I said about your age. You're a good deal younger in every way than many with less years, and I think you're the right man for it.'

'Yes,' I said without modesty. 'Thank you. I shall enjoy having a go. I didn't expect to be given the chance to Shadow and I'm absolutely delighted. Marie will be pleased. As for me, it is the only job in Government I ever wanted to do.'

'I'm afraid,' he said, 'that I cannot make you a Minister of State as I should like. They tell me that I have already appointed my full ration and I can only offer you an Under-Secretaryship. I shall, however, make it clear that you are to be regarded and addressed as Minister for the Arts.'

'It doesn't matter,' I said, not realising for a moment that it would be regarded as important by other people. 'I know my way round the arts and I shall run my own show whatever I'm called."

'Yes, he said. 'By the way, you will be surprised to know that Lord Goodman was among the many people who urged me to appoint you.'

'Oddly enough,' I said, 'I'm not surprised. We often disagreed on the Arts Council but in a manner which created respect on both sides, I think.'

'Good luck,' he said and I left without knowing that we should never be at ease with each other again until both of us were out of office, and that as a backbencher I had enjoyed an access to the PM which was to be denied me as a Junior Minister.

Marcia greeted me at the door with a smile. I kissed her lightly on the cheek.

'They'll want to see you at your office right away,' she said. 'Are you free to go?'

'Yep.' I said. 'I'm overjoyed. I must phone Marie.'

Sitting in the black Wolseley beside the driver on my first visit to 38, Belgrave Square I was suddenly seized with the conviction that I knew nothing whatever about the arts. Theatre, drama, literature: well yes, something, not all that much, critics knew much more. Films, music; liking and loving more than knowledge. Opera and Ballet; more of the first than the second, but limited even then. My background was shallow. I had no university education, and could not bring myself, like Shaw, to thank God that my mind had never been corrupted by it. I had always appreciated paintings and sculptures, and we had quite a few original works at home; but I really knew very little about the visual arts, more about museums than galleries. I was not an expert nor even a specialist.

True, I revered artists and, more important, I knew how to put the state at their service. This is what I would do. I would be Minister for Artists. I had devoted myself to actors and to the theatre: now I would do my best over the whole field. What was more, I would try to bring the world of the arts to more and more people over the whole country so that everyone should at least have a chance to know what they were missing.

I pushed self-doubt aside and walked into 38, Belgrave Square, proud and assured, and as the messengers on duty leaped to their feet, it caused me no more embarrassment then when the troops had stood to attention at the sight of my officers' uniform during the war. That's how it was; it was recognition, not of me, but of the position I occupied. I wondered how long it would last.

Inside the door a well-dressed woman with dark hair stood smiling cheerfully.

'Good afternoon, Minister,' she said, 'welcome to Belgrave Square.'

Two plaques framed the pillared door. On the left 'Department of Education and Science – Arts and Libraries Branch' – on the right 'Minister for the Arts'.

The building is early Victorian and like many such in London carries over a Georgian classic grace, the ceilings tall and the staircase curving elegantly upwards. Like all such houses it was a true 'Upstairs-Downstairs' building with splendid ground and first floor rooms, topped by increasingly mean accommodation in the higher rooms, but with a capacious basement which had housed the kitchen and scullery and servants' living quarters. In 1974 it contained the filing system and the ladies who tended it were the only members of the staff in the building, numbering fifty or so, who did not like working in Belgravia.

On the ground floor there was a Conference Room, the walls lined with pictures I disliked. I occupied a very large room which I tried unsuccessfully to change for a smaller one. When I first entered with the dark-haired woman, it was distempered in a depressing shade of green, and the pictures were on the floor against the wainscot.

'Mr St, John Stevas did not like them.' explained my guide, 'they were going back to the Tate.'

'Are you going to look after me?' I asked.

'If you wish, Minister,' she replied, 'I should like to. I was Private Secretary to your predecessor, and for a few weeks to Lord Eccles. I am Mary Giles.'

'I am Hugh Jenkins,' I said, 'Minister as much as you like to impress anyone who needs it, but not when we're alone, eh?'

There was a beautiful golden sandal-wood desk, conference table and chairs. 'Made especially for Lord Eccles,' said Mary.

Eccles indeed was responsible for the whole thing. He must have realised that if he was going to follow Jennie Lee effectively he needed everything he could get in the way of panache. Hence the splendid and separate establishment which I determined there and then to run as an autonomous republic within the Education and Science kingdom. The Secretary of State was to be Reg Prentice whom I had known and disagreed with since he was a young man; indeed his wife had been my secretary at Equity before they were married. Joan Godwin was very left-wing then, much more so than I was. I did not think I would have any difficulty with Reg and I was right – not until Fred Mulley took over was any attempt made to assert the reality that I was merely the least important of four Ministers in the Department of Education and Science.

I sat at the desk. There were three telephones. One white, one black and one red, and an internal-communications apparatus.

'These two go through my office,' said Mary, 'and I or my colleagues listen in. The red one is the Federal circuit with other Ministers. The white one is private for your personal calls.'

Cathy Maher, who became quite devoted to my wife and me entered with some tea while Mary explained that the Head of the Branch was an Under-Secretary, John Spence, but above him, partly because of the physical separation of Belgrave Square from the DES offices near Waterloo Station, was a Deputy Secretary, Willy Wright. This hierarchical structure, I later discovered, added to the status of the Branch.

'We'd better see Mr Wright,' I said. 'And I want a telephone recording gadget so that I can phone in here at any time from anywhere and leave instructions and dictate letters.'

The very slightest of frowns passed over Mary's face and was gone. After a barely perceptible hesitation she said, 'Very well. We will get one.'

A moment or two later, a man in his late fifties came in with a curious sidling gait which gave a quite wrong impression of deference. Willy Wright, now retired, was a very assured man. He smiled.

'Welcome Minister,' he said.

'Come and sit down, I said. 'Mary will be staying with me and I hope you will too.'

'I don't think they'll move me before I go altogether,' he said. 'Unless you find you can't work with me.'

'If you can work with me, there's unlikely to be a problem,' I said. 'One advantage of arriving at Ministerial office so late in life is that one is used to running things. I once had a small radar station with 150 WAAFS. Gorgeous.'

Willy smiled and I later knew that the reference had not come amiss for he had spent most of his life in the Ministry of Defence. He is a distinguished amateur geologist and a pillar of the Athenaeum – a right-winger who would fight anything which went against his beliefs providing it could be done within the rules. He could draft a better minute than anyone in the office and when necessary, would quite ruthlessly overrule John Spence, an emotional man, happily not without humour. When they were both against me they were a formidable combination, but they would carry out any policy providing they were satisfied that I had the support of the Secretary of State, of the Cabinet and of the Treasury. Unfortunately, this did not always prove to be the case.

In the days that followed I soon got used to a structured life. My week would be planned ahead, every hour of every day accounted for. the car called for me in the morning and I soon acquired a superb driver and car to myself. He was Tony Howell, black and charming, from Jamaica, who lived not far away from our Putney flat. All this I owed to Mary Giles who pointed out that, although not entitled by rank, I must have a car to myself so as to get from Belgrave Square to the House and back when required

Most mornings, except when out on a visit – and I spent a great deal of time outside London – I was in Belgrave Square; most afternoons at the House; most evenings at some function or other accompanied by Marie or Mary Giles or both.

I found that my private office included, in addition to Mary, Chris Kempson who looked after Parliamentary questions and other such matters, Jon Winkle who kept the diary and made appointments, and a remarkably efficient shorthand typist in the diminutive and cheerful Marion London.

Up to this point I had worked in the arts at many levels, had acted as their spokesman out of choice during my ten-year

Parliamentary career and had been Shadow Minister for a few weeks. Now I could actually do something for the arts. I could not have been more confident and optimistic. I plunged straight into it.

I instituted a progress meeting every Monday morning and I include an example of a progress chart on pages 98 and 99.

To the progress meeting would come not only Willy, John and Mary but also the two Assistant Secretaries, Colin Graham, who was in charge of the Arts generally and Michael Herzig, who specialised in Museums, Galleries and Library matters. There were five Principals and when particular matters were under discussion, the appropriate official would sometimes be invited for the item. After a time I managed to add Lord Strabolgi (David), who was our spokesman in the Lords and my Parliamentary Private Secretary, the first of whom was Robert Kilroy-Silk, the new member for Ormskirk.

I drove these weekly meetings through at a great rate, holding separate discussions whenever possible on subjects being handled during the current week, and I think that as a result we were able to maintain a momentum which did not slacken throughout my two years of office.

Freeing the Museums and Galleries

The Labour Party in Parliament had opposed the Tory decision to compel Trustees to charge for entry into the national collections, but there was no specific election manifesto commitment to remove the charges. One of my first utterances inside Belgrave Square was to ask to have a commitment to abolish the charges included in the Queen's Speech, which was to be delivered the following week.

Having ascertained that there was still time to get something in Under-Secretary John Spence quickly came up with the following proposal:

'My Government will review the system of museum charges.'

I rejected that, saying that the undertaking to abolish must be specific. I was then offered: 'The Government will not require the National Museums and Galleries to charge for admission.'

I decided that this was still not good enough. It was an understanding not to enforce charging, not one to abolish

PROGRESS CHART

Subject	wb 1/12	wb 8/12	wb 15/12	wb 22/12—wb 5/1	wb 12/1	wb 19/1	wb 26/1	wb 2/2	wb 9/2
ARTS COUNCIL Finance	Reply to Audit reference		Cash flow discussions			1976/77 Estimates	Cash flow discussions	Notification of 1976/77 grant	
Constitution/ Staff/Admin.									
Regions									
FILM BFI policy/ programmes	Letter on financial conduct		Case for revote	Policy on nitrate stocks. Talks with BFI				Nitrate talks with Factory Inspectorate	
BFI Admin/ Staff									
Film Industry					? PM Working Party report		Brief on Terry for S of S	PM discussion on Terry	
NATIONAL THEATRE Policy		Moving in costs settled and Spring Supplementary estimate							
South Bank Building			Spring Supplementary Estimate				Outcome of financial enquiries on sub-contractors		
CRAFTS	Consideration of Conservation Report				Future structure of CAC				Conserva[tion] Report t[o] Minister
LEVER INQUIRY	Interim Report								
WORKS OF ART Export Control									
Tax aspects				? Report of Select Committee					
NATIONAL MUSEUMS Building Programme	Imperial War Museum: Duxford site decision						Decision on Imperial War Museum presence at Duxford		
Policy					? Discussions with departmental museums on devolution				
Personnel									
Acquisitions							? Wellcome Collection for Science Museum and possibly BR relics		
PROVINCIAL MUSEUMS		Review of arrangements for assistance						Further progress [?]	
SECURITY									
BRITISH LIBRARY	Announcement on publication of site notices		Laying of British Library Annual Report 18/12		? Statutory laying of statement on BL Board Members Salaries		Laying of statement on Board members' salaries	? Joint Ministe[rial] paper on Phase of new building	
PUBLIC LIBRARIES	Meeting with LA on Bucks 3/12								
PLR Legislation	Discuss timing and arrangements for Press-Conference on TIG Report	? PLR Bill to Legislation Committee					Lord President again considers legislative timetable. Position of TIG Report publication		

PROGRESS CHART

2	wb 23/2	wb 1/3	wb 8/3	wb 15/3	wb 22/3	wb 29/3	wb 5/4	12—23 April	wb 26/4	wb 3/5	wb 10/
				Cash flow discussions							
						? Green paper on devolution to regions					
						Development of long-term policies for film archive					
						Problems raised by proposals for BFA					
				Opening to public		Outcome of financial enquiries on sub-contractors					
of						CAC Conservation Report					
								Second report expected			
			1974/5 Report of Reviewing Committee			Action on Report of Reviewing Committee					
	New conditions of grant for V & A and Science Museums			Turner Collection and Somerset House		Effect of staff savings on Departmental museums					
										•	? Formal handing over of Concorde 00 to Science Museum
				Further progress on pilot scheme for increasing loans							
				Boston Spa, Phase III of building and proposed temporary accommodation		Announcement of new Board members					
				Effect of Public Expenditure limits on public libraries							
				Draft speech and briefing for Second Reading if allowed. Issue of consultative document. TIG final report published.							

charges. A few days later, on 12th March, I went into the Lords to hear the Queen in all her panoply say:

'The museum charges recently introduced will be abolished.'[1]

I felt rather pleased with myself but how was I going to do it? The Prime Minister had made it clear that he thought I had a lengthy job on my hands and that what had been imposed by legislation would have to be removed by legislation, which, of course, would take months to prepare and carry through two Houses. But I found a quicker way. The Tory legislation simply removed impediments which *forbade* charging. The institutions had not been legislatively *compelled* to charge; the compulsion was exerted by making it clear to the Trustees that the Government grant would be cut off if they failed to exercise their freedom to charge for entry.

Willy Wright, John Spence and I had a meeting. They produced figures showing that the charges were not paying for the cost of collection and were reducing attendances at the Museums. We agreed that all we had to do was to get the Trustees of the various national collections not to exercise their right to charge entrance. I could do this by making it clear that far from having their grant reduced if they *failed* to charge; under Labour they would get no grant if they *did* charge. The legislation could stay on the statute book for I was pretty sure that once we got the charges off, the Tories, even if they returned to office, would never dare re-impose them. Furthermore, as most of the Trustees were eager to stop charging there would be no difficulty with the British Museum, the National Gallery or the Tate. The South Kensington complex was under my direct control but we might have to jolly the Maritime Museum along a bit, and the Imperial War which had been doing well out of the charges with their Colditz Exhibition might be a problem. If we played our cards carefully we could have the charges off within three or four weeks.

The first thing was to make sure that all the National Collections acted together, for only in this way could I use the eagerness of the anti-chargers to pressurise the pro-chargers. We put out the word not to stop charging until a Government announcement was made and this brought Sir Edmund Playfair,

[1] *Hansard*, 12.3.74. Col. 46.

Chairman of the British Museum, round hotfoot.

Clearly he feared that we were going to rat on our undertaking to remove the charges and said that his Trustees wanted to end charging at once. I said that we must act together and if he would be patient for a week or two I hoped to make an announcement in the House of Commons. Until then charging should continue.

I then saw the other Chairmen and only with the Imperial War Museum was there any difficulty. This, however was easily resolved by agreeing that there could be no objection to charging for special exhibitions and their Colditz show was obviously special, so long as the regular exhibition was free. Immediatley after seeing the last Chairman I asked to make a statement in the House[2] and secured leave to do so on 22nd March, just two weeks after I had taken office. Then I announced that freedom day would be Saturday 30th March, no further charges being made after closing on the preceding Friday 29th March.

This quick work received a very good press and much praise from colleagues. I was off to a good start. It also confirmed my attitude towards my civil servants. They would try to prevent me from doing anything at all if they could. The British civil servant regards the maintenance of the status quo as his main task in life; he is there to administer what already exists and to stop it from being changed if he can. But he will do as he is told and do it well if he knows that his Minister is determined and has the support of the Cabinet. In this case that was so.

The Fight for Money

In the interregnum from political control brought about by the February 1974 General Election, the Treasury, working through the officials of the Department of Education and Science, decided to whip the Arts Council into line. In 1971 the Public Accounts Committee under Harold Lever had taken the Council's side in the perennial argument about carrying over money from one year to the next. Here was a chance for the Treasury to assert its authority.

The Exchequer and Audit Department insisted that the fact that the Arts Council had a substantial cash balance held in reserve demonstrated that the grant for the previous year had been too large. On the 27th February 1974, John Spence wrote to

[2] *Hansard* Col. 1491. 22.3.74.

Hugh Willatt, then Secretary General of the Arts Council, suggesting that the Council had paid out large sums of money before it was necessary to do so in order to avoid the cash balance being even greater. The Department was determined to see that they did not get away with something similar in the current year.

At that time there was still £500,000 due to the Arts Council from the current grant which had to be paid before the end of March. Just before that, on 27th March, the Department's Permanent Secretary wrote to Willatt telling him that it had been decided to withhold £250,000 of the £500,000 outstanding, on the grounds that the Council had made payments or placed to reserve sums which were not related to the current year but to the following one. In other words they had been accumulating a reserve and had even encouraged beneficiaries to do the same.

I knew nothing of all this until Pat Gibson came to see me in a very angry frame of mind and I was soon equally angry at having been presented with a *fait accompli*. Gibson had been led to believe that a carry-over of around £500,000 would be acceptable and plans had been made accordingly

I wrote to the Secretary of State, Reg Prentice, describing the row as 'foolish' and insisting that steps must be taken to ensure that the Arts Council was not treated in such a way again. I also made it clear that I would not tolerate being kept in the dark in future and pointed out that the Public Accounts Committee was not on the Treasury's side in the argument. They had applauded the Arts Council's 'care and skill' and, even if the Permanent Secretary's face had to be saved, we must get the money back to the Arts Council in one way or another. I would see to it that an agreement was reached which would avoid any repetition of such events. This proved to be extremely arduous, for the intransigence was not all on the Department's side. Tony Field, the Arts Council's Finance Officer, was an old friend of mine who lived in the same block of flats in Putney, but although I was sure he was right in principle he adopted the emotional attitude which all good accountants bring to their tedious task and this made the search for a *modus vivendi* doubly difficult. However, I eventually had the idea of bringing the Government and Arts Council auditors together and this produced an uneasy compromise settlement. The same trouble broke out the following year with the British Film Institute and led to the resignation of their accountant, as I shall relate.

I saw my immediate task on appointment as being to do what I could to recover momentum in Arts monetary increases. In his few weeks of office my predecessor had supinely accepted the drastic reductions in the estimates which were part of the general Tory cuts in public expenditure at the end of 1973. I realised that I should never be stronger than I was at that moment, for a Minister could hardly be thrown out immediately on appointment, and so I decided to start using my elbows, and with solid support from Willy Wright and John Spence, and with no opposition anywhere else, Labour's April budget provided not only for enough money to offset the consequences of inflation but for a 3% real increase on top. At all points where I could be heard I explained that this was merely the start. I should want much more money before very long. Within the limits set by the machine, not only Denis Healey, Chancellor of the Exchequer, but also his Chief Secretary, Joel Barnett, and the Financial Secretary at that time, John Gilbert, who were all keen arts men, did their best to respond co-operatively to the continual badgering for money to which I subjected them.

In these early days I was invited by Sir Claus Moser to deliver the keynote address to a Seminar on sponsorship of the Arts at the University of Sussex, supported by the Times Trust. The occasion was chaired by the Vice-Chancellor, Professor Asa Briggs, and it gave me an opportunity to state my position as Minister on a public but non-party platform.

I said that throughout history finance for the arts had been provided by the state. Show business was a transient phenomenon stemming from the industrial revolution, and we were now returning to the norm. In the performance arts, technical invention had created new forms, recording, radio, cinema, television – leaving the original theatrical form virtually untouched in all essentials. The coach was replaced by the train and then by the car, but theatre continued to exist alongside cinema and television because it provided an intensity of experience that reproduction of performance could not match. Instead of transforming the original form the electronic world had stolen the mass audience for itself. The theatre had now

returned to its usual state of being a minority pursuit. For many
of its manifestations, to charge the real cost at the box-office
would be to exclude all but the wealthy. So we had a mixed
economy of the arts and entertainment. It was not my view that
the private sector should, could or would be eliminated. I did not
want the state to usurp the role of the impressario in revue,
musical or all dramatic theatre. Baumel and Bowen's, 'The
Performance Arts – the Economic Dilemma' had proved
conclusively that even with a static obligation – and we would
have a growing commitment for many years – the proportion of
state help must increase at a rate substantially faster than the
general rate of inflation because of the labour-intensive nature of
the arts. The offsetting of technical advance in the performance
arts into new media had gravely aggravated the problem.

Government help to the arts *in real terms* was six times as large
as it was ten years earlier and there must be no cut-back. On the
contrary, we should be in real trouble even if we tried to stand
still as was proposed by the previous Government.

All the same, the traditional arts played a small part in the
leisure of the people – 1% as against 23% on average in the case
of television. The Arts Council underwrote on average half the
cost of every ticket productions it supported and I was not sure it
was desirable for the taxpayer to shoulder the bulk of the cost of
theatrical performances. Surely it would be better to increase the
availability of the arts; for example, for the Arts Council to carry
half the cost at an increasing number of theatres all over the
country rather than move towards 75% in London.

The solution to the problem might be found in positive steps to
heal the breach between the two cultures. The arts, communications, entertainment and sport were viable and thriving
as a whole, but parts of the scene would always be in trouble until
we recognised that it *was* a whole. The state must arrange for the
popular art and entertainment forms to finance their essential
creative sources.

I sent up the argument that it would be helpful for the big
national companies to be funded separately from the rest of the
Arts Council's beneficiaries and I added that the struggle for
money was not only an annual event. Throughout the year, on

various battlegrounds and at different levels and time bases, the argument continued and was taking place simultaneously on a supplementary to the present grant, the size of next year's grant and the shape of grants to come. I finished up by talking about, business sponsorship which, in this book, is dealt with elsewhere.

Questions in the House

As a backbencher I had heard that the civil service took Questions seriously, but I did not realise quite how seriously until I had to agree or change the answers.

Each question, written or oral is given a separate file; each file has a background note and possible answers; oral questions have a series of possible supplementary questions and possible answers to them. The recommended answer originates from an Executive Officer, passes through a Principal, to an Assistant Secretary and is finally approved by the Under Secretary or Deputy Secretary before reaching the Minister through his Private Office. All this is sometimes carried out in a single day.

To the civil servants' consternation I altered most answers. I refused to evade the questions unless there was some particular reason, such as incomplete consultations, for doing so and even then I insisted on giving the real reason. I would not accept a pasted-over page giving the ultimate answer but required to see the revisions made at each stage and I often rejected the wool pulled over at the highest level, choosing an earlier and more honest answer proffered lower down the scale. However, the skill of the civil service in preparing answers must not be under-estimated. Sometimes I altered an answer only to return to the recommended version on receiving a convincing explanation of why it was essential to do so.

Written questions came in almost every day but orals were thick every fourth Tuesday when Education was top of the list to answer. Questions to departments lower down the list were seldom reached as only a score at most, with their sup-plementaries, can be covered in the 45 minutes available.

To get an oral answer it is necessary to put the question down *exactly* two weeks before the Department is top of the list. In the case of Education there would be at least sixty questions down to answer and those not reached receive a written answer unless the question is withdrawn.

The questions are printed in the order chosen by printer's random selection. The four Ministers sit on the front bench and each has a complete copy of all the questions and suggested answers; those to be answered by each individual Minister being given a different coloured tag. The Secretary of State sits opposite the Despatch Box and to emphasise that the Arts Minister was a little different I used to sit on his right while the other two sat on his left.

The civil servants responsible for drafting the answers sit in their box and the Parliamentary Private Secretaries sit behind their Ministers. The whole set-up reminded me of my days in Fighter Command during the war when the entire ground staff had one purpose in life, to get a pilot in the air, to bring him into contact with the enemy in a position and with the guns to shoot the bugger down and get back alive.

Sometimes no Arts questions would be reached orally at all, the first twenty being all on aspects of education and answered by the Secretary of State or by Junior Ministers, Gerry Fowler who dealt with higher education or Ernest Armstrong who did schools. On the other hand, occasionally three or four Arts questions would come out in the first half-dozen and I would have a field day in which to cover myself with glory or ignominy or more usually, to survive without either gaffe or distinction.

In a series of answers throughout 1974 I endeavoured to use questions to push Government policy as far as it would go. Instead of promoting friendly questions I waited for intentionally hostile ones and tried to turn them to advantage. For example, when John Hannan, Conservative, asked me to make an additional grant to the Arts Council to cover inflation I was able to say that I had already secured an extra £750,000 for them and that the current grant would restore my predecessor's cut and provide 3% growth above inflation.[3] And when the same member asked me to act on the recommendations of the Report on Provincial Museums and Galleries[4] I was able to tell him that a number of them had already been implemented and that I had increased the Victoria and Albert Museum's grant by £400,000

[3]*Hansard* 23.7.74. Col. 1280/1.
[4] HMSO 1973.

to enable them to help local museums.[5]

Occasionally I 'inspired' a question from my own side. For example, one enabled me to report that I had secured £150,000 for the Royal Albert Hall authorities to complete the restoration of that extraordinary building.[6] It was wonderfully well spent, as indeed, is most arts money.

I secured these sums of money simply by harrassing my Treasury colleagues until they gave way, and in this I received every support from my officials. As a result we finished each year substantially up on the budget figure at the beginning, but I never had any doubt about spending money on the arts and would get and give every penny I could lay my hands on. My years with the Bank Employees stood me in good stead here for, as a result, I knew the jargon and could not be frightened by big money talk.

I was not happy about the Museums and Galleries. They needed a body at their head of the same standing as the Arts Council and talking to the Directors and Trustees I found this idea was already being canvassed in one form or another. I began to discuss the possibility of converting the existing Standing Commision for Museums and Galleries into a Collections Council but I was already biting off more than I could chew and had to let this one stand over, partly because Willy Wright who had chaired the Committee on Provincial Museums and Galleries, seemed a little shy of going full out to implement what was implicit in his own recommendations.

The National Theatre

After the expected October 1974 General Election, word came round that we were to carry on and only those being translated to other jobs or fired would be asked to see the Prime Minister. My first task was to make sure that the National Theatre was finished and so I introduced a Bill to remove the Tory £2 million limit which was already overspent. I had tried to amend the Conservative Bill to remove the figures and substitute the words 'such sums as the Secretary of State may determine' and now I was moving a measure which was only required because St. John-

[5] *Hansard* 30.7.74. Col. 126.
[6] *Hansard* 21.3.74. Col. 156.

Stevas had refused to accept my amendment to his earlier Bill. For some reason, natural kindliness I like to think, but probably because I am only combative when roused, I did not rub this in at the Despatch Box. (Incidentally, there is a great advantage in speaking on the Front Bench – you can lay your notes on that Box and appear to be speaking without any.) St. John Stevas did not respond in kind. He welcomed the Bill but then launched into a virulent attack on me; so much so that George Strauss, who followed, protested. I did not reply or intervene, but as I wound up the debate there were some further exchanges which did not trouble me as I take the view that if you are a socialist Minister the hostility of the entrenched is to be expected. The time for a Labour Minister to start worrying is when he is *not* being attacked. I *do* resent sustained hostility from my own side and when I get it I exclude the person concerned and never acknowledge or speak to him. There are only two such Labour members. On this occasion I got my Bill without opposition and that was worth a few hard words.

I was and am wholly devoted to the National Theatre project and without my Bill the building could not have been completed. Quite apart from the actual construction costs, which were now provided for, there were considerable incidental expenses involved in the move from the Old Vic to the new building and especially arising from the delays which seem to bedevil all large new projects. This money would have to be found by the Arts Council.

Willy Wright drafted for me a letter to Lord Gibson, Chairman of the Arts Council, saying that the £25 millions I had secured for them was an inclusive figure and that the extra National Theatre costs must be encompassed within it. This meant that other beneficiaries would have to suffer. I point blank refused to sign any such letter. I told Wright that I would not allow the National to be seen as the robber of every other artistic enterprise in the country. If the Arts Council had failed to ask for enough money (and they had) then I would get them some more. What Willy must do was to get them to as me for it. He did so and we obtained the extra money, not without a struggle and a certain amount of juggling with monies provisionally allocated elsewhere in the education empire.

In my experience a Labour Government will find increasing sums for the arts providing the Minister is insistent and ruthless. As for the National Theatre it is an enormous success, but as I am now a member of the governing Board I am only too well aware that every new achievement brings its own fresh problems.

The Crafts Advisory Committee

The creation of this body was the best thing Lord Eccles did as Minister for the Arts. Its job is to advise the Minister on the needs of the artist craftsman; it helps promising beginners and gives grants to start new workshops. It is also concerned with conservation, exhibitions and information. They asked me for a grant of £500,000 for 1975/6 and I got them exactly half a million pounds. I visited their interesting headquarters in Waterloo Place and was served coffee by beautiful girls. The presiding genii in my time were Chairman Sir Paul Sinker and Director Sir Paul Reilly.

The only problem they had was the inadequate salary paid to the Secretary, Victor Margrie. As a QUANGO[7] the CAC had to conform to civil service levels of pay and Margrie had been put in a salary slot far below the level of the duties he was performing. It was hell's own job to get the post upgraded but we succeeded in the end and everyone at Waterloo Place was delighted and I shared their joy.

All I had to do otherwise was to go around the country seeing the fruits of their work. If all my areas of concern had been as trouble-free as this one, this would have been a shorter book.

The British Library

When I became Minister in 1974 the idea of building a library next to the British Museum had been around for a hundred years and more. In 1947 the site was designated and incorporated in the London development plan. In 1964 the Government accepted building plans but by 1967, with the growth of the preservation lobby, doubts about the desirability of demolishing good Bloomsbury houses to make way for the library culminated in an objection from the Camden Borough Council.

The accident-prone Patrick Gordon Walker, then Secretary of

[7]Quasi-Autonomous National Government Organisation.

State for Education, had let all hell loose by deciding to uphold the Borough's objections to the Bloomsbury site without providing any alternative. A Committee was set up and Gordon Walker's decision quietly reversed. When Lord Eccles came to office with the Conservative Government of 1970, preparations for building on the Bloomsbury site went ahead. By the time I succeeded as Minister, Eccles was Chairman of the British Library Board and, as I had decided that Bloomsbury was out of the question, I could see I had a problem.

The British Library had already been organisationally established by the amalgamation and re-organisation of the existing reference, lending and bibliographical services which had been built up as separate institutions over the years. The British Museum Library, the National Reference Library of Science and Invention, the National Lending Library of Science and Technology, the National Central Library and the British National Bibliography had all achieved international reputations. The lending division had been established at Boston Spa near York and was to be opened formally in 1975, but the reference libraries were spread over London, often in temporary premises.

Within a few days of my appointment I asked for possible sites other than Bloomsbury to be examined and John Spence came up with a paper with such speed that it was clear the officials were with me. I was lucky, for a site off Euston Road between St. Pancras Station and the Shaw Theatre had become available and I decided there and then that we would have it.

It was one thing for me to make my personal decision but what about selling it to everyone else? Still, if I could get Anthony Crosland who had been appointed Secretary of State for Environment, Eccles could be overcome, providing I was in a position to offer him a real Euston Road bird-in-hand in exchange for the never-never bird in the Bloomsbury bush.

How could I bring it off? It would be far and away the most expensive project I was responsible for. The ultimate cost would be well over £100 millions and the running expenses would make the price of the National Theatre look like that of a Concert Party at the end of a pier. Still, the shadow of Cromwell and the Puritans did not lay over libraries as it did over the theatre. I told

Spence to open negotiations for the Euston Road site but not to abandon Bloomsbury until we had it sewn up. Within hours of my decision to go for Euston Road I received a letter from Joel Barnett, the Chief Secretary to the Treasury, saying that there could be no announcement of a decision to proceed with a capital project of 125 million pounds. Nevertheless, after a little testiness he agreed that the feasibility of building on the Euston Road site should be examined.

Discussions took place between Camden Borough Council and the National Freight Corporation who owned the Euston Road site and within a month I was sure that the project was viable. I lunched with Lord Eccles and told him that the price of sticking to Bloomsbury would be no British Library. If he would look at Euston Road I would get the thing off the ground. I doubt if he believed me, but he had nothing to lose for Bloomsbury was stuck solid on Camden's refusal to agree. Eccles and I sparred about enjoyably, each of us knowing precisely what the other was up to without saying too much. If Eccles could hang on there might be a change of political control but meanwhile, why not let me come a cropper trying for Euston Road.

I replied to Joel Barnett sending a copy to Tony Crosland who, as Secretary of State for the Environment, was ultimately repsonsible for building matters. I also wrote to Crosland sending a copy to Barnett. To the Chief Secretary I emphasised the cost of continuing indefinitely with the present situation of having a library spread in temporary premises all over London. I said that the idea of deferring a decision, which he had floated, was unrealistic and untenable and that if he had any doubts on this score he could read the Parliamentary debates which took place when it was tried on in 1967. In all this I received every cooperation from my officials. I had no doubt that we were working on the same side and my amendments to their drafts were quite minor ones. I also took advantage of the proper desire of the Camden authority to preserve the Bloomsbury site and suggested a meeting. On this project my own officials and those of the Treasury and of the Department of the Environment were working well together. I had a word with Tony Crosland before the meeting which took place in his office at the DOE. He was in the chair and came down firmly in favour of the Euston Road site but when I received his draft for a joint paper ot the appropriate Cabinet Sub-Committee it was less positive than I would have wished. He accepted immediately and without hesitation the alterations I made firming it up.

Although Crosland and I differed politically we had known each other for years and with him I was always conscious that we respected each other. It was fortunate that all this took place before Fred Mulley who succeeded Reg Prentice for Fred would undoubtedly intervened with disastrous results. On a Ministerial level, Crosland and I got on famously. As Secretary of State for the Environment, a Cabinet post, he was near the top of the ladder while I was close to the foot. Yet he was always happy that I should take the lead in Arts and Libraries matters in which he was concerned. His responsibility was for buildings, mine for their contents; once policy had been agreed between us he gave me unswerving support. He had little patience with protocol and the paper for the Cabinet was presented as it was, joint between the two of us instead of as between the two Secretaries of State (Crosland and Prentice) or the two Under-Secretaries (Alma Birk and myself) either of which would have been more proper but less sensible, since Crosland and I were the two people directly involved. Furthermore, I doubt if I could have secured Joel Barnett's consent to the paper but for Crosland's lofty assumption that no one but a fool could fail to agree with us. I was also fortunate that in this the Permanent Secretary was on our side and he minuted Reg Prentice recommending the joint paper. Prentice agreed and by June we were ready to go to the Cabinet Home Affairs Committee.

I was fully briefed, not only on my own side of the project but about Crosland's as well which was fortunate as at the last moment he could not attend the meeting. We therefore had the unusual scene of a Junior Minister presenting a major project covering two departments to a Cabinet Committee.

All went well and the Committee agreed that we should continue the negotiations and that if I could bring them to a provisional conclusion and deliver Eccles, an announcement should be made to Parliament on the change of site and of our intention to proceed with detailed designs to enable the library to be constructed off Euston Road as soon as possible. I knew that once we had arrived at that point there could be no turning back. The British Library would be built there whether I lived to see it or not. I was delighted, for it is to libraries that I owe much of the patchy education I have been able to acquire in a life in which, when I was young and should have been told what to do, I was allowed to please myself and when older, was forced to do what I disliked.

Lena Jeger's constituency covered both sites so I told her confidentially that we were on our way. Difficulty arose about the size of the site we were to get. We wanted eight acres but Camden only wished to give us five. There was also the problem that Eccles did not believe we would succeed. I therefore stalled questions in the House while everything else was sewn up. By this time the October election was upon us and I knew that Eccles would not commit himself until after it. When we won and I returned to Belgrave Square I set up the meeting with Eccles at once. He sent me a paper beforehand emphasising that his Board were still solidly in favour of Bloomsbury. I could see that I should get nowhere unless I was in a position to give Eccles proof that Euston meant the library but Bloomsbury was death. I wrote to the Treasury urging that I be put in a position that if they agreed to change the Board could be assured of an immediate start to the project and an immediate expenditure of £15 millions on preparing the first phase. Meanwhile I ran into some difficulties about dislocating the King's Library which formed part of the British Museum.

I prepared in advance a paper for the Cabinet Sub-Committee but on the day I was due to lunch with Eccles I went down with some temporary bug which laid me out. I decided that Eccles should be offered lunch with Willy Wright instead. He accepted, but after it Wright minuted me, 'Lord Eccles made it clear that he will not go quietly from Bloomsbury.'

All the same I set up another lunch for the following week and after it Eccles wrote to me maintaining his desire to stay next door to the British Museum in Bloomsbury but nevertheless agreeing to discuss the Euston Road site with Environment officials. This was all I wanted for I knew that the Environment people could sell Euston Road to Dr. Hookway, the Director, and the other Library officials who, faced with the reality of a library off Euston

Road or none at all in Bloomsbury would put the necessary pressure on their Board.

I replied saying that I understood how disappointed the Board must be about Bloomsbury but I was sure that when they had seen the possibilities of the Euston site, which were far superior to the limitations of space available in Bloomsbury, they would decide to accept the change.

Meanwhile, I wrote to Joel Barnett again saying that there was no hope of shifting Eccles from Bloomsbury without a firm and dated undertaking that work could start on the Euston site if the examination showed it to be suitable. I said, 'Both Tony Crosland and I are satisfied that the library requirements can be met on the site and that the Camden authority are ready to meet the planning implications involved. There are points about the price to be paid and a detailed structural survey will have to be undertaken, but there is every indication that the costs of the site will be fully covered by the sale of the parts of Bloomsbury now owned and that there will be consequential savings due to a more suitable shape of the site and the absence of extreme planning restrictions which would require a large number of basements in Bloomsbury.'

On 29th November the Board of the Library decided that they could 'see no practical basis for comparison unless the Euston Road proposal was concrete in terms of land, finance and timetable.' I sent Barnett a copy of the draft paper to the Home Affairs Committee of the Cabinet in which I said on behalf of Tony Crosland and myself: 'Our judgment of the situation is that the British Library Board and its Chairman can be brought to accept the abandonment of Bloomsbury in favour of Euston Road if, but only if, the decision is accompanied by a public undertaking on behalf of the Government to start construction of the new buildings on a specified date.'

The draft paper concluded with an invitation to the Committee to agree that an announcement should be made to Parliament before Christmas which would include the words: 'The Government will authorise detailed design work for the erection of new buildings on the Euston Road site with a view to a start on construction in 1979/80 of a first phase of the new buildings.'

On 10th December, the National Freight Corporation jumped the gun by announcing that the site was to be sold for commercial development. This announcement, though this was certainly not its intention, sharpened the issue and made sure that my second visit to the Home Affairs Committee was as successful as the first and I was authorised to proceed. On 16th December I wrote to Eccles saying that Tony Crosland or I would be giving a positive Parliamentary answer within a day or two. Crosland's officials had said that he wanted to give the answer and, of course, I could not disagree, but when I saw Crosland himself he denied any such desire and on 19th December 1974 I answered Lena Jeger[8].

'The Government have been considering, together with the Board of the British Library, how further progress can best be made towards a solution of the library's longstanding and increasingly pressing needs for a headquarters with sufficient accommodation for its readers, staff, collections and services, while recognising that the intention expressed by past Governments of both parties to use the land adjoining the British Museum in Bloomsbury would involve the kind of large-scale redevelopment and disturbance towards which public attitudes have much changed.

A site on former railway land fronting on Euston Road and immediately to the west of St. Pancras Station has recently become available. It is less than a mile from the Bloomsbury site and well provided with communications. The London Borough of Camden has indicated that use of the Euston site for the library would be in accord with its policies for the development of this area. This site is now being urgently examined in detail by the Government and the Library. Provided that the outcome of this examination is that the site can effectively accommodate the library, notwithstanding that the preference of the library remains for the Bloomsbury site, the Government will authorise detailed design work so that construction of new buildings, limited initially to a first phase, can be begun on the Euston Road site in 1979-80, subject to determination of an actual starting date in the light of the economic conditions prevailing nearer the time.'

On the 2nd January I wrote to David Eccles. 'I understand

[8]*Hansard*, 19.12.74.

E

your positon and I am sorry that, for what I hope will be no more than a short time, we must seem to be on opposite sides in pursuing the common objective of getting the library re-housed.' I went on to say that it was the first time that a starting date had been named, even conditionally, and I thought it verged 'on the miraculous to be able to do this in the present economic situation.'

The site was then frozen by the Department of the Environment who told the Freight Corporation to abandon proposals to sell it commercially.

In the summer of 1975 I opened the Lending Division at Boston Spa near York. The building stands in an open field looking like an enormous barn or aircraft hangar which I suppose it was. Inside was a hive of purposeful activity which can supply a book or journal quickly from almost every country in the world. If you live in San Francisco you can often get American material quicker from Boston Spa than from New York.

The 600 people working at Boston Spa gave a very strong impression of pride in being members of the most efficient organisation of its type, although much of the work was necessarily dull and repetitive. There is something to be learned from this.

Lord Eccles introduced me at the official opening and I knew from his pleasant attitude that although the preparatory work for the great new reference library in London would take some time to complete, it was going well and the fact that the new site had advantages over the old love was coming home to him.

Early in 1976 I had to fight like a tiger to prevent the Treasury from closing the whole thing down but the work has since made good progress, the building is approved and the Euston Road site is being prepared for construction to begin in 1979. Three cheers.

Turner, Somerset House and the Theatre Museum

The inadequacy of the academic, library, research and collection facilities for the theatre in this country has troubled many people for years. Long before I became Minister for the Arts I had been involved in trying to set up a Theatre Institute and Museum in Covent Garden which had become available on the removal of the Market to Nine Elms, but the project lacked Government support and money.

When I came into office in the spring of 1974 I found that a plan to establish a Theatre Museum in Somerset House was already well advanced. The beautiful Fine Rooms in this grand old building along the banks of the Thames had been vacated by the civil service and the Theatre Museum was to occupy them under the aegis of the Victoria and Albert Museum.

That superb actor Donald Sinden, an old friend from Equity days, was Chairman of the Museum and he wrote inviting me to visit the 'splendid rooms in Somerset House shortly to be occupied by the Theatre Museum.' He said he had no doubt that I would be just as impressed by them as a home for the Theatre Museum as he was.

I had considerable doubts. The rooms were truly splendid but quite unsuitable for any museum and there was no accommodation for the proposed Theatre Institute or for any other educational or academic development. However, I decided to let it go ahead, for something better would spring from it in time to come.

So in July 1974 I told the House of Commons that a Keeper had been appointed and that it was hoped to open the Theatre Museum at Somerset House before the end of 1975. It was my private view that a much better place for the Museum would be the basement or undercroft of the Flower Market in Covent Garden. I had had my eye on this for many years and as Somerset House was without storage facilities I suggested to the new Keeper, Alexander Shouvaloff, that the Greater London Council, who owned most of it, might find him some space in Covent Garden. Shouvaloff visited the Flower Market and realised that in its wide open area he would have enjoyed a freedom totally lacking in Somerset House where he would be subjected to restrictions and hampered by operating within rooms which were themselves fine works of art.

However, the undercroft would need much money to be spent upon before it could be used as a museum and I had none at my disposal. My own civil servants were firmly committed to Somerset House, but the Department of the Environment, which was responsible for the building, was not. They had never wanted the Theatre Museum in their precious Somerset House and they told Shouvaloff that it might not be too late to switch. The Fine

Rooms, they said with some justification, were really only suitable for occasional exhibitions of such things as period furniture which would enable the rooms to be seen for themselves.

John Spence minuted Willy Wright in September 1974 referring to the 'nefarious activities' of a senior Environment official and saying that it was 'disgraceful' that a 'major policy change' was being promoted in this way. Ministers, said Spence, meaning my Tory predecessors, had rejected the Environment proposal but here they were trying to go back to it and they had already seduced a couple of our own people. This was a reference to the fact that the Victoria and Albert was under our direct control and that Roy Strong, the Director, and Shouvaloff, the Keeper to be, were therefore civil servants in the Arts Branch of the DES. Both were showing signs of wanting to ditch the confined beauty of Somerset House in favour of the spacious area known to be available in Covent Garden.

My officials exerted their authority. Strong was brought to heel; the Environment people denied that they had any intention of trying to go behind backs and on the 28th October Strong wrote to Colin Graham, his fellow Assistant-Secretary in my Branch: 'Alas I understand you are being stony-hearted over the Flower Market. Very well, Somerset House it must be for the Theatre Museum.'

However, as Environment did not want them there and Shouvaloff did not want to go there, it was hardly surprising that great rows broke out about the amount of space the Museum was to occupy in Somerset House.

All this was still unresolved when early in 1975 the splendid Turner Exhibition at the Royal Academy triggered off in the mind of Henry Moore and in many less creative crania the notion that the Fine Rooms in Somerset House should become the home of a permanent Turner Exhibition. My officials thought that the villains at Environment had fed this idea into Moore through Strong and were using the great man as a means of levering the Theatre Museum out. The Turner idea would prove to be impracticable and the Fine Rooms would return to Environment and be seen for themselves alone and for occasional period furniture exhibitions and such like. That is exactly as it eventually turned out.

However, in February 1975 when I was due to visit the Victoria and Albert Museum, everyone was still officially committed to Somerset House for the Theatre Museum. There had been some pressure in the press and I was due to see Moore, who was coming to argue the Turner case, the following day. That morning I received a letter from Donald Sinden totally reversing his previous position. He was no longer enthusiastic about Somerset House, indeed he did not want to go there at all. It would be an 'act of vandalism' to use the Fine Rooms for his purpose. I wrote on the corner of the letter 'Jesus!' and sent it to Willy Wright. My people were very angry and Spence minuted Wright, 'Mr Sinden's letter of 17th February merits the Ministerial comment entered on it.' He went on: 'We are therefore faced with a position where the Government, on the insistent pressure of the former Director of the V & A (Sir John Pope-Hennessey) is publicly committed to the present scheme for the Fine Rooms which Mr Sinden, on note-paper provided by the present Director, calls 'an act of vandalism'. It is clear from Mr Sinden's letter that Mr Shouvaloff, without clearance from the Department, has been continuing in his efforts to kill the Somerset House scheme. He is playing a very risky game because if any of the doubtful circumstances attending the use of the undercroft came to pass there would be no Theatre Museum because the Department has no money. Their game is doubly dangerous because we know that DOE officials are doing their best to undermine the Somerset House scheme for their own reasons.'

I wrote to Donald Sinden reminding him that he had been enthusiastic about Somerset House when he showed me round. I added, 'I must leave you in no doubt that you are putting at risk the possibility of a Theatre Museum in the near future. I am therefore most reluctant to agree to the Somerset House rooms being used for another purpose when it is so clear that I shall be unable to afford the alternative which you now propose. Are you sure that you are speaking for theatre interests as a whole? Let us meet to discuss the situation.'

I then wrote to Crosland saying that I could see no opportunity of making such a change at so late a date.

I knew very well what the Theatre Museum people were up to and I was not opposed to it, but I could not allow them to enlist me as an acknowledged ally at that stage. They would obviously seek to use my visit to the V & A to sell me the Covent Garden promoting the National collections as a whole, a task he would pushover for Henry Moore when I saw him the following day. I would not be played for a sucker and so I sent a letter to Roy Strong by hand ahead of my visit saying that I would not discuss the Theatre Museum with him and he could tell Shouvaloff that he would not be needed on that occasion.

This pleased my own people mightily and when I saw Strong I explained to him, as we walked round the V & A, that I was seeing Moore that afternoon and did not want to talk about Somerset House all day. He accepted this and we got on well. I felt that Strong, who often talks through his hat but always in a popular way, was essentially a publicist and should be given a job promoting the National collections as a whole a task he would perform brilliantly.

Henry Moore came to see me with George Strauss, MP. He is a much smaller man than the size of his figures leads one to expect, but energy and conviction flowed out of him. He told me that a great artist was one who lived a long life whose work was prolific and who changed the nature of artistic perception as the result of his contribution. Picasso was one such, Turner another. And Henry Moore a third, I thought.

Moore said that Somerset House was quite unsuitable for a Theatre Museum. I said I was inclined to agree about this but also thought it unsuitable for a Turner Museum. In fact, I thought it not only impossible to achieve but undesirable to attempt to house the huge Turner output in a single building. In any event, I said I could not agree to allow the Theatre Museum people to render themselves homeless unless and until alternative accommodation of a more suitable nature had been found for them.

Meanwhile, as I thought not unlikely, Crosland came back very strongly. He disagreed with my conclusion: Somerset House was quite unsuitable for a Theatre Museum. I called my officials in and they said that even if I wanted to change the official line there was no money for it. So I wrote to Crosland: 'If you can fit this pig with monetary wings I shall be happy to fly it but on the facts as they are I did not so much reach a conclusion as point to the inevitable. When I was Chairman of the Theatres Advisory Council I tried hard to get Covent Garden for a Theatre Institute and Museum. When the Museum interests were offered Somerset House they jumped at it and the TAC connived because they felt that the separation of the Museum from the Institute was no bad thing and they are still holding on for Covent Garden. At the moment this is no more than pie in the sky.' I again pointed out that I had no money for Covent Garden and continued: 'If these problems could be overcome, the question of the use of the Fine Rooms can be considered but it ought not to be overlooked that the motivation behind the whole thing stems from a notion which disregards reality even more completely than the consequential proposal about Covent Garden. The works of Turner are not the Government's to dispose of as they think best.'

I ended by suggesting that our officials should get together to examine the financial implications providing that there was some possibility of money being obtainable.

This put the ball firmly in Crosland's court. Meanwhile, Sir James Swaffield, Director General of the GLC, wrote to Willy Wright saying that there was considerable support at County Hall for the idea of putting the Theatre Museum in the Flower Market basement.

In the light of all this, when Robert Cooke, the Bristol Tory, raised the matter on the adjournment of the House on 21st March 1975 I said that I had never been very happy with Somerset House as a home for the Theatre Museum and had always favoured a combined Theatre Institute and Museum in Covent Garden and had said this long before I was a Minister. I was in touch with the Secretary of State for the Environment and with the GLC about the possible use of the undercroft of the Flower Market and would make a statement as soon as possible. I added that there were those who had some doubt about permanent exhibitions of the work of a single artist but that we were looking into all these matters.

I told my officials to be prepared to abandon Somerset House for the Theatre Museum in their discussions with Environment and Tony Crosland replied to me welcoming the statement I had made in the House. The following month St. John Stevas suggested I should call a conference and I replied: 'It is a question, not of a Conference or of priorities but of ascertaining the factual situation which is what we are about at the moment. I am not in a position to authorise any change of plan until it is established that the Theatre Museum could open in Covent Garden at least as early as it could at Somerset House, and that the Government could finance any adaptations needed, including any capital or continuing costs which might be involved. Until the factual situation has been firmly ascertained between all the parties concerned I shall not be in a position to make a further statement.'

The price of the DOE's enthusiasm to get the Theatre Museum out of Somerset House was that Crosland had to agree to pay the whole cost of the work which needed to be done at the Flower Market, which meant that there was no chance of the Museum opening there as early as it would have done at Somerset House.

The Standing Commission on Museums and Galleries weighed in on the side of the Flower Market in May and in June I wrote to Crosland accepting the change but taking care to avoid any commitment to the Turner alternative at Somerset House. I brought the GLC and the Department of the Environment together and by September of that year agreement had been reached that the Theatre Museum would be accommodated in the Flower Market as a department of the V & A. I issued a press statement announcing this and saying that the future use of the Fine Rooms would be discussed with the appropriate bodies. Privately I let it be known that I thought that the notion of using Somerset House for a great permanent Turner Exhibition was a non-starter and other uses should be explored.

Perhaps the most remarkable thing about this odd sequence of events was the way in which Somerset House suddenly changed from Shangri-La into Hades in the minds of the Theatre Museum people. A few days before he wrote to me rejecting the place with horror, Donald Sinden was quoted by the Sunday Times[10] as

[10] 2nd February 1975.

being 'totally happy' with Somerset House. 'Let the Turners go to the Flower Market' he was reported to have said. And shortly before that Shouvaloff told Betjeman in the Times[11] that Somerset House was reserved for the Theatre Museum.

After Crosland's death, Alma Birk of Environment[12] surfaced as a supporter of the Turner Lobby but as she had no command of objects but only of buildings the whole thing ended up in stalemate made no less farcical because it was entirely predictable.

The story shows how easily administrators can use public people, can cause them to change their minds and to swing about like weathervanes. The artist is particularly vulnerable. He is prone to enthusiasms, promotes causes, leaps on bandwaggons and it never occurs to him that he may be quite unwittingly serving ends quite other than those he espouses.

There was never any chance of amassing a great permanent Turner Exhibition in Somerset House. Betjeman, Moore et al were quite ruthlessly used in the rather better cause of finding good grounds to shed the Tory commitment to put the Theatre Museum in a building quite inappropriate for the permanent exhibition of art objects other than those chosen because of their suitability for the Fine Rooms themselves.

Artists were used even more ruthlessly in opposing the Wealth Tax and here they demonstrated once again that those who become wealthy are not immune from the disease of cupidity which excludes the rich from heaven and even from the brotherhood of man. However, on the present occasion the artists had been used to good purpose and the civil servants, being divided, had been overruled.

In this case I did not so much change the mistaken decision of my Tory predecessors; rather I simply allowed it to be changed and then adopted the Environment solution, which I personally supported from the beginning, in my Ministerial position, taking the Department with me. Environment still have Somerset House and it is being used for occasional exhibitions of a suitable nature. The preparations for the Theatre Museum in Covent Garden are taking an unconscionable time but when the work is

[11] 15th January 1975.
[12] Lady Birk, Under-Secretary of State.

eventually completed it may be hoped that, at long last, the premises will be able to house and display the history, collections, records and costumes in a manner worthy of the dominant role the theatre has played in helping our people to get to know themselves.

Cinema Films – Art and Industry

Jennie Lee's White Paper's call for coherence in the arts and entertainment cannot begin to be answered until Governmental responsibility is co-ordinated. As it is, the whole area is full of absurdities, not least among them the division of departmental responsibility for the cinema film between the Department of Trade – responsible for the industry, and Education – responsible for the art. In practice this means that a Junior Minister in Trade takes an occasional interest in film production when one of his officials tells him that some decision has to be made and the Arts Minister looks after the British Film Institute and the National Film School.

To do him justice, Harold Wilson was conscious of this muddle and his first attempt to do something about it was to give me what he described as a 'general co-ordinating role in relation to artistic and cultural matters' and an 'effective interest both in the work of the film industry and in ancient monuments and historic buildings'.[13] Unfortunately, neither at this nor at any other time did he consult me on the matter and I was given neither means nor authority to make my co-ordination and interest effective in any real sense of the word.

I did better with Environment than Trade – with Buildings rather than the Film Industry. In neither case was there any formal co-ordination process apart from an occasional meeting, and I spent little time on trying to set up any such structure. For one thing I lacked the rank to carry weight with Cabinet Ministers, and for another, what was needed was not co-ordination but a transfer of responsibility. If I did not represent the Government in relation to the film industry there was little I could do. So long as the civil servants concerned with the industry were located in the Department of Trade I could give no instructions and Ministers refused to surrender any part of

[13] *Hansard*, 14.3.74. Col. 4.

their empire. They were incapable of absorbing new ideas, not through lack of intellectual stature but because of preoccupation with, to them, more important matters. They simply held on and said what their civil servants told them to say. I had no executive concern with the film industry as such. I could express opinions but no one need take any notice. One of the few points where I could exercise pressure was for the National Film School which was primarily my responsibility, but with some Trade concern.

A year after he had given me the non-existent co-ordinating role the Prime Minister laid on a dinner at Downing Street for leading film people. It was on the 13th May 1975, and after the main course Harold Wilson said that he hoped there would be a general discussion of the problems of the film industry. He then invited John Terry, Managing Director of the National Film Finance Corporation, to open the discussion. Terry supported my line that Ministerial division of responsibility was unhelpful. He went on to ask the Government to release to the NFFC funds that were frozen by the previous Government. The Chairman of the Cinematograph Films Council was pessimistic about getting money out of the television programme companies and other people spoke at greater length than the substance of their contributions justified. None of the film producers seemed to me to have any constructive contribution to make, but it went on until 11.45 pm when the PM stood up, as I thought to close it, but he suggested an adjournment of 15 minutes to attend to the calls of nature!

After that, more and more people supported my ideas about Ministerial responsibility and the need for a film authority. Harold Lever said nothing quite briefly and departed. Richard Attenborough supported my line. Sir Don Ryder, Peter Shore and others contributed in a rather non-committal fashion. At last the PM saw my waving hand. I said that the infrastructure of the film industry was created for a market that no longer existed. Changes in the structure would not create prosperity, but there could be no prosperity without such changes. The PM had floated the idea of a Royal Charter and I supported this, although nothing came of it. I urged that the industry and the art must be unified and, in turn, must be recognised as a part of the cultural and entertainment complex. I was getting tired and suggested that we should all think on these things and meet again. After several other speeches, Harold summed up saying that there was remarkable unity of opinion. If they agreed he would appoint a small working party to develop proposals and report back. He seemed to have inexhaustible stamina and to be ready to go on talking all night, but it was nearly 2 in the morning and everyone else was tired.

A short statement was issued and here it is:

'The Prime Minister gave a dinner for representatives of the film industry at 10 Downing Street on Tuesday 13 May. The Secretary of State for Trade, the Chancellor of the Duchy of Lancaster, the Financial Secretary, Treasury, the Minister for the Arts, the Parliamentary Secretary, Department of Trade (Mr. Deakins) and Sir Don Ryder were also present.

There was a full discussion of the needs of the British film industry and of its relations with Government. On behalf of the Government it was said that, subject to the availability of Parliamentary time, the Government was prepared to provide for funds to be made available from the British Film Fund for production of scripts and for pre-production expenses on lines recommended in the recent report of the Cinematograph Films Council and elsewhere. It was also agreed that a small working party of those present on behalf of the industry should be set up to develop the ideas advanced in the discussion in consultation with others concerned and to report back with specific proposals within a time table to be agreed.'

The British Film Institute had originally been established in 1933 arising from a discerning recognition of the value of film among scientific and educational bodies. Its aims were 'to encourage the development of the art of the film, to promote its use as a record of contemporary life and manners and to foster public appreciation and study of it from these points of view.' Government help was minimal in the early days, but the Labour Government of 1949 found £66,000 and when Jennie Lee came to office, the aid shot up to £475,000 in 1968/9. The BFI runs the National Film Theatre and two dozen or more regional film theatres; it is responsible for the National Film Archive, has excellent information and documentation services, a film availability service, a Production Board, educational and other

services. Its Board. of Governors is appointed on the recommendation of the Minister for the Arts and it has a small but
devoted staff who quarrel a good deal among themselves.

Early in 1975 Willy Wright told me that the British Film
Institute was bucking the Government accounting system. They
were, he said, behaving worse than the Arts Council and this was
because their accountant was even more emotional about
commercial accounting than Tony Field, the Arts Council's
Finance Officer.

At the end of the previous financial year they had drawn the
balance of their grant in a lump sum and were believed to have
paid money in advance of need. This year they had been more
closely examined and could only establish a need for £400,000.
As there was £650,000 of their grant unclaimed, this meant they
would have to lose the remaining £250,000, in accordance with
the rule of public accounting which lays it down that money must
not be advanced before it is needed. It could not be drawn and
carried over for future needs, for the Treasury did not allow
balances to be held by recipients of public money all over the
country. They felt that interest should accrue to the general
public and not to aided bodies.

The result of this decision was to bring the Chairman of the
BFI, Lord Lloyd of Hampstead, to see me in a state of great
concern. Lloyd, short and slight, a distinguished academic, was a
devoted Chairman and a good one in many ways but the BFI was
a difficult assignment and I felt that his heart was really in the
Film School, of which he was also Chairman. Willy Wright
explained that the Deputy Director, Alan Hill, was running the
show. He was also the Accountant, and Keith Lucas, the
Director, devolved all such matters to Hill in association with
one of the Governors, Robert Camplin, who was also a
commercial accountant, as well as very knowledgeable and
experienced in the film trade. Hill, said Willy, was openly
contemptuous of the Parliamentary system of accounting and
was refusing to co-operate. He was advising that if any part of
the grant was withheld, the Governors should threaten to resign
en bloc.

At the first meeting Alan Hill was present and tended to
dominate. I decided that I would encourage Lloyd and Lucas to

accept their responsibility and since I did not want to lose the lot of them, I would isolate Hill.

At the next meeting I had no officials present and saw Lloyd and Camplin alone so as to disabuse them of the idea, which they clearly held, that on this I could be separated from my civil servants. Whether we liked it or not, until such time as the Treasury system of accounting was changed, we all had to operate within it. I would negotiate a reasonable carry-over from one year to the next but would not waste my time trying to impose commercial accounting on the Treasury.

Then Lloyd threatened to resign. I asked him to defer a decision and called Wright and Alan Hill in and asked them to see if they could find a compromise. Thereafter I refused to see Hill and there was soon a story in the Guardian that he intended to resign. I saw Lloyd and Camplin again and agreed a solution proposed to me by Willy Wright. They had found a need for £100,000. We would only withhold £150,000 and this we would try to get back for them the following year if they could demonstrate a need for it. This compromise was accepted by the Governors and Hill resigned.

On 16th April Dennis Lloyd wrote me a very nice letter and it was clear that, for the moment at any rate, the resignation of Hill had solved the problem. The Accountant did not actually leave and was still present when I toured the BFI some time later, but I gave instructions that Hill was not to be among the party and he departed physically soon after. A capable man, I believe, certainly a forceful one, but in the wrong job at the BFI.

Lloyd applied for the re-vote of £157,000 at the end of the year. The case was contained in a six-page letter and I wished that the BFI could manage to express itself more succinctly. My wish was granted all too soon for early in the New Year Dennis Lloyd wrote again. He had clearly heard that my officials had uncovered the fact that the case for the re-vote had collapsed and he wrote a short letter in which he said that he found it 'impossible to contemplate that any Minister with responsibility for the Arts, least of all yourself, would be a party to a decision' which did not grant a re-vote of the full £157,000. Unhappily the BFI's books showed that they had no immediate need of the money and in my reply I pointed out to Lloyd that our undertaking to apply for the re-vote had depended on their statement that they had been unable to carry out their full services for lack of funds. In fact they had carried out these services and they had already paid for them in the previous financial year. Nevertheless I would try to get £50,000 which would provide the Institute with a reasonable working cash balance to carry over to the next year.

The Exchequer and Audit Department had demonstrated that the BFI had operated with an intention to beat the system and when Lloyd showed no signs of accepting the position I had to write a rather strong letter pointing out that the responsibility for the situation which had arisen was that of the Institute in that the expenditure for which they were claiming the re-vote had already been met from their own resources. After a meeting of the Governors I received a much more conciliatory note from Dennis Lloyd and my instructions on this were 'reply with cordial and terminal brevity.' This was done and perhaps I should say here that I have always liked and admired Lord Lloyd and was always satisfied that he acted in the best interests of the BFI as he saw them.

In my experience the endeavours of everyone in the arts were always on behalf of the cause they had at heart but there are right and wrong ways of squeezing the maximum out of Government, and I made it clear that I would enthusiastically support the first and sit firmly on the second. Dennis Lloyd and I had lunch together soon after that, and when I was fired, his was among the warmest of the vast number of letters I received regretting my departure.

I think Keith Lucas might well be ready to agree with me that proper devolution of responsibility may entail the risk that arguments, reasonable in themselves, are taken, without adequate re-examination, to a point at which they are exposed as impracticable. The following year the BFI made out a good case and within the rules I was able to get them some part of the extra money they so badly needed. It seems to me that the National Film Theatre alone is a superbly successful operation and those responsible for it do not get the credit they deserve.

On a lighter note, from time to time I received anonymous letters which were said to be written by members of the staff of the BFI. These alleged (inter alia) that intimate favours from junior female staff members were enjoyed behind a filing cabinet. I enquired about these pleasures but it seemed that they were illusory.

In August 1975 I received a Minute from Willy Wright saying that the Factory Inspectorate had issued a warning that the old nitrate-based film stock held in the BFI archives was probably unsafe in the current hot weather. A collection of old films had recently exploded in Latin America. Houses had been built near the boundary of the BFI vaults at Aston Clinton in Buckinghamshire and it might be necessary to move the film stock. The Ministry of Defence had been alerted. I commented on this Minute; 'We should take no chances. What sort of a watch is being kept and how long notice will there be of an emergency?'

The reply was a further Minute saying that Willy had seen the Factory Inspectorate and they recommended 'No panic action'. At the same time they also recommended that access to the archive should be restricted, which meant in effect that it should be closed. It also transpired that it was not considered safe to move the stock. My comment on this was 'to avoid risks is not to take panic action. I repeat, no chances must be taken'.

The possibility of evacuating nearby houses was then looked into and the closure inevitably leaked; Ken Gosling had an accurate piece in The Times on 16th August. An immense amount of toing and froing then took place between officials, and each Monday at the weekly 'Progress' meeting I asked about the state of play. The long process of transferring old films on to new acetate stock would take years, even if more money was found to hasten it, for the news of the instability of the old stock had spread and commercial holders of old films were busy unloading their stuff free of charge onto the Archive which was torn between a desire to have everything they could lay hands on and the knowledge that it might all blow up in their faces.

As summer passed into autumn, the heat diminished in every way and without it actually being said, the feeling was that the original report of the Factory Inspectorate which had caused all the fuss had been unnecessarily alarmist. However, I was not satisfied and demanded to go and see for myself, but it was not until November that the visit was arranged.

I found that the vaults at Aston Clinton were completely full and that the surplus was held in hired vaults at the National Film School at Beaconsfield or elsewhere. I was unhappy but not surprised to discover that the fact that they had been believed to be in danger had been concealed from the workforce consisting largely of local part-time ladies. I saw a very alarming film showing what could happen and said that unless I received a report from the Health and Safety Executive to the effect that the danger could be eliminated I would recommend to the Secretary of State and to the Cabinet that the archive be closed and nearby houses evacuated. Meanwhile the Ministry of Defence had discovered a couple of possible places where the film could safely be stored if it could be moved. I also asked for an estimate of the cost of speeding up the 'duping' process on to modern acetate film.

By the end of the year the Executive had decided that there was, after all, little danger of explosion; the problem was a smoke one. It could be toxic. Steps were taken to reduce the overheating of the vaults, alterations were made to vents and doors which reduced the risk of fire and explosion to an acceptable level and a little money was found to cope with the fume problem.

One beneficial result of the alarm was to accelerate the process of transferring nitrate to cellulose. It is to be hoped that the impetus has not been lost and that the problem is now well on the way to resolution.

A curious incident occurred late in 1975, John Huntley, formerly a senior official of the BFI, had resigned in 1973 in circumstances which had left much bitterness on both sides. Huntley had been accepted as a candidate for one of the seats on the BFI Board which are the subject of a ballot by members of the Institute and had topped the poll.

The curious incident was that I was recommended not to appoint Huntley but Nicholas Garnham who was second. Garnham, a left-winger, and an existing member of the Board had been accepted with reluctance but had proved to be a good member and now the Establishment wanted me to prefer him over the choice of the membership! The poll is technically advisory but there had been no previous case of failure to appoint an elected candidate. On the other hand, I well understood that Keith Lucas, the Director, would not want on his Board a man whose employment at the BFI had been terminated in strained circumstances. They were not only strained but strange for it was a part of the leaving agreement negotiated by the Association of Supervisory Staffs, Executives and Technicians that no statement should at any time be made by anyone as to the cause of Mr Huntley's resignation.

I decided not to appoint Huntley on condition that it was made a general rule that ex-members of the staff were not eligible for election to the Board and that no further such candidature should be accepted. Mr Huntley came to Belgrave Square and we had a very civilised talk in which I made it clear that I had made my decision with reluctance and thought he had just cause for complaint. If he wished to air his anger publicly he should feel free to do so and I would make no response.

It speaks of the unsatisfactory nature of the organisation of the BFI that no effective action was taken; that Huntley stood again and my successor was placed in the same position as I was, and did as I did. Whatever the cause of the rift, the manner in which Mr Huntley was subsequently treated did the BFI no service. It also damaged me in some eyes as a small but virulent bunch of letters made all too clear.

It could, of course, be said that as Mr Huntley was a party to a leaving agreement containing a vow of silence all round, he had strained that agreement by standing. But I took the view that the Minister's veto should be removed and that in future the BFI should be forced to put up with the consequences of their own actions or lack of action. They should no longer be in a position to be bailed out by a Minister forced to choose between creating an impossible situation in the BFI and violating his own sense of propriety. In sum, whenever a measure of democracy is introduced by giving a group elective powers, those eligible for election must be determined before the event and the result must be absolute.

At a function at the National Film Theatre I was the subject of one of John Gielgud's famous gaffes. We met with signs of mutual recognition and he said at once that he was delighted to see me.

'I do so enjoy your television show,' he added. I must have looked non-plussed for someone hurried him away and I heard later that he thought I was Joseph Cooper whose 'Face the Music' I also enjoy but he doesn't even have a beard!

The last time Gielgud and I had had any extended conversation, was more than thirty years ago when I was running English Programmes at Rangoon Radio. I have a clear recollection of the stuffy little studio with its single tulip mike and of how, as he read from 'A Shropshire Lad'. the sweat running down our faces was augmented by tears.

In March 1975 I had a letter from Dennis Lloyd in his capacity as Chairman of the National Film School, inviting me to visit their place at Beaconsfield. I was interested in the school as I had been a little involved with Jennie Lee in starting it off in 1970, shortly before the Tories came into office. Before going I had a look at the finances of the School and recalled that it had originally been funded mainly from a contribution from the 'Eady Levy,' an obligatory deduction from cinema exhibitors' box-office receipts intended to support home film production. 80% of the cost of the school had been found from this source, but with the decline of the cinema, not only were more and more of the graduates going into television but the cinema's share of the cost had declined to 25%. The prosperous television industry, however, was paying only a miserable 5% of the cost of its skill input from the School while the remaining 70% now came from the public purse through my Department.

On my visit I took Eric Deakins with me who was then responsible in the Department of Trade for the commercial film, among many other things. Eric is a film buff and he was receptive to my argument that under the Tories (nothing is more spurious than their reputation for knowing about money) the financial proportions here, like everywhere else, had gone all to hell. The outcome was that the grant from the Eady Fund was upped for the first time in years, to £120,000.

The Director of the School, Colin Young, had been there from the beginning and was widely regarded as a first class man. Deakins and I were most impressed with the Film School, a workmanlike outfit existing on a shoestring without excessive complaint, no grand buildings, just a grotty collection of huts inhabited by people who knew what they were about and loved it. While there I received a petition from the students about their grants and was able to help a little.

Early in 1976 Dennis Lloyd asked for a grant of £490,000 for the National Film School. This was substantially higher than any previous grant and I think he was astonished when I wrote to him on the 15th March saying I would be getting him the exact sum he had asked for. I was nearly always able to do this for most of the recipients of state money during my two years which, perhaps, is why I received so many sorrowful letters when I was fired. Both my Secretaries of State, Reg Prentice and Fred Mulley, supported me and allowed me access to Treasury Ministers on my arm-twisting expeditions. Both found me a little Education money when I was short and neither raised any objection to my playing around with my own 'vote', such as meeting an urgent call by using funds earmarked for another purpose but not immediately needed.

In this Willy Wright and John Spence were my willing accomplices for all of us were eager to support the arts with the largest amount of money we could secure from any source.

John Terry was appointed Chairman of the Working Party set up after the Downing Street dinner and other old friends of mine, Richard Attenborough and Alan Sapper, General Secretary of the Film Technicians Union, were members. Its recommendations were published in January 1976[14] Fred Mulley, now Secretary of State, had said that I was not to minute the Prime Minister direct but I did so, including Fred in the circulation. I thought I was on safe ground as Harold Wilson respected my knowledge of the film industry but, of course, what I did not then know was that Wilson had already decided to go.

[14] *Cmnd.* 6372. HMSO.

I told the PM that I agreed with the Working Party that a British Film Authority should be set up but advised that the Film Institute should remain separate and that co-ordination should be achieved ministerially. I continued:

'You were good enough to invite me to perform a coordinating role in films. I failed to achieve anything useful at all because the problems were far beyond the coordinating capacity of a Junior Minister and I think your decision to establish the Working Party recognised this.

What is happening in films is, *mutatis mutandis*, what happened to the theatre a score of years earlier. The theatre was replaced by the cinema as the daily bread and butter entertainment of our people just as the cinema has now been replaced by television.

The retirement of the cinema from its primary role to a secondary one does not mean that it will die any more than the theatre died. It *does* mean that the British film industry will only be able to operate profitably on a reduced scale and that if we wish it to reach its highest possibilities we shall have to sustain that effort with public funds just as we sustain the theatre with public funds.

We allowed the commercial thatre to die except in those areas such as the West End where it could sustain itself profitably. We should do the same in the case of the cinema. There is no case for the artificial prolongation of the commercial cinema beyond its natural life but there *is* a case for the support of the British production industry.

There is also a case for the partial substitution of the commercial cinema by the publicly owned cinema; for the growth of the British Film Institute into an Authority carrying out functions not dissimilar to those of the Arts Council.

In these last paragraphs I have referred to the cinema separately from the Film Industry. This raises the question, is the British film industry more than the production end of the British cinema – has it an export potential? The answer is, yes, of course, but it must primarily serve the British cinema. The days in which our film producers were the main international source of the superfilm, selling all over the world while the home market steadily declined, are long over.

In the light of this, should the recommendations of the Working Party be viewed favourably? Yes I think so. I agree that the normal stance of the official is, perhaps properly, to advise against change; to foresee the snags in any proposal and to throw cold water on it. But I also agree that we cannot leave the film industry where it is and do nothing.

Apart from anything else, the state is already involved to a much greater degree in the film industry than it ever was in the commercial theatre and the atmosphere of our time is different. To-day the Government is held responsible for everything. A decade of theatrical starvation took place between the collapse of the commercial theatre in the fifties and the growth of the regional theatre in the sixties. In the cinema we cannot allow this to happen. We have to build up the supported cinema as the wholly commercial cinema declines for there are fundamental differences between the theatre and the cinema.

The cinema has never been mainly British. It is an American form and it remains American-fed. It will not die out altogether as the theatre died out in the regions, even if we do nothing. What will die is the British Film Industry.

I remain concerned about the British Film Institute and about the question of Ministerial responsibility. I believe that, at least for the time being, the BFI should remain separate from the BFA and should continue to be funded and appointed directly. But if the two parts of the industry are to be brought into closer harmony Ministerial responsibility should no longer be divided and the Minister or Ministers responsible for the arts and entertainments, including the film, should *not* be located in the Department of Trade.'

Hugh Jenkins.

1.3.76

On the 4th March I was called to a meeting at 10 Downing Street. The PM was in a very relaxed mood and told me that my Minute on the film industry was the best he had received, not excluding that of the responsible Minister, Peter Shore. This was probably because I agreed with him more than did Shore. He was determined to implement as much as possible of the Working Party's Report in spite of objections from Joel Barnett, Chief Secretary to the Treasury, which he swept aside. Harold Lever intervened but had obviously not read the papers and he tried to bluff by saying that as his contribution was rather long, he would put it in writing. Wilson said he was glad to hear this as on Friday afternoon 23rd January 1958 Lever had spoken in the Commons from noon until 4 pm. He was relieved to know he did not intend to get started to-day.

The meeting continued in this amiable fashion, the assumption being that with his Prime Ministerial authority Wilson would come to the rescue of the film industry and would implement the recommendations of the Working Party. Although he had already decided to go I do not think that the then Prime Minister could have appreciated how utterly powerless he would be to do anything at all once he had stepped down. As it is, more than two years later, very little has been done. Wilson himself became Chairman of what was called an Interim Action Committee which has reported in its turn, but, as I write there is still no British Film Authority; Ministerial responsibility is still divided and as a result both the industry and the art fail to play in this country the significant role they fulfil in the trade and in the culture of other nations.

Business Sponsorship

Soon after I was appointed I asked to have the Arts Council's papers for each of their meetings which enabled me to keep in touch with developments without relying on Willy Wright's periodical reports which were necessarily selective and transmitted through a very shrewd but quite idiosyncratic mind.

Early in 1976 a lengthy report from the Officers recommended that the Council should become the coordinating body for commercial sponsorship of the arts. I minuted Willy Wright; 'this is highly undesirable and cannot be permitted. The Arts Council is already too all-embracing and must become less, not more so.'

The Arts Council document was not only wrong in principle but quite inaccurate. During the previous two years I had spent a lot of time encouraging commercial sponsorship and was well advanced towards an agreement with the CBI under which, with Government launching money, they would establish a body to encourage commercial patronage of the arts. The Arts Council document appropriated these developments, in which it had had no hand, to itself. I concluded my Minute to Willy Wright: 'Business sponsorship must be seen as complementary to and even, in some cases, in competition with, Government sponsorship and not something which the Government seeks to place under the aegis of its own patronage agency. The less business sponsorship is seen to be associated with the Arts Council the better it will be and the more likely business men are to find the money.'

By this time I had had several meetings with the CBI and the project would have been launched but for Harold Wilson's ill-advised decision to ask Harold Lever to carry out an investigation of sources of finance for the arts. The CBI had initially seen in this some possibility of operating at a higher level and it took them some months to discover that Lever was not going to do anything and to return to me.

A further meeting took place in February 1976 which was attended by Lord Drogheda, Sir Campbell Adamson and Anthony Garrett and C. G. Knowles of the Imperial Tobacco Company. After that, the association for Business Sponsorship of the Arts was established with Lord Goodman as Chairman. A press statement was issued and, as I expected, one outcome of this was a letter from ASH (Action on Smoking and Health) complaining about the association of Imperial Tobacco with the new body. I had already insisted that ABSA should move its address, which was in the offices of Imperial Tobacco, and should get a secretary other than Mr. Knowles who was on their staff and so was able to reply accordingly, but I added that I saw no reason why the arts should refuse money coming from any legal source providing there were no strings attached. I did not regard a note in the programme saying that the production had been sponsored by this or that Company as objectionable. If Durex wanted to sponsor the National Theatre that would have been fine with me.

I had a note circulated to the Arts Council which read as follows:

> 'Since the election of the present Government the Minister for the Arts has been pressing on the Confederation of British Industries and the Trade Union Congress the desirability of encouraging commercial and industrial sponsorship in a more substantial and systematic way. The importance of these efforts has been emphasised by the Prime Minister's request to Mr Lever to carry out a thorough investigation of the future needs of the arts and the possibility of support from sources other than central or local government.
>
> 'In the climate created by these initiatives a number of

organisations are ringing up with the intention of increasing the amount of sponsorship.'

I then listed these bodies and said that I hoped that ABSA would grow into a coordinating or umbrella organisation for business sponsorship.

In reply to a question in the House I said: 'I see no ground for dissuading any industry from increasing the total resources available.'

I attended officially a number of sponsored occasions including the Boston Symphony Orchestra's concerts at the Royal Festival Hall in March '76 and the Midland Bank's Prom season at the Royal Opera House a few days before I was fired.

One of my last actions as Minister was to write to Lord Goodman on 2nd April 1976 suggesting that ABSA should be reconstituted as a Government/CBI/TUC body and to act as a coordinating organisation for the encouraging and planning of business sponsorship. I reminded him of the £15,000 I had put aside as launching money for such a body.

CHAPTER EIGHT

Late Rise and Early Fall

The Wealth Tax and the Arts

Back in August 1974, Denis Healey, as Chancellor of the Exchequer, presented to Parliament a Green Paper[1] setting out the Government's proposals for a Wealth Tax. The Paper said that taxes on wealth were common throughout the world and suggested that in Britain they should only be levied on fortunes exceeding £100,000 or perhaps £200,000 beginning at 1% and rising to $2\frac{1}{2}$% or 5% over £5 millions. It was made clear that these were discussion figures only and that no final decisions had been made, but the Government felt that the tax should be levied on individuals and should be chargeable on all property above the levels determined.

There was a special section on what was called 'The National Heritage' though this was nowhere defined. This lacuna enabled the enemies of the tax to use the term to suggest that the totality of the national treasure, including that large part already publicly owned, was threatened by a wealth tax and that all of it, including those private treasures deep in bank vaults, in some way belonged to the many who would never even see it. The Green Paper said that there were 'forcible arguments' against outright exemption of works of art but that it would be necessary to ensure that a wealth tax did not lead to the dispersal of the 'National Heritage' but to it becoming 'more readily available to the public generally.'

The Green Paper continued:

> Accordingly any special arrangments which are made for historic
> houses or works of art etc. should be conditional on the house

[1] Cmnd. 5704 HMSO.

being open to the public or the work of art etc. being on public display, whether in the owner's house or on loan to a public collection, with such modifications as might be appropriate for delicate objects or research material.

After suggesting that payment of the tax might be deferred until the death of the owner in appropriate cases, the Green Paper went on:

> For some categories of works of art there might perhaps be exemption from the interest accruing on deferment (though not from the charge itself). This could be combined with arrangements to take the works into public ownership in satisfaction of accrued wealth tax liabilities.

Months before the Green Paper was published the arts plutocrats and their minions sprang into action. The National Arts Collections Fund in the person of Sir Anthony Hornby was very quickly off the mark, writing to Denis Healey on 9th April. Simultaneously, Ernle Money (Tory, Ipswich) was asking questions in the House and the Earl of Rosse, Chairman of the Standing Commission on Museums and Galleries was equally active. Fortunately, their letters were sent to me and I replied non-commitally as did John Gilbert, the Financial Secretary, in the Chamber. I also wrote to Healey making it clear that I favoured special arrangements for owners of art property, short of exemption. The Reviewing Committee on the Export of Works of Art is serviced by the Arts Branch and Lord Perth, its Chairman, wrote from 38 Belgrave Square to the Chancellor. The Duke of Grafton raised the matter in the Lords. I had a reply from Denis Healey and at that stage we seemed to be at one.

Letters to the press from Hugh Leggatt, a dealer, from George Levy, President of the British Antique Dealers Association, from Denis Mahon, a collector and a Trustee of the National Gallery, and from sundry stately home owners continued throughout the summer of '74 and among others I received a *cri-de-coeur* from the Earl of Crawford and Balcarres. I told him that the Green Paper would, I thought, set some of his fears at rest. I met Sir Geoffrey Agnew at the Hazlitt Gallery and I agreed that he should come in for a talk after the publication of the Green Paper.

The Scotsplutes were equally active and I received copies of dozens of letters to their Secretary of State, Willie Ross.

My officials were all in favour of exemption and I was relieved when the Green Paper was published and held the position open with a bias *against* exemption of the arts. I was satisfied with the Green Paper as it seemed to me to be in accordance with the draft I had seen and approved. I did not realise until I was looking through the papers again in preparation for this book that the original draft from the Board of Inland Revenue had contained the words 'exemption would not be an appropriate way to help'. Willy Wright had altered this to the wording which actually appeared in the paper 'there are forcible arguments against exemption'. Thus a firm rejection of exemption had been modified by my pro-exemption senior official and in approving the draft as amended I had accepted and endorsed the beginning of the watering down process which ended in the abandonment of the tax. Nevertheless, at the time I was happy with 'forcible arguments' and determined to present them to the Select Committee which was to consider the tax in greater detail.

In the second General Election Campaign of 1974 I shared one of the Transport House Press Conferences with Harold Wilson and the official Press Release quoted me as saying among other things:

> 'If we are going to do something to redress the shocking maldistribution of ownership in this country we cannot exempt the arts, paintings, antiques, and other valuable objects. To do so would be˙ to create a tax haven and the present retreat from equities and other forms of investment would be encouraged. At the same time it is the Government's intention to cushion those owners of artistic objects who are prepared to make them available to be seen by members of the public.
>
> 'The impact of what is proposed has been greatly exaggerated and in any event there will be very full discussions with representative persons and bodies. Like VAT, this is ultimately a matter for the Treasury, but of course I am concerned and involved and discussions will also take place between departments and between Ministers.'

In December 1974 Airey Neave (Tory) moved a Motion

arguing that the Wealth Tax was a threat to the arts. What he seemed to imply in the motion was that it was a threat to the *owners* of works of art. Throughout the whole debate the Tories plugged the idea that anyone who possesses a valuable work himself becomes precious and must be treated as gently as his possessions. Neave painted a moving picture of gallant souls hanging on by the skin of their teeth to objects handed down throughout the generations and by a daring leap carried us to Leningrad where our brave Russian allies were fighting to keep their collections from the Nazi hordes.

There was a tribute to Mr Hugh Leggatt who was already working away in the cause of enabling the rich to stay wealthy although he believed himself to be fighting against what he called 'Marxism'. The fact that a Wealth Tax exists in the United States, but not in the Soviet Union, in Federal Germany but not in Eastern Germany, in several other Western European countries but in no Eastern European country; that the Tax is essentially a capitalist tax, none of this deterred the plutes and their spokesmen. One must admit that they were remarkably successful in recruiting to their side thousands of people, perhaps millions, who would never pay the tax and who could only benefit from its application to the top group of property-owners.

Neave was followed by Andrew Faulds (Labour) who complained that the Chamber was empty and proceeded to leave it himself after he had fulsomely praised St. John Stevas as the best Arts Minister we had ever had. How this Tory's ten languid weeks elevated him over Jennie Lee's six splendid years was not revealed to us. Patrick Cormack, (Conservative) took right off into a stratum of poesy which Mrs Dunwoody (Labour) who followed him was unkind enough to call 'emotional claptrap', and St. John Stevas made one of his speeches. Replying I was lushly complimentary to John Gilbert, the Financial Secretary to the Treasury, who was sitting by my side and I pointed out that the arrangement for gifts to all the National Heritage bodies still existed so that the tax was really a voluntary one. If one did not wish to pay it, one simply gave the valuable work away. Furthermore, works of art could be accepted in lieu of estate

---

[2] *Hansard* 13.11.74. Col. 1045 et seq.

duty. A Select Committee was to be set up which would make recommendations on detail.

Behind the scenes the most efficient and successful pressure group was hard at work. Lord Perth, the charming Chairman of the Reviewing Committee on the Export of Works of Art came to see me together with one or two of his colleagues. They expressed grave forebodings about the combined consequences of the capital transfer and wealth taxes on the national heritage. My officials agreed with them, especially Willy Wright, and indeed I had already received from him a recommendation that I should give evidence to the Select Committee on the Wealth Tax calling for artistic property to be exempted from the tax.

I told Willy that I would do no such thing. On the contrary, I would give evidence that a Wealth Tax which exempted art property would be disastrous for the arts and for artists and I instructed him to prepare a document to this effect. A long silence ensued.

I felt very isolated. It was rumoured that the Chancellor was under pressure to back-track on the Tax and I had no doubt that the wealthy were as influential in the Treasury as they were elsewhere. My senior civil servants were against me; where could I find allies? Senior colleagues in Government were uninterested; they had their own problems and in any event not all of them could be trusted to back me. The Parliamentary Labour Party could not be brought in at this stage because of the absurd convertion which excludes backbench MPs from the Governmental process.

It occurred to me that I might find support from Professor Maurice Peston who had recently been appointed by Reg Prentice as his political adviser; if he was an ally I could bring him in on discussions as he had access to all papers. I telephoned Maurice and he came over to Belgrave Square. We had a preliminary talk and he immediately agreed that to exclude art property from a wealth tax would be to bring about a withdrawal of investment from other areas into the arts with consequences damaging to the economy and to the arts. The only people to benefit would be owners of treasures, dealers and their spokesmen.

Early in 1975 I received a new draft of the proposed evidence

to the Select Committee which moved considerably in my
direction, but I was still unhappy with it and amended it
substantially. In February I called a meeting with Willy Wright,
John Spence and Maurice Peston and began by saying that the
draft should be re-written again and should begin by making it
clear that it concentrated on the *Arts*. It would assume that a
wealth tax was to be introduced and would express no view
against that policy. This was accepted reluctantly and it was then
discovered that Peston had not had the third draft of the
document containing my own amendments. Nevertheless, we
found a copy for him and ploughed through it. Willy and John
accepted amendments which I think they would have resisted
more strongly but for the helpful presence of Professor Peston and
the general consequence of these changes was to move the
document away from acceptance of the alarmist prognosis which
was being peddled on behalf of the owners of art property.
Nevertheless I was still unhappy with the draft and asked
Maurice Peston to prepare his own written commentary upon it.
When it came it blew a wind of fresh air through the sullen
resistance which was spoiling my hitherto good relationships with
the civil servants.

Peston's document did not change the basic attitude of my
officials, but it certainly affected their outward stance. Professor
Peston urged that our submission to the Select Committee should
be based upon the assumption that the introduction of a wealth
tax was a desirable reform. He found no such assumption behind
the paper as at present drafted. Willy then commented on
Maurice Peston's note and after this the draft was again
completely re-written in a form I found entirely acceptable,
containing much of my own material and some of Peston's. It
produced a balanced view indicating that owners of art property
would need special treatment within a wealth tax but providing
this was done, the tax would be a beneficial one. It would be a
further stage in the long process by which over the years more
and more objects of artistic value had become accessible to the
public.

In the files, to which I was given access in preparing this book,
I found a note from John Spence sending a copy of the final
version to his Under-Secretary counterpart in the Treasury. He

said that most of the substantial changes were the consequence of 'Ministerial directions' and he added, 'Mr Jenkins may well decide to attend the Select Committee himself.' He was dead right I would. I did not see how I could expect my civil servants to give convincing oral evidence in support of a case which had been forced upon them.

Much later I learned from Harold Wilson that by this time he had already gone off the Wealth Tax (if indeed he was ever on it) and that if he had been aware of my intention to give oral evidence personally, he would have stopped me from doing so.

I had decided that the Arts Council must be allowed to give its own evidence to the Select Committee even though Lord Gibson had made it clear that he was not on my side. Willy Wright who represented the Department on the Arts Council was no help here and Gibson wrote a letter to Denis Healey directly opposing me.

I substantially altered the draft reply typing an addition of my own which ended as follows:

> 'It may be that the real problem is not among those which have been identified, for they can be ameliorated, but rather in that art objects may be sold to pay for the tax falling due on the general wealth of the richest families in the land. Lord Perth has made no secret of the fact that he wants "The Heritage" excluded from the tax altogether. If that were granted, the next step would be an attack on the tax itself for it could be cogently argued that "The Heritage" was still in danger.
>
> 'I am for the Government encouraging the maintenance of our vast collection of valuable, beautiful and antique objects and I shall do my best to help in that, but not at the cost of preserving privilege and the vast differences in ownership which disfigure our society and which the Government is pledged to reduce.'

On receipt of this, Gibson circulated widely a reply in which he asserted that it was my view that the preservation of 'our artistic heritage' must take second place to the reduction of privilege and inequality. I replied sharply to this, so much so that I allowed Willy Wright to tone the letter down a little before despatch, but it still slapped Gibson down hard. It proved impossible for the wealthy to accept that the exemption they sought would be disastrous for the arts and the reason they could not accept it, although it was quite obvious, was that for them exemption was not an end in itself but a weapon in the real struggle. This, as the honest Perth made clear, was to put the Government off a wealth tax altogether and to use the arts as a lever in that cause.

In the files I also found that before being sent to the Select Committee my draft had been submitted to the Permanent Secretary, who objected strongly to much of it. Willy Wright's response was: 'A good many passages in the paper were express additions or amendments made by Mr Jenkins after discussion with Professor Peston. Mr Jenkins has decided that he will attend the Committee himself as the paper includes expressions of political opinion. Some of the passages you have queried or to which you have proposed amendments are among those insisted on by the Minister. I have therefore felt obliged to retain some of the phrases you suggest omitting.'

It was suggested to me that the Treasury were unhappy about my idea of self-valuation (i.e. that the owners could value their treasures themselves rather than submitting to an outside valuation) and so I took the opportunity of a visit to John Gilbert, then Finanical Secretary to the Treasury, to deal with the matter. I had created a great fuss by opposing VAT on the arts. I was on a loser there because the Government's Common Market stance was quite subservient at that stage and the requirement to 'harmonise' taxation meant that we would not act unilaterally even though technically free to do so. So when Gilbert broke the news to me that all my pleas were in vain it came as no surprise, but I simulated shock, horror and despair, and when I had recovered, said, 'Well there it is. There's one thing you can do for me. Write me a letter saying that the Treasury has no objection to my self-valuation proposal on the wealth tax, will you?' He said he would and did.

All the same, Willy Wright came back again trying to get me to accept the Permanent Secretary's amendments. I rejected them all, writing at the foot of his Minute, 'You have altered the heading of the Memorandum to make it one from me rather than from the Department. This means that I decide what goes in it. It is no longer Departmental evidence. I will accept no

F

amendments. Send to Select Committee unaltered.'

He did so but there was one alteration. The heading was changed back to make the document a departmental one. So in the end, if you insist they accept it.

This entire episode shows, however, that I totally under-estimated the strength of the owners. I believed I would achieve what I was working for: to make the possession of works of art within a wealth-taxed society sufficiently attractive to encourage retention but not so attractive as to increase hoarding. I even contemplated treating existing owners more favourably than prospective ones, but the dealers, who depended on trade and who were flogging the stuff abroad while prating about the 'National Heritage' were, I was told, opposed to it. Nevertheless, I determined to submit the idea privately to the Chancellor. I was over-confident and devoted myself too exclusively to the arts and thus did not realise that the wider objects of the wealthy were being achieved. While I was determined that artstic property should not be excluded from a wealth tax, the Labour leadership's enthusiasm for the tax itself was waning under the blandishments and warnings of the plutes. The Select Committee on the Wealth Tax with Douglas Jay in the Chair began its proceedings at the end of 1974 but it was not until May 1975 that I appeared before them with Willy Wright, John Spence and Maurice Peston.

The Select Committee contained very few supporters of a wealth tax. The Chairman, Douglas Jay, was lukewarm while other Labour members, Colin Phipps, Neville Sandelson, and Brian Walden, for example, ranged from the doubtful to the hostile. If the Committee had been chosen to ensure that there would be no wealth tax its membership could not have been better selected. Perhaps it was.

My written evidence had described the system of protection of works of art as it existed and had explained how under it there had in recent years been no serious losses abroad. Throughout the piece there were phrases I had insisted on; for example, that it was not undesirable for objects to come on to the market if they finished up in public ownership. The arguments of the critics of the application of the tax to art property were fairly easily disposed of, and I was particularly proud of my own idea of self-valuation with the safeguard that the Government should have the option to purchase the object at the valuation!

At the hearing, Robert Cooke, the Bristol Conservative, immediately questioned me on two phrases in the memorandum: one, that a wealth tax could increase the availability of works of art to the public and another that it 'would assist in separating fine art from its traditional associations with exclusiveness and personal wealth'.

Were these my views? I said that they were.

Mr Sainsbury, the Hove Tory, asked me if I planned to hold discussions with interested bodies on the application of the tax to which I replied that it would be useful to do that once they had accepted that there was going to be a wealth tax and that it would apply, with safeguards, to works of art.

The Liberal, John Pardoe, pressed me on public ownership. What made me think it was a good thing for works of art to be publicly owned? I replied that so long as they were available to the public I had no objection to them remaining in private ownership but to put one's money into art could not be allowed to become the standard means of evading a wealth tax.

Nigel Lawson (Conservative) asked me about the object of a wealth tax and I said it was to diminish the large differences in ownership which disfigured our social and economic relationships.

I came away from the hearing feeling that the Committee had grasped the case I was making and providing the Government were firm in their intention to introduce the tax, might accept it.

The position of at least one of my officials, Miss Nichols, was peculiarly difficult, for she was secretary to the Reviewing Committee presided over by Lord Perth and also a member of my staff and thus answerable to me.

Roy Strong, Director of the Victoria and Albert Museum, a Government owned collection, is also a civil servant and I was astonished to see his name on the notepaper of the anti-wealth tax outfit, 'Heritage in Danger'. I gave a direct instruction that he was to resign from it and this was obeyed but that did not, of course, affect his views which, on this issue, were suprisingly extreme.

I found in the files a draft of the evidence to be given to the

Select Committee by 'Heritage in Danger' under Lord Cottesloe, from which it appeared that my office was in closer touch with my political enemies than I suspected at the time. I also found a letter from Roy Strong to Willy Wright in which the Museum Director ludicrously called for the abandonment of the entire Green Paper. Strong quoted a number of objects which had recently come on the market as evidence that even before its implementation the tax was having what he called 'disastrous' effects. Willy Wright, in a note to John Spence, thought that his attitude to the tax was still the opposite of mine. Instead of saying that the Government intended to introduce a tax and that it was his duty to advise how it might be applied without harm to the arts and, if possible, with advantage, his settled aim remained to demonstrate that the tax would be damaging and to illustrate why this would be so. However, he also described the letter as 'having some elements of fever' which I felt to be about right on the assumption that the fever had reached the point of delirium.

The media were almost wholly opposed to the tax. Even the Guardian and the New Statesman carried prejudiced articles and letters. Some of the most opaque came from quite repectable bodies such as the Museums Association. I was beginning to be subjected to personal attacks. In the Financial Times I was described as being 'swayed by my doctrinaire beginning to be subjected to personal attacks. In the 'Financial views'. An aspect of these views was correctly quoted in the same paper, 'To exclude works of art from a wealth tax would be to create a tax haven and the present retreat from equities and other forms of investment would be encouraged.'

This view I also expressed to the critic, Peter Fuller, who came to see me about an article he was proposing to write on the subject for The Times.[3] It was one of the few pro-wealth tax articles to appear. It is significant that the arts critics were my chief supporters. In this they differed from the sales-room correspondents and I think it important to note that the tax was supported by those who look at pictures without monetary considerations in mind.

The evidence of the Board of Inland Revenue to the Select

[3] *The Times,* 10th May, 1975

Committee on the subject of 'The National Heritage' was on similar lines to my own, and I was impressed by the way in which the officers of the Board handled the Committee in oral evidence. I doubted whether my own people would have done as well.

In general the other witnesses to the Committee were opposed to the tax. The committee then set up two Sub-Committees and I was invited to give more detailed evidence to one of them, presided over by the Tory, Robert Cooke, who was virulently hostile to the tax and especially to its application to the so-called 'Heritage'. In parenthesis, one of the best points of the Board of Inland Revenue's evidence was the manner in which the idea that all art property in private ownership should be regarded as belonging to the nation even if never seen by the public, was punctured. In my own memorandum I had pointed out that the term included objects acquired by various means, some of which might reasonably be (and in some cases were) regarded by other nations as more properly belonging to *their* 'National Heritage'. I had also insisted on the inclusion of a sentence saying that if the tax brought objects on to the market, this would not be undesirable if the outcome was that they ended up in public ownership. Another of my sentences read as follows: 'It is further asserted that the effects of the wealth tax on the arts have been greatly exaggerated in an endeavour to discredit the tax and in the cause of privilege and inequality of ownership.'[4]

I advanced with unabated enthusiasm towards the Sub-Committee. Before doing so I wrote to Chairman Jay, saying that I wanted to emphasise that works of art which we ought to retain as a nation constituted about one-half of one percent of the total trade.[5]

All the same I was concerned that I was almost alone in advocating to the Select Committee that the arts should not be allowed to become an inshore tax-haven. Peter Fuller, who had interviewed me for the Times had told me that most of the leading art critics shared his view that it was essential not to exempt owners of treasures from the tax. He then got together a group of seven leading critics who subscribed to written evidence to the Select Committee in support of the view that art-wealth should not be excluded.

[4]*Select Committee on a Wealth Tax*, H.C. 696, Vol. 11, 384, HMSO November 1975
[5]Ibid. Vol. IV, 1708.

This evidence, beginning on page 1451 of the fourth volume of the Select Committee's documents, takes up just under seven pages and is a well argued piece buried among mountains of irrelevance. Indexed under John Berger, for alphabetical reasons, it was also signed by Guy Brett, Richard Cork of the Evening Standard, William Fever of the Observer, Peter Fuller and Paul Overy of the Times and Caroline Tisdalle of the Guardian, beyond any question seven of the leading art critics. This memorandum was submitted on the 26th June but when I appeared before the Sub-Committee on 16th July it had not been circulated to the Committee.[6]

I was asked whether, in view of the weight of the evidence for exemption, I had changed my mind. I said I had not, and pointed out that the Committee had not called any of the seven distinguished art critics who shared my views. Individual members of the group were then described as Marxists by Mr Skeet, the Bedford Tory. I agreed that John Berger had written an important book on art from a Marxist point of view but said that this did not seem to me to invalidate the evidence. I pointed out that almost all the evidence which had been given was beside the point as much of the significant art in the country was already in public ownership and most of the privately owned stuff was of little importance and could be exported without loss to the nation and with benefit to the balance of payments. What needed to be stopped could be stopped without difficulty.

At the end of the hearing – and I re-read it in preparing this work without any diminution in my doubtless excessive self-esteem – I reached the conclusion that the Select Committee had been established not to examine the Wealth Tax but to destroy it and the composition of the Sub-Committee B with the anti-wealth tax Cooke in the Chair was for the purpose of ensuring that, if anything went wrong and a Wealth Tax could not be avoided, at least the tax should be so shot full of loopholes as to be no menace to the wealthy and of little benefit to anyone else.

Looking at the files I also found that after I had given evidence Roy Strong had again written excitedly to Willy Wright only to get put down quite firmly. As a pukka civil servant, Wright knew that once the Minister had committed himself in public he had to

[6]Ibid. Vol. III, 1183 et seq.

be supported. Wright's reply to Strong concluded: 'Officials, of course, have to take the instructions of their Minister on this, as indeed, on all policy matters.' But although I could beat my own officials I could not overcome the pusillanimity of my senior colleagues in Government. The Cabinet seemed very frightened of the media.

There were other pressures. On the file there was a letter to the Prime Minister from the Earl of Crawford and Balcarres saying: 'The Minister for the Arts is impervious to arguments. His purpose is quite clearly to destroy the private ownership of works of art.'

The Crawford and Balcarres letter came from the PM's Private Secretary to mine with a request for a comment on which a reply could be based. Mary Giles prepared an admirable reply containing such sentences as 'Mr Jenkins remains of the view that it is undesirable that works of art should be wholly exempted from the tax but that special arrangements will be necessary to encourage the retention of important objects in this country.' I added another sentence as follows: 'In the opinion of our Minister, many of the objections which purport to be dealing with the impact of the tax on the arts are arguments against the tax as such and it seems probable that this is so in the present case. If it is not, the special arrangements suggested by Mr Jenkins should enable Lord Crawford to continue in the same public spirited way as he now proposes.'

But Wilson's eventual reply to Crawford said none of this and indicated the way things were going. He wrote on 19th December 1975: 'the Minister for the Arts is stating his personally held view that deferment would be more appropriate. He lends his support to one of the solutions which the Green Paper canvasses as a possibility. I can assure you that we have yet to take a final view and when the Select Committee has completed its examination we shall pay careful attention to what they have to say in their report.'

In a speech to the Museums Association at Durham University I had summarised the case presented to the Select Committee by the seven art critics. They had argued *inter alia* that the tax would bring about increased public access to valuable objects in private ownership. Two days later I gave my final oral evidence to the

Select Committee and this was the signal for a series of wild personal attacks on me in the press. One of these was several columns of abuse in the Sunday Telegraph in which, among other things, I was called a 'barbarian'. I was legally advised that this was actionable but decided that the writer was not worth powder and shot.

There were several attacks in the Evening Standard and the Guardian joined in talking of the 'horrendous consequences' of the tax being applied to the fat arts cats and quoting Andrew Faulds as wondering 'if the doctrinaire and dogmatic Jenkins is working for the arts or for Moscow.' 'Och, aye, to that,' said the Guardian thereby rendering itself actionable.

The Guardian returned to the attack in a piece by a member of its staff named Donald Wintersgill but this article, although mistaken, was not abusive, as distinct from the letters the paper printed and there was another quite laughable piece on 8th August by an unnamed reporter. Meanwhile, I was receiving calls from various art critics explaining that they were bitterly ashamed of their philistine colleagues but could do nothing about it. The policy of their papers was against the wealth tax and this was the way to attack and discredit the tax itself. However, Art and Antiques Weekly gave a fair report of the position taken by the seven critics which I had summarised in my Durham speech to the Museums Association.

Keith Nurse, the Daily Telegraph arts reporter in one of his articles said† that demands for my resignation were growing in arts circles. Nurse afterwards admitted that he was talking exclusively about collectors and dealers, indeed the actual person quoted as evidence of the call was George Levy, president of the British Antique Dealers Association and as I said to Nurse, a Minister called upon Levy to resign *must* be doing his job properly.

Leggatt surged up again in the Daily Telegraph and Hornby of the National Arts Collection Fund referred to 'the Minister and his like'. in a column in the Guardian. I wondered if he would tell me where I could find a few of my like as I felt I could do with them!

By August the uproar had reached New York where the New

†*Daily Telegraph*, 24.7.75

York Times quoted Leggatt taking his usual line, but the report was balanced and fair. Too little of this sort appeared in the British press. Peter Fuller did another interview with me which was published in the Guardian. Among generally cool and factual responses I allowed myself to say: 'Concern comes unconvincingly from those who, wearing other hats, are engaged in flogging the stuff to Arab sheikhs'. I have no doubt that this remark infuriated where the cap fitted uncomfortably closely and kept the anger bubbling. It was therefore unwise, perhaps, to quote, Lord Clark of 'Civilisation' as allegedly saying that art collecting was a form of gambling and tax evasion, and Lord Eccles as referring to the 'brute force' of the instinct. I also agreed that the Wealth Tax might be the thin edge of a wedge, saying that no one but a fool would try to insert a wedge at the thick end.

However, Richard Cork came to my aid in the Evening Standard, thus demonstrating that some of the critics were able to write against the policies of their own papers. Leggatt came back in a letter and was heard in a brief interview on Radio 4 claiming that he would have to sell one of his own pictures to an American buyer. He went right over the top on 15th August in the Daily Telegraph quoting Andrew Faulds again, this time as saying 'I am never sure whether the Minister is working for the advancement of Moscow or the Arts.' The piece was headed 'A Minister and his Motives' and went on to say that 'this disquiet as to the true motives of Mr Hugh Jenkins, MP, is being voiced by many moderates of all political parties.' The article went on in the high pitched way peculiar to Mr. Leggatt but this time I decided that something had to be done about it. Not everyone, I was warned, treated Leggatt and most of the press with what one of my Parliamentary colleagues called my 'amused and condescending disdain'.

In a way, the article was as rude to the seven critics as it was to me. It implied that I had written their evidence to the Select Committee for them and even their entitlement to the description 'distinguished' was put in doubt. So I was not surprised to see that Peter Fuller replied in a letter published by the Daily Telegraph a few days later. Describing Leggatt's piece as 'irrational', he said that the wealth tax would advance the interests of people who enjoyed looking at works of art rather than trading in them. He went on: 'It is the duty of the Minister for the Arts to act in the cultural interests of the majority in this country and to extend and encourage public access to the best works of art situated here. This is precisely what Mr Jenkins is doing'.

Leggatt then forecast in the Guardian that I was about to be dismissed by Harold Wilson and I was told that the Prime Minister was being urged to replace me.

Andrew Faulds wrote to the Telegraph replying to Peter Fuller's letter and inviting me to clear myself of guilt by association with Berger and Fuller by declaring myself a non-Marxist.

I was being consistently advised by my officials to reply to none of the press attacks, but Lord Goodman once again expressed the view that the Leggatt piece in the 'Telegraph' was actionable. He was in difficulty himself; as Chairman of the Newspaper Proprietors' Association he was against me on the issue Leggatt was writing about and, indeed, had given evidence to the Select Committee himself, accompanied by Leggatt as a member of the Heritage outfit, which Leggatt served. He recommended that another firm of solicitors should take the case. I had a discussion with them and said that I did not want to sue. I did not want money, I simply wanted to stop them from frightening Harold Wilson into dismissing me. I was popular in the art world and it would be absurd if my departure was to be engineered by a few members of the Parliamentary Labour Party, a bunch of dealers and the Tories. With the solicitor's agreement I wrote to Bill Deedes, the Editor of the Daily Telegraph, whom I knew and aksed him to print an article from me. Deedes agreed and I wrote the piece. Willy Wright read it and suggested an alternative approach. He also reminded me that I must get the Prime Minister's approval. I put together Willy's piece and my own and we agreed to this repudiation of Leggat/Faulds:

> 'As there have been considerable misunderstandings about how the Wealth Tax might affect works of art, I welcome this opportunity to set out the main facts and arguments.
>
> The alternatives are broadly to exempt works of art from the Tax, or to make special arrangements in the application of the Tax which would ensure that massive losses of the most important works of art abroad are avoided.

Obviously exemption would certainly have the effect of avoiding sales on the market at a rate which the country could not afford to purchase for the public collections. But this would be at the cost of making an exception for a particular form of wealth, would erode the broad basis of the Tax, and would give rise to other claims for exemption. It is not the purpose of this article to deal with the general social issues raised by the Tax, but it is relevant to point out one likely effect of total exemption – particularly if works of art were the only significant form of private wealth to be so exempt.

There would be intense speculative pressure on the limited number of major works of art still in private hands and this would further inflate their value: to the disadvantage of the serious collector and scholar, and the public collections.

Incentives for theft and smuggling would be increased and the cost of maintaining and displaying to the public would also rise bringing back a call for entry changes. Those scholars and critics who so passionately advocate total exemption can hardly have thought about the consequences of such a tax haven. They would be seeing their treasures through bullet-proof glass only, or, worse still, only reproductions and replicas would be thought safe enough to display to the world. The only people to benefit would be the speculators and the law breakers.

The alternative is to make special arrangements which will ensure that most owners see benefits in retaining their works of art and to ensure that when disposal is decided upon there are advantages in disposal to a public collection. My views on this subject were clearly set out in the evidence submitted to the Select Committee and printed with the Minutes of Evidence given on 7th May and 16th July 1975.

How can these objectives be achieved without the exemption of works of art other than in the case of an artist's stock of his own works? One way is to ensure that, provided that certain conditions are met, the Tax can be deferred. These conditions could require display to the public or an undertaking either to make the works of art available to scholars and students by arrangement or to lend to public collections either for extended periods or on demand.

The nature of the deferment of tax would require careful study in order to preserve the general incentive to retain notwithstanding the costs and responsibilities of ownership. It would be reasonable to provide that the amount of tax payable on works of art during any one life should be less than the tax payable on any wealth realised by the sale of such works. At the same time it would be necessary to ensure that the public collections as a whole were enabled to buy at least the most important of the works of art which did come on to the market.

When the Report of the Select Committee is received the Government will decide. It is my concern as Minister for the Arts to ensure that whatever decision is taken should be in the interests of the public at large. This means that more and more people shall be given the chance to see a growing number of the finest examples of the artistic achievement of mankind.'

This draft article was referred to the Attorney General, and when I went to see him Sam Silkin implied that he could think of no reason why this had been done. Perhaps it was hoped that I would forget about it. It then went to the Chancellor of the Exchequer. Nothing transpired; time passed until 18th November when Mary Giles received a letter from the PM's office. In it the Private Secretary said that the best way of dealing with the situation *'which should not have been allowed to arise'* (my italics) would be for me to prepare an article which would not advocate what I had submitted to the Select Committee but would set out the various alternatives without coming down on the side of anything!

I refused to do this and tried to see the Prime Minister about it, but his office simply ignored my Private Secretary's attempts to make a date. I approached him in the Lobbies but he immediately fell into deep conversation with whoever happened to be near him. Once I got him and said, 'Harold, I've been wanting to talk to you for weeks.' He looked hunted and said, 'I'm very full just now. I'll fix something.'

Nothing happened and by chance I saw Tony Benn and told him I was getting no support. I could not even persuade the PM to see me and was considering whether to stay in a Government which had lost its will for socialism or even for reform.

'You will not get to him,' said Tony. 'You are getting the treatment. Don't resign. Think whom he might put in your place. Just hang on. But I agree, the system is fundamentally wrong.'

I thought about it. The joy and certainty of my early days had evaporated. I still knew precisely what had to be done, but now I also knew that I was not going to be allowed to do it. Given the necessary freedom and authority, I could set in train a series of changes in relationships which might help to modify our society and foster creativity, but I would not be permitted even to try. I was a Junior Minister, the most ignominious position open to any MP other than that of Parliamentary Private Secretary. It would be better to recover the freedom of the backbenches. I had a feeling that I could not last long anyway. Would it not be better to go now rather than wait to be pushed?

Yes, but given another year I could get Public Lending Right started and do something about the Arts Council. I could make the Treasury pay hard money to the Arts as the price of their part in forcing a retreat from Socialism.

Under pressure from Cledwyn Hughes, Chairman of the Parliamentary Labour Party, Andrew Faulds withdrew his libellous allegation privately. I thought of insisting on a public withdrawal but decided that such matters were not worth spending further time and thought on. I might as well let the whole thing go and concentrate on areas where there was still hope.

I was under instruction not to submit my article for publication because the Prime Minister did not want any Junior Minister to say anything at all about the Wealth Tax at that time. I did not know it, but it had been decided not to proceed with the tax in that session of Parliament. Instead, I asked Deedes whether he would accept a general article from me about the Government's policy on the arts as a whole but he refused even to look at such a suggestion.

I reflected that one of the most bitter things had been a letter to the Times[7] signed by many of the leading artists in the country. The signatories, who included people thought of as progressives or even socialists, demonstrated that they had fallen victim to propaganda and did not understand that far from harming them, the tax would benefit artists. I thought that instead of exposing their misinformation publicly, I would invite them to Belgrave Square for a talk and did so in the columns of the Times. The outcome was an extremely rude and public rejection of the invitation, again in a letter to the Times. I was angry and sad.

[7] *The Times*, 10.9.75., 31.10.75.

Sad, that once again, artists had shown how easily they could be used; that distinguished artists should not only join with their exploiters to attack their devotee but should do so in a manner unworthy of their distinction. I was angry at the humiliation of a public rejection of my invitation by people, some of whom I had thought to be my friends. I was furious, because I believed that if I could talk to them I could win them over; not all of them, for I knew that judgment could be corrupted by wealth and some of the artist signatories were among the richest in the country. Nevertheless, as the writers appeared to believe that, for example, artists would be charged wealth tax on their own stock of unsold works, a proposal which existed only in the fevered imagination of the opponents of the tax, it would not have been difficult to explain that they had been deceived. When I considered that these people preferred to nurse such mistaken beliefs rather than risk having them dispelled by a visit to my office, I was suffused with rage at such ill-natured prejudice.

It occurred to me that among some of the dealers there might be more rational ground for opposition to the application of a wealth tax to art treasures. It would have helped to expose the international art racket. People of high reputation in that world would have been revealed as having 'dirty fingers' as Paul Levy put it in an Observer review of two books published in 1975.[8] Mr Levy had said that, taken together, these two investigations had demonstrated the sordid nature of the trade, adding that art dealers and collectors were priests and worshippers of Mammon: 'The dealers get even richer and the art loving public, awed by the price tags of the objects they venerate, have their aesthetic sensibilities blunted.'

I agreed. The international art trade had become nothing more than speculation and gambling as was later confirmed by the Chairman of Sotheby's honest and modest description of himself as 'a sort of amiable croupier'.

I did not allow myself to be silenced but on public platforms asserted that one reason for the vicious attacks which were being made upon me was that the racket could not be defended by reputable means. Some dealers feared that the application of a

[8]*Observer*, 17.8.1975., *The Double Market* Keith Middlemass (Gordon & Cremonesi) *The Arts Crisis* Bonnie Burnham (Collins)

tax would open up the smelly corners of their scene. 'Some of those who defend this set-up clearly think they can only do so by seeking to blacken, or perhaps redden, those of us who are concerned with art rather then with selling and speculation,' I said.

On 11th November the Select Committee on the Wealth Tax published their report and revealed that they had been unable to come to any agreed conclusion! The Chairman's draft had been rejected as had other drafts proposed by the Liberal, John Pardoe, the Tory, Maurice Macmillan and Jeremy Bray, a good example of a strong supporter of the Wealth Tax from the Labour centre. For Bray, the Chairman's report was not strong enough; for the others it was too strong. Jay proposed a conditional exemption for art treasures which might have been made reasonably watertight if it had been applied only to existing owners at the time of the publication of the report. The Tories proposed very slightly qualified exemption. Pardoe weakened Jay a little further. Bray rejected special treatment for the 'Heritage' altogether. He was much more extreme in the matter than I was – so much for the 'Marxist' nonsense for it would be hard to find anyone less vulnerable to such a charge, or compliment, then Jeremy Bray.

The fatal blow came on 18th December 1975. In a written answer to Douglas Jay, Denis Healey announced that there would be no Wealth Tax in that session of Parliament.

My whole struggle had been in vain. I might just as well have gone along with exemption and had I done so I would still have been everyone's blue-eyed old man. As I said it to myself, I knew that this was nonsense. I was a socialist and had to fight for what I believed in, whatever the consequences. What I did not know at the end of 1975 was that Harold Wilson had already decided to go and that his successor would dispense with my services long before the further year I needed was out.

If a Wealth Tax is eventually introduced by a Labour Government I trust it will include art property. If it does not, an area will be preserved where the deodorised connoisseur inadequately masks the stink of capitalist corruption. These dealers correctly identified their enemy in me, for if I had been given the necessary authority I would have forced them to operate in the open to the benefit of the arts and to the advantage of the living artist. The sale room stands between art and the people and it is not to be admired.

Looking back, the course of events seemed to have a strange inevitability. I could have modified developments in detail but not in general. Why should I imagine that a Junior Minister could have any such power? The individual who had aided me most had been Maurice Peston. As Special Adviser to Reg Prentice he had access to all papers and I was able to bring him in. No person and no committee without such access, CAPAG*, for example, could be of any value. All the same, I ought to have put the Arts Sub-Committee of the Parliamentary Labour Party into the picture at an earlier stage. Because their Chairman was George Strauss, a wealthy man and a notable art collector, I had thought they might be against me. I was wrong. Strauss was among the fifty-eight signatories to a motion which Raymond Fletcher put down at the end of 1975 which read as follows: 'That this House congratulates the Government on its increased grants to the arts, to crafts and to museums and galleries; supports the moves to make the Arts Council more democratic and more representative of those working in the arts; welcomes the Minister's evidence to the Select Committee on the Wealth Tax seeking to weaken the link between the visual arts and private wealth and urges the Government to persist in these policies and to regard the hostility of certain sections of the arts establishment and the press as a tribute.'

Public Lending Right

When I became Minister for the Arts in 1974 the campaign by authors to be paid for the lending of their works by libraries had been waged off and on for more than a quarter of a century. One of the originators was John Brophy, the novelist, who proposed in 1951 that borrowers of books should pay a penny per volume to the library which would pass the money to the publishers for distribution to the authors.

Various schemes were tried and abandoned as impracticable or undesirable, including Arts Council proposals and ideas to

*See page 178.

amend the Copyright Act. The authors themselves were divided on method and a group including the novelist Brigid Brophy, daughter of the originator, broke away from the Society of Authors in 1972 and formed the Writers' Action Guild. This group rejected the Society's decision to settle for a scheme which would have based payment on the libraries' purchase of books and held out for one based on payment related to the number of times a book was borrowed.

Jennie Lee made it clear that Labour would not countenance any scheme which breached the principle of the free library service and Lord Eccles tried to tie the proposal to the Copyright Act. My predecessor, Norman St. John Stevas, supported the notion in principle.

When I came into office I found that there were immense complexities in implementing PLR and that none of these had been resolved. I also discovered that the office was strongly in favour of a scheme based on the number of book purchased by libraries as against the loan-sampling basis favoured by the authors. Under pressure, the office worked on proposals for legislation but these left out the vital questions of where the money was to come from and how it was to be paid and to whom.

Nevertheless I decided to force the issue and gave instructions that we should bid for a place in the immediate legislation programme for a PLR Bill. I then invited all the interested parties to meet me in Belgrave Square. In preparing for the meeting I began to understand for the first time the perils of the voyage I had so gaily embarked upon.

The PLR enthusiasts were influential and vocal rather than numerous; this was not something that would benefit the masses, on the contrary it would take from the many and give to the few. The many have never objected to this, providing the few are deserving, but they like the rewards to be distributed according to need, and this is where PLR fell down. It was a plan to add to the wealth of the haves rather than one to rescue the have-nots, for however one re-jigged it, the essence of the scheme was that the most popular authors would get the most. PLR had to be sold on the more difficult proposition that this was a *right*. The entitlement was that of writers as a whole and the lesser known authors wanted the more popular writers to receive their larger share. The claim was for the craft of writing rather than for the individual writer.

The meeting was attended by Michael Holroyd and Mr de Freitas of the Society of Authors, by Maureen Duffy and Brigid Brophy of the Writers' Action Guild and by Lord Goodman. Graham C. Greene, nephew of the writer and director of Jonathan Cape, was there from the Publishers Association and there were representatives from the Library Association and a small posse of my officials. The meeting began stormily which I always regard as a good sign. The Library Association came out dead against the whole idea, withdrawing from a tacit acceptance of a principle which they had seemingly adopted on an earlier occasion. Others, led by Lord Goodman, tried to suggest that the Branch was also withdrawing and it is true that if they had been in a position to do so my officials would have scuppered PLR. Not for nothing were they the Arts and Libraries Branch of the Department of Education and Science, and the library people were precisely those who were being instructed to produce a scheme they regarded as inherently dangerous in that it diverted money into the pockets of authors which librarians felt would otherwise go into the purchase of books. This fear was unfounded since this would be fresh money legislatively raised for this specific purpose, but unfounded fears do not go away.

The Branch knew that PLR could not openly be opposed since the politicians were wedded to it, but their attitude was very different from the relative enthusiasm they brought to the removal of museum charges. There they were going home, back to the good old days before the Eccles error; here they were being asked to strike out into new country and they hated it. This vigorous dislike had become personalised on to Maureen Duffy and Brigid Brophy and was just as vigorously returned.

I set up a Technical Investigation Group which began to carry out, for the first time, a dispassionate appraisal of the relative merits and possibilities of the two methods of implementing PLR. It was clear that it was going to take a long time, so I pursued the idea of introducing a Bill which would give me powers to implement either or both, at a later stage, by secondary legislation.

As early as April 1974 I had secured from the Branch outline proposals for legislation on this basis and these were widely circulated among those concerned. The proposals were not liked by the WAG. They felt that the document was biased in favour of the purchase-based system and against the loan-basis which they passionately supported. Michael Herzig, the Assistant Secretary, who was in charge of PLR at this stage was wholly in favour of a purchase-based scheme if PLR *had* to come and this view was shared by the Treasury. However, I presented a paper to the Cabinet advocating a Bill which would leave the issue open and would give authority to introduce either or both by statutory instrument at a later stage. I gave the authors a firm assurance that the legislation would not favour the introduction of a purchase-based scheme more than that of a loan-based one.

By the end of April I had established that the source of finance would be central government funds and that no local government money would be affected. This broke the main objection of the librarians but failed to remove their anxiety that at some future date some other Government would rob them. I pointed out that this could be done anyway, but it was like trying to assure a Tory that a Labour Government will do him no harm. I then had to calm the Department of the Environment who were looking at the idea from the local authority point of view and the Department of Trade who were involved from the angle of copyright and of relations with publishers.

Kenneth Baker, a youngish Tory MP, was proposing to introduce a private PLR Bill but he agreed to withdraw his Bill providing I could give him firm assurances about the Government's intentions.

I went to the Cabinet and a crucial meeting of the Sub-Committee on Home Affairs took place on Friday, 3rd May. Roy Jenkins was in the Chair and he read a note from Ted Short, then Leader of the House, which was less than enthusiastic. However, I pointed out that Kenneth Baker would get the credit if the Government failed to come out with a firm undertaking. This was eventually authorised and on the 9th May I answered an inspired question from George Strauss saying that the Government hoped to introduce a Bill before the end of the year. In doing so I pinned myself firmly to the PLR cross.

The Library Association made it clear that if they *had* to have a scheme they favoured the purchase method of counting entitlement. In June New Society published a story saying that the scheme to be introduced would certainly be purchase-based and as writers tend to believe what they read, this frightened both the authors' organisations into a state of frenzy. By this time I had myself decided that I would not introduce anything other than a loan-based scheme and when I received a furious letter from the two bodies signed by Brophy, Duffy, Michael Holroyd and Antonia Fraser I decided to give them a clout and I finished my letter as follows: 'Meanwhile, it would be helpful if it could be assumed that we are all seeking the same end. I cannot prevent you from believing otherwise but it does not make for the mutual trust without which the value of communication is debased. To blame those who are trying to grapple with difficult problems is to behave like the king who beheads the bearer of rough tidings.'

This encouraged the office and from then on they started to work harder to produce a feasible loan-based scheme. I told the authors that when I received an interim report from the working party I would ask them to come to the office to discuss it. I then commissioned an independent survey by an excellent body called 'Logica' and they worked with the office people and reported to the Technical Investigation Group. I announced this to the press in August and received quite a large pro-PLR post.

Well before the end of the year, the TIG had shown that the loan sampling system would be no more difficult or expensive to administer than the purchase scheme. I was much impressed with the interim report of the Group but the Chairman, W. H. Harvey, seconded from Education, complained that the authors' technical representatives at the time were not playing a full part in the work and tended to speak with forked tongues. I decided that the only thing to do was to put Maureen Duffy herself on the group. I liked her and respected her fine mind. From that moment on we had an author who understood the reality of the problems to be solved.

PLR was accidently omitted from the Labour Party Manifesto for the October Election, but in a press conference with Harold Wilson at Transport House, I said that Labour was committed and that we planned to legislate before the end of the year. We had experts working on the technical problems but even if we did not resolve them all, this would not be allowed to hold up the Bill, for we would seek powers to introduce a scheme, the details of which could be determined subsequently.

My undertaking, which I repeated in a letter in the Times, without qualification and perhaps unwisely, was circulated by the Writers' Action Guild in their Newsletter. They pointed out, however, that it was still open to Government to introduce a purchase-based scheme which they did not regard as PLR at all. When I returned to Belgrave Square after the Election I found that the office had accepted, at last, that PLR was coming and that even a loan-based scheme might be possible. John Spence minuted me to the effect that it was hoped to get the Long-Title of the Bill down before the end of the year even if drafting was not completed by then. I commented: 'Congratulations!'

Although I did not fully realise it at the time the incident demonstrated how the civil service works. In the early part of 1974 I could be thought of as a transient nuisance and foot-dragging was the order of the day, but after October, when I was clearly going to be there for some time the staff began to do their best to implement those aspects of policy which were judged to have general support in the Government.

The Library Association maintained their opposition but I replied, 'I would only mislead you if I were to give the impression that the principle of creating PLR is still open to useful discussion.' I pointed out that PLR figured in the current Queen's Speech and I said that it would be introduced during the forthcoming session.

I had got the Bill into the list as Category 1 Top Priority and had minuted the Prime Minister, 'It may be necessary to confine proceedings on the Bill before Christmas to a First Reading with production of the Bill in full and Second Reading early in the New Year.' It was, I thought, merely a question of clearing up the details. Ominously, however, as I discovered much later, John Spence had put it on record on 29th October in a Minute to Willy Wright that the commitment to legislate had been made by me without consultation with the Branch, which hardly tied in with his concurrent Minute to me in which he had appeared to adopt the commitment without protest.

By this time I had got the interim 'Logica' survey, and I really had no doubt that we could make it, although the librarians were still being difficult. After the next meeting of the Technical Investigation Group, the Chairman, a very cautious man, had gone so far in a report to me as to accuse the librarians of indulging in 'niggling filibustering'. He regretted that as a result of this I would not have an agreed report within the time-scale I had drawn up. He further described the librarians as 'obstructive and obtuse'.

It was clear that I could not make a final decision between purchase or loan as the basis of the scheme before Christmas. In fact, I was quite determined that it should be loan-based but the Parliamentary draughtsmen refused to produce a Bill until I could demonstrate to them beyond doubt that what I was legislating for was practicable, and for that I needed the final TIG Report. I therefore decided to go ahead with the Bill giving powers to introduce a scheme based on either or both methods; an 'enabling' Bill.

On 21st November Willy Wright minuted me adhering to the Departmental view that the purchase-based scheme was best. By this time I had the draft report of the TIG and it was clear that Willy's recommendation was not in accord with their findings, for they were neither recommending one nor the other. It was my Department itself with its library orientation which was pushing the purchase-based scheme.

I issued a consultative document to the interested bodies setting out my proposals for legislation and by the end of the year I had secured the agreement of the Cabinet Home Affairs Sub-Committee to proceed. In the consultative document I said that I proposed to vary payments to authors according to the published price of their books. This was in accordance with the advice of the office and at the same time I issued a press notice and made a statement in the House in the form of a written answer to Bruce Douglas-Mann[9].

WAG reacted strongly against the decision to relate payments to the purchase price of books. I invited them to the office and Duffy and Brophy soon convinced me that they were right by producing a number of books proving that the cheaper ones represented a much greater effort on the part of the author than some more expensive 'coffee-table' volumes.

[9]*Hansard* Col. 232 28th November 1974.

WAG did not like the inclusion of the purchase-based scheme at all and wrote seven pages of detailed refutation of it. I explained that to legislate at all before the end of the year I had no alternative but to proceed as I had indicated. Assistant-Secretary Michael Herzig still maintained his preference for the purchase-based method but I was able to convince the authors that I did not share it and that the decision would be mine. I had a number of technical discussions with library and publishers' representatives and then saw the Association of Municipal Authorities and the Association of County Councils.

On 11th December I wrote to Ted Short, then Leader of the House, asking for formal permission to introduce the Bill before the end of the year. I said: 'As you know, we promised in the Queen's Speech to legislate on this topic and I am circulating a paper. I hope you will authorise an immediate approach to Counsel to draft the Long-Title of the Bill.'

My paper to the Home Affairs Committee of the Cabinet ended: 'I therefore seek agreement, providing for the entitlement of authors to payment as specified above and to proceed with preparation of the proposed legislation.' Attached to the document were the actual proposals for legislation. On the previous day, the Permanent Secretary had minuted Reg Prentice to the effect that he had serious misgivings about the proposal. Prentice minuted me, 'We have a clear commitment to proceed but I am inclined to share the Permanent Secretary's scepticism.' John Spence wrote a surprisingly strong reply making it clear that the Permanent Secretary was talking from sheer ignorance. By this time I knew that all I could get before the end of the year would be a Long-Title describing the Bill, with drafting to take place in the New Year. Ted Short wrote to Roy Jenkins on 12th December saying that he was reluctant to accept the idea of putting down a Long-Title before a complete draft of the Bill was available. On 19th December I wrote to Ted Short saying, 'if we are to fulfil our undertaking, confirmed several times in the House to introduce this legislation before the end of 1974, we must draft a Long-Title by 10 pm this evening for presentation to Parliament tomorrow. Parliamentary Council require your authority to draft the title by 5 pm today.' This went round by hand and I asked to see Ted Short in his office in the House. The

First Parliamentary Counsel was with him and they both firmly rejected the idea of proceeding with the Long-Title without the draft being completed. I was deeply dejected and thought of resignation, but I believed then that I would get the Bill early in the new year and I decided to draft a written answer for a PQ to be put down by John Tomlinson (Labour) the next day. The reply was: 'For technical reasons it has not proved possible to produce the legislation as I had hoped before the House rises. The Bill will be introduced as soon as practicable in the New Year'.

On 31st December I wrote to Antonia Fraser and to Brigid Brophy saying, 'As I cannot get a Bill drafted until February I have decided not to put down a Long-Title before the end of the year.' The decision was explicitly accepted by the Society of Authors and implicitly by WAG.

Looking through the files, the weight of public support for a loan-based PLR scheme, much of which I never saw while in office, was surprising. The letters included some from constituent-writers and even at this distance I feel sad that I was not allowed to fulfil their hopes. There were hundreds of others; from well-known authors, members of the public and personal friends.

In February I asked for a job description of the Registrar to be set up under the Bill. His powers would be considerable and the proposal was that he should be a lawyer of some standing. In March, the Cabinet Legislation Committee decided that they were not willing to let the Bill proceed at all in the form I had proposed. Short was against it and the Leader of the Lords (Shepherd) had refused to introduce it there. I had therefore had no alternative but to agree to complete the field tests and to present a Bill *either* on a purchase basis *or* a loan basis later in the year. At that time there was great pressure on Parliamentary time. One reason for the decision was that everyone else round the table saw the deferment of my Bill as presenting hope that his or her own baby would be allowed to come to life.

On 21st March the Technical Investigation Group met again. They had been working on the problem of reference books, on the bar codes which were to be read by light pens, patterns of payment, methods of computer measurement, and other preparatory studies. I was pushing the pace so hard that even the

Chairman began to protest. The new decision that we could not legislate until the scheme was worked out in detail meant that every stage had to be re-checked. At this point the cost of the 'Logica' investigations had amounted to £28,000 and I was ready to spend the same again.

On 11th April I sent a Minute out: 'We should be frank with the authors and with Parliament and say that the Government has decided that we need a decision on method before drafting the bill and that therefore introduction will be delayed until the autumn. Arrange a PQ accordingly.'

When I broke the news to the authors on 15th April they expressed dismay and shock. On 23rd April there was a demonstration organised by the authors outside Belgrave Square. I went out and spoke to them from their own platform and got a fairly rough reception. They believed, not unnaturally, that failure to implement my undertaking was due to the disregard of electoral promises which the public have learned to expect from politicians, but which I hope they will never learn to tolerate. I got no support, even from those authors who knew the failure was no fault of mine. I thought that my personal commitment would show through; that they would see that I had committed the Government and myself in order to achieve what otherwise would not be achieved at all; that I had given a date which I had genuinely thought could be met at the time and that the reason I could not do so was because the problems of implementation had turned out to be much more severe than had been expected and that I had to show that they could be solved in a way which would convince not only those eager to be convinced but the uncommitted and even the hostile.

I was wrong. They did not want to know. What they wanted was a scapegoat and I was it. Nevertheless I broke through to understanding and faith among a few and left the platform to scattered applause and with a bunch of roses presented to me by Maureen Duffy which was, I supposed, to demonstrate the support she could not or would not express for fear of losing solidarity with her angry fellows. There was some sort of a St. George and the Dragon theme about this demo. I thought I was playing the Saint but was seen as the reptile.

My first year of office had not only been successful but it had been seen to be so. My second year, which began about this time, was characterised by hostility in the press and by loss of confidence among those whose support I needed. My undertaking to introduce PLR before the end of 1974 was rash but it was a gamble which would have paid off if I had been given another three months of office. For that I would have been prepared to endure a temporary loss of popularity. As it was I had to put up with the unpopularity and was deprived of the recovery of esteem which would have accompanied the successful implementation of the PLR Bill, which was lost in the end because there was no Arts Minister in the Commons to see it safely on to the statute book.

I wrote to the authors' organisations after the demonstration and added a postscript: 'Many thanks for the lovely roses. I gave one each to those who have been working hard on PLR and who have hitherto received little but suspicion and contempt for their pains. It is my hope that you will have reason to feel that your gift was not misplaced.'

By that time, with the politicians' readiness to make a virtue out of necessity, I had reached the conclusion that perhaps it was as well that I had been forced to complete my tests before drafting the Bill. As a result I might well be able to exclude the purchase-based scheme altogether and legislate only for proper PLR. The decision to defer legislation had been imposed upon me but once it had been taken it was the Government's decision and I had to adopt it as my own and justify it.

The Times on 3rd June reported that I had been going round the country seeing practical tests of loan-based and purchase-based schemes being carried out at various libraries. It said that I went to Welwyn to see the loan-based scheme demonstrated and to Tottenham to see the purchase-based scheme. What they could not say was that the tests confirmed my decision to legislate on the loan basis only and demonstrated that there was no good reason why I should not have been allowed to introduce my enabling Bill six months earlier. I also found that library people on the ground did not appear to share the hostility of their spokesmen to PLR.

The truth about loan-based PLR is that throughout the years when it was being advocated it was, in fact, impracticable. It only became practicable when the invention of modern sampling and the computer and the application of these and other inventions to PLR by the Technical Investigation Group and 'Logica' made it so. It was always quite impossible to count all loans. The British on the whole do not buy hardcover books, they borrow them, and the 600 million loans a year our public libraries make would have cost at least £5 million to count. The universal adoption of International Standard Book Numbering, ISBN, was another necessity. An electronic light pen can recognise a bar code which translates such a number; it does not know authors and titles. As all loans could not be counted a reasonably accurate sample had to be determined. We discovered that a 72 point sample would reduce error to 4% providing it was rotated. That was the basis of our system, but we measured not books borrowed, but books returned; that way the borrower was not held up and the operator could count the books at leisure and put them through the machinery before returning them to the shelves. The ISBN number fed on to the computer by the light pen gave us all the information we needed for PLR and, gave the operating library quite a useful amount of additional knowledge about its patterns of lending.

The cost of all this would be about £400,000. As I had only been able to get £1 million promised to start PLR off in the first year the authors would have to share £600,000, ranging from a minimum of £10 to a cut-off figure of about £1200. However, once PLR was established, the cost/benefit ratio would improve year by year.

At this time I committed the office to the loan-based system by saying that I would not introduce any other system and wrote to the authors' organisations making it clear that I intended to get PLR on their basis or not all. As I pointed out to the staff, the only people we were going to please by introducing the loan-based scheme would be the authors but the purchase-based sceme would please no one at all and we would do better to forget the whole thing. So from then on it was loan-based or nothing.

I decided to publish the first report of the Technical

Investigation Group[10] and for those willing to know it was an impressive account of the solution of real difficulties and a description of problems still to be resolved. The press release which summarises the Report is at Appendix Six (p. 258).

When it became clear that we were not going to legislate in the 1974/5 session of Parliament I encouraged Bruce Douglas-Mann to put down a motion on the Order Paper regretting this, and calling upon the Government to legislate early in the next session. The motion only attracted about 50 signatures, almost all Labour, and would have been better had it been approached on an all-Party basis.

Marcia Falkender wrote asking about progress and I replied on the 18th July: 'I hope to be able to persuade colleagues that we should get everything ready to introduce the Bill at short notice so as to be able to take advantage of any gap in the Parliamentary time-table that may occur early in the session. It is, of course, essential that our undertaking on PLR is repeated in the coming Queen's Speech.'

I sent a copy of that to Michael Foot who, although at that time Secretary of State for Employment, had almost alone among Cabinet Ministers shown a personal interest in the Bill. Roy Jenkins was, alas, a total loss.

This continuing narrative about PLR, the delays and disappointments spreading over months and years makes clear, I hope, how heartsick the authors must have been. At the time I did not feel it so much myself because of my constant preoccupation with other matters. Reading a diary kept at the time I see that I remained cheerful and confident and because I had no doubt of the ultimate outcome I treated setbacks as minor irritations to be overcome in a very short time. I was also, I am afraid, quite intolerably cocky. For example, my diary note on the Belgrave Square demo reads as follows: 'I went out into the Square and spoke to them through their own loudspeaker. This satisfied the intelligent among them but did nothing for the twerps. Next day I was sad to read in the papers that these apparently included my old friend Ted Willis, who was quoted as saying that my speech was a 'disaster'. I have arranged to see the

[10]*Public Lending Right: An Account of an Investigation of Technical and Cost Aspects*, HMSO March 1975.

chump in a few days to put him right.'

When I saw Lord Willis, he said that he had the impression that I had the feeling that my friends were deserting me. I confirmed that I had exactly that feeling and he said he wanted to correct it because I was greatly loved and everybody wanted to keep me where I was until I had done what I wanted to do. I said that they had a very funny way of showing it and reading the press, the PM might well take the view that I had lost all my support in the arts world, in which case I might as well be dispensed with as a troublesome and unpopular Minister. There were plenty of other people about who wanted the job. I was glad that I was loved but also wanted to be understood and I went on to explain to him in detail the problems we had come up against and how I hoped to overcome them.

This interview took place in the House of Commons and afterwards I walked out of my room and over to the Abbey where I spent an hour. I came across the effigy of a 13th century bishop over his tomb and stood staring at his calm face. The windows nearby had been blown out during the war and replaced by new stained glass inscribed in memory of those killed in the bombing of London. I found this reminder of the long continuity of the people to which I belong curiously refreshing and sustaining. My breath was taken by the extraordinary beauty of some parts of the Abbey and at that moment I think I ioved everyone and everything.

One Sunday that June of 1975 Marie and I drove over to Chislehurst to see Ted Willis and his wife. Maureen Duffy, Brigid Brophy; Michael Levey and Gerald Kelsey were also there. Over dinner in the local pub the talk came round to PLR and I had to explain that I could not support a Bill Ted was introducing in the Lords to implement PLR.

I made it clear that although I would have to kill it, I had no objection at all to the introduction of the Bill since the presentation of a private Bill would help to firm up the resolution of some of my less enthusiastic colleagues in Government. It would, moreover, assist me in getting an early Government Bill, for I would be able to give as our reason for rejecting Ted's Bill the fact that our own Bill would be ready for presentation in the next Parliamentary session. None of them understood, or perhaps wanted to

understand, why this was so, but they were resigned to it
except Brigid who talked about blowing up the Ministry and
shooting me. In the end I had to slap the table and point out to
her that while we both had the same aim, she knew about as
much about the realities of Government as I knew about writing
novels.

When the Legislation Committee of the Cabinet met on this I
said that, in opposing Ted's Bill, our spokesman in the Lords,
David Strabolgi, would have to give a firm undertaking about
our intentions. Ted Short, in the Chair, intervened at once to say
that Strabolgi would not be able to give any such undertaking. It
was not possible to say in advance what would be in the next
Queen's Speech. As PLR was in the current Queen's Speech I
said that Strabolgi could point to this and, without specifically
saying that it would also be in the next one, could indicate that
the Government's resolution in the matter had not weakened.
This was accepted but I felt very uneasy about the Cabinet's lack
of enthusiasm. I decided to see if I could get the new Secretary of
State, Fred Mulley, on my side but at our first meeting there was
no opportunity to raise the matter. Fred slapped the Permanent
Secretary down pretty hard once and my immediate impression
was that he would be much more interventionist with me than
Prentice had been. When I got him on PLR he seemed reasonably
receptive. Mulley decided to hold his first lunchtime beer and
sandwiches meeting at Belgrave Square. He made it clear that
Bryan Davies who was to be appointed as PPS to replace Kilroy-
Silk (who had given up the job by mutual agreement) would be
an additional Parliamentary Private Secretary in the Department and not solely concerned with the Arts Branch as Kilroy-
Silk had been. I came to the conclusion that the change from
Prentice would be likely to be for the worse. This view was
confirmed when Mulley told me that the committee to consider
the Queen's Speech had laughed when he had said that I had a
Bill ready. I told him that there was nothing to laugh about as I
had a Bill ready months ago and it was not my fault that I had not
been allowed to introduce it. I asked him whether I could attend
the next meeting of this committee myself. He was non-
committal.

I had breakfast with Arnold Goodman and he agreed to make

a PLR speech in the Lords. Harold Wilson had just appointed Harold Lever to investigate the financing of the Arts, and as this had been done without consulting me it raised rumours in the press that I was about to be fired. I gathered from Goodman that several candidates for the attractive job of Arts Minister were being pushed, but that he was continuing to advise the PM that I was still the man for the job and as this was the view of Jennie Lee as well he thought Harold would not go further than the present 'initiative' with Lever which Goodman agreed was a pointless absurdity.

Meanwhile, it seemed that Mulley did not like me going to Cabinet committees except when he was unable to go himself and so I had to provide him with a brief about PLR which I hoped he would use effectively. When I read the Cabinet Minutes it was clear that he had done nothing and PLR was very likely to be dropped from the Queen's Speech for the coming session of Parliament as a result.

It was not really Fred's fault. The Government had proposed too much legislation in the last session and there was a panic to reduce it to a minimum in the present one. Every Cabinet Minister was determined to keep his pet piece of legislation in and there was no one there who regarded PLR as very important. If the Minutes were to be believed, which we know from Crossman and others they are not, then PLR was dropped without discussion. I rushed around talking to any Cabinet Minister whose ear I could get; to Tony Benn, Barbara Castle and others, but they all looked surprised and returned to their own preoccupations. Clearly, they had never given a thought to PLR – and why should they? What an absurd mockery of Government this is, I thought. I wrote to the Prime Minister and hoped for the best. In the letter I put just the slightest hint of resignation. It would be better to get out if PLR was to be abandoned. I got hold of Elizabeth Thomas and told her to get Maureen Duffy to mobilise the PLR big guns to sign a letter to the 'Times' calling for PLR to be retained in the Queen's Speech.

I went to the Tribune meeting where I found Dennis Skinner trying to persuade Michael Foot to resign from the Cabinet. As this would have let the Tories in, it seemed to me to be mere foolishness except on a longer term estimate than I was prepared to indulge in. The meeting was drowned in conflicting statements on economic policy and clearly it was impossible even to mention the arts. What a bunch of philistines the PLP are and the Left is as bad as the rest, I muttered to myself and came away feeling once again that the position of Junior Minister was suitable only for the lickspittles . If PLR was going to go, I would bloody well resign.

But on the 14th July I made my speech on the Wealth Tax to the Museums Association in Durham and was so attacked in the press as a result that I immediately felt like a socialist again and not just a trimmer. If I resign, they'll have a lot worse than me, I thought. They'll have someone who really believes in trimming or doesn't know he's doing it.

At this time I had a meeting of a group I had got together and which I called CAPAG, Current Arts Policy Advisory Group. I was not allowed a Political Adviser so I had decided that I would have an unofficial group to keep me socialist. They included Maureen Duffy and PPS Bryan Davies, Doug Hill of Tribune, Peter Fuller, Caroline Heller and Nicholas Garnham, Catherine Itzin, Elizabeth Thomas, Maurice Peston, James Curran, Jean Seaton and Alan Brownjohn. At this meeting we had some talk about PLR but spent most of our time discussing the composition of the Arts Council.

Soon afterwards Maureen Duffy and Brigid Brophy asked for a meeting with Fred Mulley. They did this without consulting me and Fred accepted, equally without consulting me. Of course, Mulley's brief for the meeting was prepared by my officials and when it was shown to me I was shocked to find that the office was still bitterly hostile to Brophy, Duffy and WAG and to loan-based PLR. I sent the brief back and had it re-written in a quite opposite sense – and in the end Mulley was briefed to accept the loan-based system. To safeguard against the possibility that the office might still send their original brief I wrote my own brief for Mulley and took it to the meeting but no fast ones were pulled and all was well. However, as my note summarised the position more frankly than the official brief, I handed it to Fred after the meeting and include it as an appendix to this book (p. 261).

Fred seemed pessimistic about getting time for the Bill, so I got in touch with Maureen Duffy and recommended that the authors should seek an interview with Ted Short who held the key to Parliamentary time. I also got hold of Michael Foot and he agreed to fix a meeting with Ted Short for the two of us. I think Foot must have done some preliminary work on Short, for although I arrived early and alone, the Lord President saw me right away and it was immediately apparent that there had been a sea-change. Gone was the calm, sad assertion that nothing could be done (which seemed to disguise an inward satisfaction that such was the case) and instead a relaxed Ted Short told me that he thought there would be no difficulty in re-stating the commitment to PLR in the coming Queen's Speech, and he accepted without hesitation my assurance that the Bill would be ready. When Michael turned up he repeated his co-operative attitude without prompting and as we went down the stairs Michael said, 'He's not a bad chap'. I felt he was talking about a new Ted Short whose acquaintance I was glad to make.

When the draft Bill was ready, early in September, Fred Mulley telephoned me to say that it could go to the Cabinet Sub-Committee providing I agreed to the deletion of a clause which provided for an advisory committee. I had no alternative but to accept, and at a meeting of the CAPAG group soon after I had to explain that we must settle for what we could get as a PLR Bill, providing it contained the essentials.

The next day I had a hell of a time at the Cabinet Sub-Committee. Roy Jenkins introduced the subject of PLR by saying that legislation was not necessary. We could simply announce our intention to proceed and then legislate at some later date. It seemed that this idea had emanated from Ted Short, back to his old obstructive form, in a letter to Roy Jenkins a copy of which did not reach me until after the meeting. The Leader of the Lords agreed and I had a struggle to make it clear to all present that this would be utterly disastrous; indeed I could not accept it and would be forced to consider my position. (This is the accepted euphemism for a threat to resign.) The situation was saved by Lady Llewelyn Davies who suggested that the Bill should be introduced in the Lords in view of the congested state of Commons business. In the end Roy Jenkins summed up by saying that the Committee somewhat reluctantly gave me their consent to proceed. John Silkin and Elwyn Jones were on my

G

side, but most people were indifferent, and some actively hostile, not to PLR as such, but to any Bill which might hold up their own brainchild.

Nevertheless, by the autumn of 1975 it was clear that I had won. A Bill to take loan-based PLR through Parliament was in course of preparation in spite of the personal opposition of Michael Herzig, the Assistant Secretary in charge of the project. At that point Herzig was replaced by Harold Rackham who came over from Education. Rackham was a personal friend and married to an active member of the Putney Labour Party, but he arrived too late. Nevertheless, it was a relief to feel that there was no longer any need to fight on two fronts. The earlier opposition within the Branch had delayed PLR but the Bill was killed by my dismissal. Rackham put his heart into the PLR Bill, and when it was lost he shared my bitter cup of disappointment.

During the Party Conference in October 1975 the headline 'Hugh Jenkins To Go' appeared across the front-page of the Evening Standard. A few days later I received a copy of a letter from the Prime Minister's Secretary to Fred Mulley's Secretary. It asked that 'no new policies should be publicly announced nor should any new policy decisions be taken with respect to the arts without prior consultation with the Chancellor of the Duchy of Lancaster.' I wrote to Mulley: 'I have just seen a letter from the Prime Minister's Private Secretary to yours. What is all this about? So far as I am aware no one is contemplating new policies. Perhaps we could have a word on your return.'

And I congratulated him on his performance as Conference Chairman which really had been very good.

Next day there was a piece in the Guardian saying that Marcia Falkender was going to take over my job. Marcia rang up to assure me that the story was nonsense. She was very angry and was writing to the Guardian to protest. She also said that other stories about my job were bunk and we arranged lunch together.

Once again I contemplated resignation. I talked to Marie about it. She said that anyone who resigned was forgotten the next day and advised me to lower the profile. Next day Ted Short, back to Dr Jekyll form, told me that PLR would definitely be in the Queen's Speech and I decided to stay and see it through. When I attended the next Tribune meeting I found them up in arms at the thought that I might be fired. Someone suggested a Motion on the Order paper and I agree that this would do good rather than harm.

When Parliament resumed in October we had some late nights and I was answering questions in the afternoon having been up until three the night before and busy all the morning. After answering one from St. John Stevas I thought the Speaker called 23 which was my next question and I got up to answer. It turned out to be 25 which was Joan Lestor's and she pushed me aside amid some laughter. Wilson had just come in and he handed me a file saying that I might like to take his questions too. This jokey exchange was the first time I had spoken to Harold in months, but I decided that I was not going to be fired and would not resign.

The St. John Stevas question was on PLR. He asked if I would try to get the measure on the statute book before being replaced by Marcia. I replied that we could easily have introduced a purchase-based scheme as he intended. Pressed further by Robert Cooke I said the Bill would provide answers to his questions.

On 9th November Philip Oakes in the Sunday Times wrote a very hostile piece accusing me of cant and saying that the Government had no intention of keeping its word. The next day, Ken Gosling reported that loan-based PLR was to appear in the Queen's Speech. Gosling was right, Oakes wrong. All the same, I was a little uneasy when I heard the Queen say that 'proposals for Public Lending Right would be put forward'. I would have preferred 'Legislation' or just 'A Bill'. 'Proposals' could mean a White Paper and my resignation. I was particularly apprehensive because the draft I had seen weeks before had contained the words 'A *Bill* will be introduced . . .' (my italics).

Nevertheless, I proceeded to complete the Bill and on the 16th of December I presented it to the Legislation Committee of the Cabinet just a year after my abortive attempt with the original enabling Bill. The 1975 Bill was committed to the loan-based system and on 16th February it was published. I sent copies of the Bill to all the interested bodies together with a consultative letter. I was still fighting off some last minute wrecking attempts but they were half-hearted and at that stage it was thought that the battle was as good as won.

A little before this, New Review published a symposium on PLR. In it, Dannie Abse, said: 'We've got a Philistine Government. Hugh Jenkins is a Philistine himself. He should resign.'

Another writer, A. Alvarez said: 'Anyway, he (the Minister) is a complete idiot. They're all a lot of fucking Philistines. Wilson's never picked up a book in his life. He spends his spare time with business men. He doesn't give a damn about the arts. Nor does Hugh Jenkins. Jennie Lee was the only Minister who was keen to do something about the position of the arts.'

Kingsley Amis, in the same symposium, rather to my surprise, took my side. 'Hugh Jenkins is all right,' he said. On the other hand, someone called Desmond Bagley, announced with an air of authority that I was not at all enthusiastic about PLR. Jennie Lee said, 'All I know is that Hugh Jenkins has worked very hard, and it is in the Queen's Speech.'

The First Reading was in the House of Lords on 18th March 1976 with a Second Reading debate on 5th April. When I was dismissed on 20th April the Bill was still in the lords where the new Minister, Lord Donaldson, was resisting Ted Willis's attempts to extend it to cover reference books and to make one or two other desirable but not immediately practicable improvements. It returned to the Commons at the end of May when an attempt was made to avoid a Second Reading Debate in the Chamber by referring the Bill to a Second Reading Committee. This was stymied by more than 20 members standing up and objecting, and the Second Reading was moved in the Chamber by Margaret Jackson, Under Secretary for Education and Science, on 26th May 1976. As the Minister for the Arts was now in the Lords, one of the Education Ministers had to take on the chore in the Commons, but it was unfair to lumber the most junior and most overburdened one with it and this, in itself, indicated that the Government felt that now that I was out of the way the Bill could be regarded as of little consequence. It was not even allowed a Second Reading debate at prime time and was put on at 10 pm, after the Bail Bill, at the end of ordinary business. The motion to extend time was opposed and eventually carried by 115 to 12 but the debate was halted by points of order raised by Michael English (Labour) who proved to be one of three implacable opponents of the Bill. The Government evidently believed that the Bill would get an unopposed Second Reading but at 11.34 pm they adjourned the debate, to my dismay and astonishment, on the grounds that there were not enough members left in the House (100) to secure a closure, and that if they did not adjourn then it might drag on all night. I was furiously angry, for in another hour or so Second Reading could have been obtained. What was lacking was will and enthusiasm. Had I been Minister I would never have agreed to adjourn and we would have obtained Second Reading that night.

In the debate I said: 'I believe that the importance of the Bill cannot be over-estimated. We are establishing a principle the future of which will fundamentally affect the whole craft of writing and many other things as well. We live in a society in which we pay for use. We pay for the use of our houses, for the use of our television and for many other things . . . Is there anyone in the House who thinks the creative artist is unimportant? Is there anyone on the Socialist side who thinks the creative artist does not matter in society?'[11]

The truth was that most Members on both sides of the House were not present and did not give a damn about the creative artist, and neither did the Government.

In spite of my constant pleas, nothing more was heard of the Bill until 5th July and then it appeared once again after 10 pm, and once again there were fewer than 100 members present. At 11.40 pm Margaret Jackson again moved that the debate be adjourned. I was not alone in finding this totally incomprehensible. I went to see Michael Foot and agreed to support the adjournment on condition that the Bill would be brought before the House again at a time when its passage could be secured. I reported this in the Chamber.

Nevertheless, the Bill did not return until 14th October, now desperately late in the Session and, once again, at 10 pm. This time, as on its first appearance, there were just over 100 members there. At 11.18 pm the Government attempted to close the debate and failed by one vote – 99 to 7. It was said that the failure was deliberately arranged by Government Whips hostile to the Bill.

[11] *Hansard*, 26.5.76. Col. 586.

So the debate continued and eventually at 1.17 am Second Reading was secured by 99 votes to Nil, the two opposers being the two tellers against the Second Reading, the Tories, Sproat and Moate. So, on 14th October we obtained a Second Reading which could have been secured on 26th May.

There were those who believed that the Bill was subjected to deliberate sabotage by the Whips and particularly by the Chief Whip, Michael Cocks, who was said to be personally hostile to the measure. Others took the view that the Whips were correctly interpreting the feelings of Members by giving the Bill a low priority. It was also suggested that the authors' organisations should have mounted a massive protest to give Michael Foot the power he evidently lacked to raise the Bill in the Cabinet's order of priorities. Others believed that my own dismissal indicated that the Government would be happy for the Bill to expire with my period of office. Nevertheless, we had got a Second Reading at last and I determined to do my utmost to see the Bill through its Committee Stage.

When the Committee met on 26th October the presence upon it of the three main opponents, Sproat, Moate and English (I used to call them Stoat, Grope and Foolish) was uncompromising; even the Committee of Selection did not seem to be on our side.

It was immediately apparent that wrecking tactics were going to be employed as Michael English straight away started raising points of order. Whatever had been the Government's previous attitude to the Bill, it was now apparent that they were belatedly going to try to see it through, for Margaret Jackson moved that there should be four sittings a week, Tuesday and Thursday mornings and afternoons which meant nights.

English opposed this at length but my own contributions made up in brevity what they lacked in elegance.

I said: 'Sit down and shut up.'

And later: 'Belt up.'

And later still: 'You belt up, too.'

We spent the whole of the first morning discussing when we should sit and finally Margaret Jackson's motion was approved by twelve to three. No prizes are offered for guessing who the three were. Once the Chairman, Mr. Costain, reproved me and I was surprised to find myself banging a bunch of envelopes against my desk in sheer frustration.

'The Hon. Member must not use his envelopes as a gavel', said the Chairman and as he did so I remembered Khruschev and thought I should have used my shoe.

The Committee discussed amendments to Clause 1 of the Bill all day on Thursday, 28th October. One of these was serious – a decision by the Government to remove the word 'works' which had been inserted by amendment in the Lords and to restore the word 'books' which had been removed. I understood the desire to extend the bill to records and cassettes but felt we must settle for books in order to have any chance at all of getting the Bill. However, it was clear that the Government amendment would be carried comfortably and so I abstained to indicate my support in principle of future extension of PLR.

At 10 pm Margaret Jackson moved the adjournment of the Committee. I opposed this as I wanted to sit there all night and wear the three opponents down. Unhappily the adjournment was carried by eight votes to six, which greatly disappointed me.

The outcome was that we continued to discuss amendments to Clause 1 on the following Tuesday and I voted against an attempt to include reference books in the Bill, as no effective means of implementing this had been discovered.

The sitting was suspended at 7.30 for dinner and when it resumed at 9 pm, the Tories failed to turn up. Some of our own people connived with them, and although present in the House had not returned to the Committee Room by 9.20. The sitting was suspended and yet another opportunity of breaking the back of the opposition was lost. I think it was at that point that Brophy and Duffy, who alone among writers were present throughout, at last realised that in politics the 'moderates' are moderate in their enthusiasm and in their conviction. Small wonder that Oscar Wilde felt that moderation was a thing to be avoided.

On Thursday 4th November 1976 Clauses 1 and 2 were agreed and it was rumoured that the Opposition were willing to let us have the Committee stage as they believed that it was now so late in the Session that they could kill the Bill when it returned to the Chamber. This proved to be the case and on the following

Tuesday it was agreed that the Bill, as amended in Committee, should be reported to the House.

This took place on 16th November. Again the Bill was subjected to a series of amendments. The debate began by Margaret Jackson again moving to leave out 'works' and to restore 'books'. In the chamber the three regular opponents were joined by another Tory, Nigel Lawson, whose objections to the Bill were even more confused and contradictory. It was opposition for opposition's sake and St. John Stevas revealed that the Tories had refused to be whipped on the issue.

In this debate Sproat unsuccessfully tried to defend the practice of the Tories in Committee in which even the alleged supporters of the Bill among them had refused to come into the room, although standing outside, to make up a quorum. When the first vote was taken at 7.30 pm, the Government amendment was carried by 154 to 23 and it was clear that there were very few Tories in the House. The debate continued on Tory amendments to bring reference books within the ambit of the Bill. These had been selected, although a similar attempt had failed in Committee and, surprisingly, the Deputy Speaker who was in the Chair at the time allowed discussion on all sorts of irrelevant issues. I tried to persuade him to keep discussion on the rails but he was either unable or unwilling to rule anything out of order. The vote on this bunch of amendments was taken at 9.30 pm, and this time the Government carried the day by 125 to 33 – Labour members were beginning to go home and a few Tories had returned after dinner.

The debate continued with a Tory attempt to extend the Bill beyond public libraries. The Motion to continue the debate after 10 pm was carried by 140 (Labour) to 9 (Conservatives). At that point it seemed possible that we might get the Bill through but soon it became clear that a handful of Tories were determined to wreck it. Without any attempt by the Deputy Speaker to stop him the House was treated by Moate to dissertations on Cornish folklore and, helped out by interventions from his friends, he spoke for an hour from 11 pm to midnight ending by saying that he did not wish to speak at great length. After a brief intervention by Margaret Jackson, Sproat took over and carried on an entirely irrelevant discussion with his friends for some time without intervention by the Deputy Speaker. About 1 am Michael English challenged the Government to move the closure saying that there were not the necessary 100 members in the House. I went to see the Whips and they confirmed that almost all the Tories other than one or two Frontbenchers and those opposed to the Bill had gone and there were not 100 Labour members left – the debate could therefore go on all night and tomorrow's business be lost and still we should not have the Bill. There was an anguished discussion in Michael Foot's office with Duffy and Brophy present, while I fumed and raged and swore, but when I got back into the Chamber Margaret Jackson was moving the adjournment yet again and PLR was lost a little before 2 early in the morning of 17th November. I was too sick at heart to make any comment. A few days later the Session ended without the last minute rescue attempt which I urged on Michael Foot. And that was that.

Why did we fail? We failed because I was dismissed as Minister but also because there was no one else in the Government who shared my own view of the importance of the arts. If it had been given a three-line Whip the Bill could have been obtained easily but on a weak two-liner and with an unwhipped opposition, Members simply went home. And that at a time when two hours' more work would have seen the measure on to the statute book. Sadly without my presence on the Front bench to drive the measure through, to rally the troops, to talk to them, to urge them to stay and fight – all of which are actions not open to a newly dismissed ex-Minister – the lot of writers fell in the level of priorities of almost all members of the House to one of those things one believes in but is content to leave to others to look after.

Why did we fail? We failed because there arose three determined opponents of the Bill who saw in the general lack of enthusiasm for PLR an opportunity to make a mark. In the case of Sproat it was general opposition. Any other Bill on which the Government could be defeated would have done as well. Moate represented the library interests but with that motivation he combined a natural tendency to talk at length against anything. English was more complex. He was against the Bill in toto, seeing in it the thin end of library charges but he was also against it because it failed to reward the good author more than the bad. Because it sought to remedy a general injustice to a group rather than to benefit the artistically worthy. He was against it because there are wealthy authors who have no need of it – the classic Tory case against the Welfare state.

Why did we fail? We failed because politics is not yet about the arts in Britain. We failed because my period of office saw the high water mark of Government intervention and support and my departure was the sign of a temporary withdrawal. At that time PLR was too closely associated with a dismissal Minister for the Government to take it seriously.

Early in the new Session, in the spring of 1977, Ted Willis, at my suggestion, put down exactly the same Bill in the Lords and with the support of Lord Donaldson it was carried through all its stages and was ready to come into the Commons on 3rd March. I tried to bring it into the Commons but as it was a Government Bill and a Money Bill at that, only the Government could do so. All that session I tried to persuade the Government to pick it up until Michael Foot seemingly became embarrassed at the sight of one he had sponsored into the House thirteen years earlier. Devolution was postponed and Europe deferred. Great gaps were torn in the Government's legislation programme but no attempt was made to fill a couple of days of Chamber time with PLR. I offered to see the Bill through its Committee stage from the backbenches but the offer was rejected. Never in the history of Parliament has there been a Bill to which the House was so totally committed in theory and so totally indifferent in practice.

The authors' organisations seemed defeated and gone to ground. And so compared with the struggles of the previous years 1977 was inactive but towards the end of it I sought from the Government an undertaking that the commitment to PLR should be repeated in the Queen's Speech. I did not get that undertaking and one thing is certain; if Labour intends to implement PLR, it must do so now and the Bill must be taken at prime time on a three-line Whip. If the next government should be Tory – and I do not think it will be, but if it should – they could and would implement PLR like a shot. Labour in opposition would be very keen and the Tories have at last learned a lesson from us which we seemed temporarily to have forgotten:

It is that this country is in an arts phase – anything to do with the arts is popular and Labour lost more than it knew by a decision to reduce its support for PLR to a hypocritical lip-service.

The Irresponsibility of the Arts Council

I know of no one who carries weight in Parliament who wishes to bring the Arts Council under political control in the sense of subjecting its artistic decisions to questioning in the House of Commons.

The Council is already under financial control and always has been. Every penny it spends must be accounted for to the Minister for the Arts and his officials. The grant is handed over in a miserly fashion and the Council has to show that it has been properly spent before the next instalment is forthcoming. 'Properly' means properly within the functions and duties of the Council and those duties include that of artistic decision-making. The exercise of artistic judgment is not the function of the Minister and he will do well during his period of office to conceal his own opinions so as to avoid the chance that someone might think they are of some consequence. They are not, except in the very widest sense. For example, the Minister may properly express the opinion that more money should be spent on this or that art form or in this or that part of the country, but he does not advise, still less direct, the Arts Council.

The Arts Council is therefore technically irresponsible (i.e., not responsible to anyone), answerable for its decisions only to itself. This fact has long worried Parliament which has reasonably taken the view that although MPs do not wish to set themselves up as arbiters of taste, the Arts Council ought to be accountable in some way to a wider constituency.

This view was expressed as early as 1949 by the Select Committee on Estimates.[12] The Committee had received a memorandum from Equity which complained of the lack of

[12] *House of Commons Paper 315*, HMSO, 1949.

contact between the Council and employers and those employed in the arts. The memorandum continued: 'This lack of contact springs, we believe, from the fact that the members of the Arts Council and of its advisory panels are nominated individuals responsible to no one but themselves. In practice this makes for the autocracy of a small group of officials.'

The complaint was voiced that the Drama Panel exercised no control over the Drama Department and it was proposed that 'the Drama Panel should include a proportion of members elected by theatrical organisations and responsible to those organisations. Each panel in turn should elect at least two representatives to the Arts Council itself.' Equity concluded by suggesting that the Panels should be given more influence over the work of their relative departments and in the functioning of the Council as a whole. Thirty years later, no change has been made. If anything the Panels are less influential, for the scale of the operation has multiplied nearly a hundredfold and the Panels are not even allowed to elect their own Chairmen.

Equity said that their proposals had been endorsed by their Annual General Meeting and in support of them they brought to the Estimates Committee not only their brilliant General Secretary, Gordon Sandison, who was sadly to die young a few years later, but a distinguished group from their Council including Sir Laurence Olivier who complained that the Arts Council never consulted Equity's opinion about anything. At that time Sir Laurence was himself a member of the Drama Panel and he made the point that he was there as an individual and not as a representative of Equity. He agreed with the criticism of the lack of power on the Panels saying that the Drama Panel was 'neither a representative body nor a powerful body. They are simply a body to make suggestions. They have no power of driving a suggestion home.' He thought it both desirable and possible for there to be a Drama Panel which would have the confidence of both the profession and the public. Michael Denison, himself on the Arts Council, supported him arguing that a Committee decision was preferable to the individual view of any one person.

The Theatre Managers' Association took a remarkably similar view complaining that they had been asking in vain for years for more formal and closer links with the Arts Council.[13] On behalf of the Musicians Union, Hardie Ratcliffe pointed out that representation on the Council or on the Music Panel had both been requested and that they had put forward two names but neither had been selected.[14]

In its conclusions and recommendations the Estimates Committee referred to these complaints and requests for representation on the Panels and suggested that the trade unions and other bodies should be consulted with a view to establishing closer relations with the Council

Nothing came of this recommendation; the Arts Council, on the contrary, gradually established élitism as a virtue and in the following decades began to confuse oligarchy with independence.

When the Arts Council appointed me a member of the Drama Panel in 1962 I was Assistant General Secretary of Equity and Joint Secretary of the Theatres Advisory Council which I had helped to bring into being. It was made clear to me that I was chosen in a personal and not in a representative capacity but, of course, I did seek the views of both Equity and the Theatres Advisory Council on matters of importance and as the Arts Council was represented on the TAC as an associate member, they were fully aware of this first breach in their patrician seclusion.

In 1968, twenty years after the earlier report, the Estimates Committee again decided to look at the Arts Council and once again came up with a recommendation that the Council should become a more representative body. The Council was told to carry out a study 'in conjunction with the bodies representative of artists', but no such study was ever carried out. Once again, the Arts Council thumbed its nose at Parliament and pursued its increasingly exclusive course.

At the time of the 1968 report I was on the Arts Council itself, Jennie Lee, as first Minister for the Arts having insisted upon my appointment. The Chairman, Lord Goodman, and I disagreed totally about democracy. Relations between the Arts Council and other bodies in the arts were by this time much closer than in

13 Ibid. p. 84.
14 Ibid. p. 118.

earlier days, partly as a result of the work of the Theatres Advisory Council, but the Council as a whole still believed in the curious proposition that to retain its independence *from* Government it was necessary for it to be appointed *by* the Government. There was also a more rational objection. Appointment ensured that the Arts Council consisted of persons dedicated to the arts. When the Arts Council emerged from CEMA there was no demand for democratic control. The idea of state support for the arts was new and the sums deployed were minimal. It was not until the Council had grown into a great influence in the land and Government patronage was taken for granted that complaints began to be heard that this enormous power, this decisive influence, was exercised by a small group of appointees answerable to no one but themselves. By that time the Council had become a part of the establishment and tradition had converted defect into virtue.

When I first became Minister, the then Chairman of the Arts Council, Pat, now Lord Gibson invited me to his home in Chelsea where an enjoyable dinner was served by his charming and efficient wife to a dozen leading members of the Arts Council and myself. We sat at a round table and afterwards continued there, talking seriously about arts problems and relationships for quite a time. I recall The Marchioness of Anglesey, Lord Balfour of Burleigh, Professor Baldry, Viscount Esher, Jack Lambert, among others.

They plied me with questions which I enjoyed trying to answer, for I felt myself to be among people with whom I shared a common purpose, but after a while I began to see that the questions were all directed to ensuring that the Arts Council remained exactly as it was and simply went on doing more of the same. So just before we rose I said,

'May I ask a question? What is wrong with the Arts Council? What changes need to be made?'

There was no answer so I pressed them. 'You mean it's quite perfect. Nothing at all needs to be done except to get more money?'

There was still no answer and I knew that if I sought to introduce constitutional changes I would get no help from the Council.

In June 1974 I visited the Arts Council, meeting the Chairman, Pat Gibson, again, but this time with the leading officials rather than the lay members of the Council itself. I raised the question of democracy, floating the idea of a combination of election, of nomination by interested bodies, and of appointment. I also asked them to think about the possibility of making the Arts Council's decisions less subjective; more amenable to public justification, perhaps by some kind of points system. I said that the allocation of housing by local authorities was a very sensitive matter and Councils had to be able to explain why this person was housed and that person was not. Was artistic merit incapable of expression in terms more exact than 'We all think he's good?' Or perhaps it was 'All his peers think he's good,' Or the critics? Or our officers? Or the Chairman and I think he's good. Was that really it?

I suggested that the Arts Council had become the prisoner of its own past. Pat Gibson replied that he was sceptical about democracy but he agreed that they would try to evolve some system of measurement and I proposed that they should try it out for a time against the time-honoured method of peering into their own artistic entrails. Gibson agreed to recommend the Council to open up membership of the Advisory Panels so that any person or body with ideas on the subject could put forward names for consideration.

Summing it up, I said that it remained my view that the sense of unfairness often felt by applicants who received little money or none at all would be decreased if their representative bodies were given a say in the distribution of the financial support of the state. I added that such feelings of injustice would be further reduced if any method could be thought of to demonstrate an element of consistency in the Council's judgments.

Back in Belgrave Square I wrote large numbers of letters to every organisation I could think of in the whole arts area inviting names for consideration for membership of the Council, for the position is that the Minister recommends the membership of the Arts Council itself while the Council appoints all its own Advisory Panels.

I had a hand in ensuring that the October 1974 General Election Manifesto of the Labour Party included the words 'We shall bring forward proposals to make the Arts Council more democratic and representative of people in the arts and entertainment'. Getting something into a Manifesto is one thing but to carry it out, even if the Minister concerned is eager to do so, is quite another.

In replying to a debate initiated by Bryan Magee, MP, in the House[15] on 10th February 1975 I blew the arts trumpet a bit and incidentally said that we had 'started the process of drawing the membership of the Arts Council and its committees from a wider spectrum'. And on 17th March,[16] replying to Robert Cooke, MP, I referred again to the Manifesto undertaking, making it clear in doing so that 'we do not want and will not have a Minister of Culture who lays down a Government line on the arts which all who wish to be financed must follow.'

I soon found out that there was no support in the office for changing the constitution of the Arts Council and told Willy Wright that when he attended Arts Council meetings, as he did as the Department's assessor, he should put forward Labour Party policy and not his own views which I understood was his practice. I also upbraided him for failing to brief me properly about a row which had arisen as the result of an Arts Council decision to chop the Phoenix Opera Company. The management of the company, supported by Labour MPs Laurie Pavitt and Bryan Magee, believed that they had lost their grant because of favouritism. They were convinced that another small company was chosen for other than purely artistic reasons.

Willy Wright drafted me a letter of denial to Bryan Magee who took it to the Chairman of the Arts Council. Gibson admitted that one of their officials had agency interests. However, the Arts Council were satisfied that these interests did not influence decisions at all and that, in any event, the official concerned did not determine the Phoenix matter. Pavitt reported this back to me and I found that John Spence had relied on a telephone call from the Arts Council denying the story. Wright had translated this into a Minute to as a result of which I had been led to deny what Gibson had subsequently admitted to be true. I blew Wright and Spence up in front of Gibson whom I called over to

---

[15] *Hansard*.Col. 103.
[16] *Hansard*. Col. 1355.

Belgrave Square and told him that this sort of thing would continue to occur from time to time so long as the Arts Council remained a secret society.

I never believed and do not now believe that his agency interests, which were subsequently disposed elsewhere, had any effect on the work of the official concerned, but while there is no element of representative democracy on the Music Panel or on the Arts Council, who can persuade Phoenix Opera that everything was above board? Personally I regarded the withdrawal of their grant as perhaps unwise, even unreasonable, but not corrupt.

My first four appointmnets to the Arts Council were Vic Feather, Ann Clwyd, Elizabeth Thomas and Jonathan Miller. The two women, especially Elizabeth Thomas, were more successful than the men, both of whom resigned. Feather because of the illness which led to his death and Miller because I persuaded him to accept appointment, misguidedly, at a time when he was no longer interested.

Later in 1974 Willy Wright raised the question of further vacancies which would occur at the end of that year. By this time I had received hundreds of suggestions. I hoped that these would be the last appointments and that I would persuade Gibson to accept a system of nomination and election during 1975. Willy Wright's note headed 'Arts Council membership' said: 'You wished to discuss this with Lord Gibson.' I had expressed no such wish. In the case of the first four appointments I had simply told Gibson of the recommendations I proposed to make and he had accepted them, some with more reluctance than others. Wright went on to say that Gibson would have some suggestions to put forward and that it would be right for me to listen sympathetically to them and to agree to discuss them with Reg Prentice.

I thought that Wright and Gibson had probably cooked up this approach between them, but I had no objection to discussing the matter with the Chairman and, indeed, thought it proper that I should do so. However, to be on the safe side, as I particularly wanted Raymond Williams to be a member, I wrote to him and told Gibson that the invitation had been sent when he arrived. He countered with the suggestion of Roy Fuller. I had heard that Fuller had little use for the idea of working in committee as a member of a team but as the Oxford Professor of Poetry he could not be rejected and Elizabeth Thomas supported the idea. Gibson may have thought Fuller was a tame cat, but when he came to see me prior to his appointment I sensed the tiger in him and was not surprised that his contribution until his resignation was said to be more sparkling than constructive.

Gibson agreed to my suggestions of Richard Hoggart, Martin Esslin and Laurence Harbottle although he jibbed a little at the last. He may have known that Harbottle was the unanimous recommendation of the Drama Panel and that in appointing him I was practising a little informal democracy. I did not know Harbottle, but when I met him I was much impressed. The other two had also been widely recommended and I knew them both to be splendid choices. I wanted Marina Vaizey to go straight into the Chairmanship of the Arts Panel but Gibson would not have that. However, he accepted her readily enough on to the Council and in return I agreed to his suggestion of Annette Page for the vacant ballet seat. One of the few people to refuse my invitation to join the Council was that great character Ed Berman, so I put forward Malcolm Griffiths and Stuart Hall and a large number of other names. Gibson agreed to consider them for membership of the Panels with a view to some joining the Council later.

This decided me. Gibson was clearly ready to try to work with me, so I would try to work with him. If I had had available a Chairman after my own heart and yet acceptable to the Prime Minister and the Cabinet, I might have engineered Gibson's resignation at that point. But Roy Shaw, the ideal choice, had already accepted the job of Secretary General. It was a pity, for I could have worked with Shaw as Chairman and between us we could have revolutionised the Arts Council. As it was Gibson not only stood between us but won Shaw for the anti-democratic cause. I did not know in 1974 that this would occur; that Gibson, that pleasant man, would stick his toes in as soon as he had prepared the ground; that he would get into a strong enough position to appeal over my head and that he would prevent me from carrying out my Party's policy of reforming the structure of the Arts Council.

Nevertheless it is bound to come. Scotland and Wales will want to run their own Arts set-up and Scottish and Welsh Arts

Councils will follow devolution. They are unlikely to continue as sub-committees of the Arts Council of Great Britain and will contain some nominated or elected members. Whether the ACGB remains the residual body or an English Arts Council is established with a UK Council to co-ordinate, appointment as a principle is doomed.

There are many ways of making the Arts Council less objectionable than it is without subjecting it to Government control. For example, the Council could be enlarged, meeting quarterly and an Executive Committee could meet monthly. The Advisory Panels would include people elected by appropriate trade unions, managerial associations and interested societies. Each Panel would elect its own Chairman and Vice-Chairman who would represent them on the governing body and act as their spokesmen. Regional Arts Associations and local Government arts committees would choose persons to represent them. The period of office should not exceed two years but people should be able to be re-elected. Not less than a third nor more than a half of each body, Panels, Council and Executive should be appointed as at present but by a Minister for Arts, Communications and Entertainment, who would be in the Cabinet, from among nominations submitted to him each year by the electing bodies. The Council would choose its own Chairman and Vice-Chairman and might be permitted to go outside its own ranks for either, but not both, of these office holders. All members would be allowed to charge actual out-of-pocket expenses and loss of income involved in carrying out Arts Council business.

Thus the Arts Council and its Advisory Panels would consist of persons placed there by organisations of artists of all kinds including trade unions, managerial associations and specialist and interested bodies plus a strong element appointed by the Minister from among persons recommended to him.

There are other possibilities, but it is essential to get away from the present position in which the Government appoints a group of all-powerful poodles and then throws away the lead. Like the House of Lords, such a group is so conscious of its own incongruity that it tends to avoid unpopular decisions. On the rare occasions when the Council upsets a strong group or acts against the advice of one of its own Panels, its position is at once shown to be indefensible for it does not derive any part of its authority directly from artists or the public. The Council is a group assembled by a series of chances, a collection of random choices made by a very tiny and ingrown electorate advised by the Council's own bureaucracy and finally approved by a Secretary of State or Prime Minister who knows little about the people concerned and naturally opts for what he is told is safety, which means the arts establishment.

Such a body operates out of consciousness of its own worth: it has no other justification. The Council avoids any method of evaluating its decisions on the grounds that artistic judgment cannot be measured. When I asked for a system to be worked out and tested the Council took no action. Perhaps their lack of enthusiasm might be explained by the consideration that if a system showed their judgment to be faulty, the whole basis of an appointed Council would have been brought into doubt. How can an establishment be justified once its infallibility is questioned?

It may be that this is why I was replaced by Jack Donaldson. He was a figure acceptable to the establishment while I was acceptable only to artists, to their organisations and to the artistic left, which includes most of the critics. I was on friendly terms with a number of establishment figures but they did not like my policies and why should they? I aimed to take their power, their influence, their authority from them and who would not wish to get rid of a fellow who wanted to do that? The Fabians were too right about 'the inevitability of gradualness' in this country but although I was not allowed to make the necessary changes in my time, they will come gradually but inevitably.

In the spring of 1975 I gave a dinner for the Arts Council at which I pushed the idea of democracy again and for the first time I had the sense that some members of the Council were taking the matter seriously. At this time there was a great deal of groaning in the press, notably by Jack Lambert, who wrote a 'Requiem for the British Theatre' in the Sunday Times. This was offset, to some extent, by Helen Dawson with a much more balanced piece in the 'Observer'.

Lord Gibson had taken things into his own hands by publishing a claim for £25 million as against £19 million, in his introduction to the Arts Councils' report, as being the sum needed for 1974/5. An increase of £6 million in a year was a large sum but I should have gone for more had I not been hamstrung by the publication of his claim. Gibson never trusted me to secure the largest amount possible and was always going above my head, writing to Healey or seeking interviews with the PM. If he had left it to me I should have got the Arts Council another million, possibly more. I knew long before Gibson that the demands of the National Theatre would increase and, combined with the effect of inflation, would soon turn his £25 million from a splendid dream of affluence into an inadequate reality.

While all this was going on I was travelling about the country each week opening things, making speeches and keeping in touch with the arts people in the regions who were all much more cheerful, satisfied and confident than the London moaners.

I wrote to Gibson on the 5th August 1975 proposing that, as a gesture towards democracy, the Drama and Literature Panels should be invited to choose their own Chairmen whom I could then appoint to the Council. I hoped he would agree to co-operate in carrying out a trial on these lines. I then left with Marie for a visit to Wales and at the Eisteddfod in Criccieth, I discussed democracy and devolution with Ann Clwyd and Aneurin Thomas, Director of the Welsh Arts Council. Both were in favour of both these proposals. Then to Liverpool where, not unexpectedly, I found a strong feeling that the Arts Council was too London based and that local authorities should have a say in the distribution of its funds. On my return I spoke to the Progressive League about Democracy in the Labour Party which the media interpreted as a tremendous attack on Harold Wilson. In fact it was an advocacy of representative and party democracy and for a Cabinet elected by the Parliamentary Labour Party.

Gibson did not reply to my letter until 21st August and it was clear that he had explored the ground in the meantime and had come to the conclusion that he could safely defy me. For he retracted from his earlier attitude of reluctant readiness to move a little in my direction. He said that I was asking him to change the character of the Arts Council and this he point blank and quite brusquely refused to do. Until such time as the Charter was changed he would not co-operate with me. My proposals were ill-advised, for the Charter did not provide for Panels to elect their own Chairmen who would then be appointed to the Council.

I was angry. I knew that I could not get Parliamentary time to change the Charter and the only thing to do would be to get rid of Gibson. I drafted a letter designed to bring about his resignation, but Willy Wright reminded me that I had no power of appointment and could only send a Minute to the Secretary of State and he provided me with a draft for the purpose. I refused to accept my powerlessness and sent a curt note to Gibson saying that I was sorry he did not feel able to co-operate with me in fulfilling my Party's election undertaking. I would be making a statement about the Government's intentions in the matter. I sent a copy of this letter to Fred Mulley together with Willy's Minute which explained the background. I said that the Charter would have to be revised with devolution, but that in the meanwhile we should seek to make the interim modifications I was proposing.

Mulley replied that we should go slowly. He was surprised I had proceeded so far without consulting him. I said that I *had* been taking it slowly and that I had been trying to get the Arts Council to move in the direction of Party policy with little success for more than a year. I now needed his support.

I knew that things were going on which affected me and my task, but I did not know what they were and the Prime Minister resolutely avoided me. I was also anxious about the deterioration in my public image. I blamed my Public Relations Officer and eventually had him transferred. Now I see I did him an injustice for it is clear that he was not being allowed to put me into a good light and the media very sensitively pick up these areas of dissent in a Department. He was not independent, being seconded from the Education Public Relations Office at Elizabeth House who were more successful with their publications work (they turned out an excellent glossy pamphlet about the arts in the regions which I called 'Arts with the People') than with the media.

Wilsonry, Leverage and Mulleydom

On the 24th June 1975 I received a copy of a note from the Prime Minister's Private Secretary enclosing a letter from Wilson to Harold Lever, Chancellor of the Duchy of Lancaster, giving him the job of assessing the possibility of raising money for the Arts from other than Government sources. A draft press statement was enclosed which said that the assessment would be carried out in consultation with the Minister for the Arts.

I was greatly put about by this as I was almost ready to bring off a deal with the CBI on business sponsorship and any intervention at this stage would be positively unhelpful. I went to see Fred Mulley who said he knew nothing about the proposal and we agreed to write separately to Wilson asking for an interview before the press statement was released. I wrote on the 26th June saying that I was surprised to learn that he had asked Lever to undertake 'a thorough assessment of the financial position of the arts'. I enclosed a copy of a letter I had sent on the 19th June to Campbell Adamson of the CBI confirming an offer of £15,000 as the Government's contribution towards the setting up of a new organisation for business sponsorship of the arts which had been under discussion for some time. I also pointed out that Lord Redcliffe-Maud was currently undertaking a full examination of financial support for the arts. There was nothing for Lever to do and I asked for an interview at which I would persuade the PM to drop his unfortunate idea.

There was no reply and I hoped that the foolish notion would be quietly forgotten.

However, on the 9th September I heard from Lever's office that he was going to issue the announcement about his investigation of arts financing. I telephoned him and told him that I had asked for a meeting with the PM before this statement was published and that no such meeting had taken place. Lever said he was sorry about that, but the PM was not available and the release could not long be delayed. I wanted the statement that the investigation would be carried out in consultation with me given greater prominence in the release. He seemed surprised that the announcement, which he clearly had not read, contained any undertaking about consulting with me at all. He was not proposing to work in association with any one. I said I had all the information he needed and I presumed he did not wish to deprive himself of the facts. As for me, I welcomed assistance from such a high source. He said he did not wish to embarrass me and I said I did not wish to embarrass him. He said I could not embarrass him and I said I was trying to help him. He was just leaving for Holland but agreed to look at the statement and telephone me in the morning. He did not do so, but I telephoned his office and found that they were proposing to release the statement leaving out any mention of my involvement in the investigation. I erupted and eventually agreed to withdraw my objections to the release on condition that it gave prominence to my part in the proposed investigation. Nevertheless the press hailed the announcement as the appointment of an 'Arts Supremo' and once again forecast my imminent dismissal.

All this was in the middle of the row about the Wealth Tax and at this point I had the greatest difficulty in getting letters typed in the office on either of these two issues. I had to harry and press my Private Office staff who were clearly in conflict with the rest of the office and in the end overcame the difficulty by taking some notepaper home, typing and posting a letter and presenting the office with the copy for filing. My leading officials seemed to me to be stone-walling, perhaps in the belief that I would be replaced at any moment by some one less insistent on the fulfillment of Party policies. They knew very well that on these key issues I had little support in the Cabinet.

I took the opportunity of a speech to my own General Management Committee in Putney to list the things we had achieved in the arts in my 18 months of office: The removal of museum charges, getting the British Library out of Bloomsbury and into Euston, the Theatre Museum out of Somerset House and into Covent Garden and finding enough money to keep all the important works we needed in this country and getting the Arts Council, the Crafts Advisory Committee, the Museums and Galleries, the Regional Associations and the Film Institute and School all much their largest grants ever. It was not a bad record. I also took the opportunity of arguing the Wealth Tax case and talked about the opening of the National Theatre and Public Lending Right. I kept silent about the Arts Council, for although I would not give up, I could see no way of winning that one. I had a feeling that my tenure of office might be coming to an end and reflected that the Labour Party would be a more effective instrument for wresting control from the capitalist establishment if its leadership had the will to do so.

During the Blackpool Labour Party Conference Robert Carvel, an Evening Standard lobby correspondent came up with an announcement that I was to go and that Harold Lever would 'become the Cabinet Minister with specific and continuing responsibility for the arts. No doubt Mr. Jenkins will fairly soon get the sack,' he said.

However, in the week after Blackpool Mary Giles, my Private Secretary, put in my box a copy of the letter I have mentioned earlier from the PM's Private Secretary to Fred Mulley's PS. It said that the PM had asked his man to arrange that no new policies should be publicly announced nor any new policy decisions taken with respect to the arts without prior consultation with the Chancellor of the Duchy. The PM also wished to be consulted in advance on all ministerial appointments in the arts which should come to him from Fred Mulley. The PM's PS would be grateful if Mulley's PS would arrange for the Prime Minister's wishes on these matters to be met forthwith.

What a way to go on, I thought. My old friend Harold Wilson whom I have known for twenty years and supported for Leader of the Party will not see me. Instead he tells his Private Secretary to tell Fred Mulley's man to tell Mary Giles to tell me something I do not wish to know.

I nobbled Fred Mulley in the House. He told me he had no idea of what the PM thought he was up to. He confirmed this in writing on 16th October but said that we must both abide by the PM's wishes, and he added: 'I do not think that this is the right time to press for constitutional changes in the method of appointing members to the Arts Council. I think it better not to proceed as suggested in your Minute of 23rd September.'

Since there was no proposal for any procedure in that Minute but simply information of what I had already done, I decided to let Fred have it. I wrote to him on 21st October saying that we both ought to know what the PM imagined he was doing. We did not know why he had asked Harold Lever to investigate something which was already known. We did not know why Harold Lever had to be consulted about new policy decisions when there were none in hand or contemplated. I had asked Harold Lever at Blackpool, and he did not seem to know either. The policy of making the Arts Council more representative and democratic was an existing one and I had made no appointments without consulting him and none of them were controversial, so what was it all about? I knew one thing; the Chairman of the Arts Council, Lord Gibson, had seen Harold Lever immediately prior to the sending of the letter from the PM's office and I added: 'I must therefore assume that Gibson made some complaint to Lever which had this effect. This would be in character as from the beginning Gibson has sought to go over my head, but this is the first time that he seems to have succeeded.

'For the last eighteen months I have been trying, not without success, to loosen the grip of the snobocracy on the arts scene. They are a small group, very influential but entirely without support in the country. Now, at the moment when I am beginning to undermine them, I find myself being undermined.

'When we meet I will explain what has been going on. The arts establishment seems powerful but is, in fact, highly vulnerable for their only friends are in the media and they rely on public veneration for the arts to preserve their privileges. The attitude of artists towards them is confused, for deference and fear is mixed with outright loathing.

'These Tories must be beaten or they will beat us and the struggle can be won, but not if I am deprived of the full confidence of the Prime Minister without explanation or discussion just when I am moving towards developments which will hearten the arts and entertainments world, give them confidence in the radicalism of the Government and in doing so strengthen the morale of our troops all along the line.'

I subsequently met Fred Mulley by appointment in his room in the House of Commons. We had our Private Secretaries with us.

Fred said that before going to see the PM he wanted to know what I meant by making the Arts Council more democratic. I explained again and said that I had been gradually implementing our election manifesto undertaking to 'make the Arts Council more democratic and more representative of those working in the arts and entertainment.' This policy was opposed by our civil servants and by the Arts Council. That opposition had until recently been expressed in terms of delay and minimal cooperation. Now it was overt and bold and this meant that the leading opponent, Lord Gibson, Chairman of the Arts Council, had got the support of the leading members of the Party in the Cabinet, including the Prime Minister, in what looked like a successful attempt to prevent me from implementing Party policy. Although the Establishment appeared to have suborned the loyalty to our own policy of leading members of our Party, I should still do my best to implement that policy whether they liked it or not, so long as I remained in office.

I did not, in fact, succeed in getting out this exposition in the reasonably coherent form I have outlined above for Fred constantly interrupted me with irrelevant questions and so I cannot be sure that he allowed himself to hear what I was saying. My impression was that the questions were intended to put me off my stroke and prevent me from making my case. His response was not entirely clear either. He was going to see the PM but his concern seemed to me to maintain his own position against that of Harold Lever. He said he did not mind if the PM wanted to hand over Cabinet responsibility for the Arts to Lever but he, Mulley, must know where he was. He was unenthusiastic about my ideas, regarding them as unimportant. He did not appear to understand, or perhaps did not want to understand, that I was trying to make progress by pressure, pending larger constitutional change.

The next day Mary Giles showed me what purported to be a note of this discussion which she had received from Mulley's Private Secretary. It bore slight relation to what had taken place but did set out my proposal that the Panels should elect their own Chairmen whom I would then recommend to him for appointment to the Council.

The note asserted that the Secretary of State had said that he was opposed to this proposal which was described as 'oligarchical'. It would mean that appointments would be influenced by panel members appointed by the previous Government. Fred Mulley had presumably read and agreed this note, but in fact, during the discussion, he had uttered no such blather. He had not described an attempt to break down the present oligarchy as oligarchical in itself and he had not said that the Panels were appointed by the Government when, in fact they were appointed by the Arts Council. Fred's PS was clearly not very well informed and I was surprised that the Secretary of State should have allowed such a rigmarole to be attributed to him.

The note went on to say that Mulley had said he would prefer a fully democratic system and noted my reply that this would need a constitutional change in the Arts Council. My proposals were intended as a move towards democracy and the note correctly stated that I had promised to send Mulley a paper setting out the details. It attributed to the Secretary of State the statement that he 'much preferred the present appointment procedure' and said that I 'agreed that no action would be taken' without consulting Mulley. The note added that there had been a short discussion on the Wealth Tax and claimed that Fred had said that neither he nor I should have become involved. As I was already involved up to my neck this would have been a pointless remark and I did not recall it being made.

When I read this farrago I typed a note to Mary Giles putting it on record that it did not correctly set out what had taken place, as she knew. I said it would be difficult to argue that the Secretary of State had not said what he and his Private Secretary had attributed to him. Therefore, instead of correcting the Minutes, I went on to give instructions that Mulley was to be told that insofar as it referred to statements attributed to me I did not accept the Minute and neither had I any recollection of some of the remarks it attributed to him. Mary minuted that she had spoken to Fred's PS on these lines but whether my disclaimer reached Mulley I do not know. Certainly he never repeated any of the nonsense on any subsequent occasion.

I then sent Fred a letter making it clear that I intended to do my best to implement Party Policy both on democracy in the Arts Counicl and on the Wealth Tax. It did not actually say that if you and the PM don't like it you will have to fire me, but that was the implication. I also again asked to meet the Prime Minister in spite of the conviction in my Private Office that he would only see me if he intended to deliver the bullet.

Things were now hotting up in the press. The Arts always arouse strong feelings, and I was not spared either personally or in my capacity as Minister. But some letters of support were printed in The Times, notably from John Trevelyan and Ed Berman. Trevelyan said the constant criticism was unfair and

Berman argued that I was being pilloried for trying to implement Labour Party Policy, and was getting precious little support. However, a Motion on the House of Commons Order Paper in my support gathered a large number of signatures. I warned CAPAG that a confrontation was developing but that I intended to pursue my course unless and until dismissed. I had to make a formal speech to the Contemporary Portrait Society and without the pre-knowledge of my office, spatchcocked into it a protest at lack of support from artists who should have known that I was their man and could be relied on not to agree to taxing the stock of living artists. I said that one of their members was painting my portrait and I could see no signs on it of the horns and tail which ought to be there if half of what was said about me was true.

At a recption following a Gala Concert at the Royal Festival Hall in honour of Sir Robert Mayer's 96th birthday, Lord Goodman drew me on one side and told me he thought I was safe until the end of 1975. Harold Wilson would make no changes even if I persisted in the 'mistaken policies' to which they were both wholly opposed. Wilson had decided to go himself and would leave questions of Ministerial changes to his successor. I accepted that Wilson would be unlikely to dismiss me while I enjoyed Jennie Lee's support, but I made it clear that I would not be deflected and I could not understand why Goodman continued to support me when I was pursuing two lines of policy – the Wealth Tax and democracy in the Arts Council – to which he was vocally hostile. Furthermore, I could not believe that Wilson would retire. 'As to the first,' said Goodman, 'I shall fight you all the way on policy but I still believe you are far and away the best man for the job. As to the second, we shall see.'

Goodman was probably well aware that I was going to get nowhere with either of my attempts to implement a measure of democratic socialism in the arts and, since I knew my way about, was a better man to have in nominal charge than the probable alternative. Nevertheless, it was odd that I retained Goodman's support for I made no bones about my basic hostility to his political outlook. Perhaps Jennie Lee was the real link between us.

Meanwhile, while all this was going on I continued unabashed. I lunched with chameleon Richard Marsh and sold him the idea of inclusive tickets for British Transport Hotels and theatres; went to Deal to see the Royal Marines School of Music and next day Marie and I dined with the Attenboroughs, Richard and Sheila, privately at the House of Commons. I saw Max Rayne and suggested Joan Plowright for the National Theatre Board, but he strongly resisted the idea and said she would not accept anyway. I decided not to put the matter to the test. I told Rayne that if Peter Hall's term of office was to be extended it must be on condition that he reduce his extra-mural activities. Raymond Williams agreed to join the Arts Council, but his contribution could have no immediate effect.

Renée Short put down a question asking about consultation with the Panels in making appointments to the Arts Council. I crossed out the evasive answer I was given and substituted a straight affirmative. Back came the file from Fred asking me to give the draft answer. I refused unless I was also allowed to give my own answer, so in the end the answer said nothing and something, and I explained the reason for this to Mrs. Short. Ultimately it was as follows: 'A variety of confidential discussions take place before appointments are made to the Arts Council and the views of many people and organisations are sought. Those consulted are likely to include members of the Panels of the Arts Council.'[17]

I then asked the Secretary General, Roy Shaw, to come and see me and gave instructions to my officials that all members of the Drama Panel were to be consulted on Council appointments. I told Professor Shaw that the Government was displeased with the Arts Council's action in seeking to bring pressure to bear through the media prior to a full discussion with me (Shaw had given a press conference at which he had done just this) and especially because he had given the impression that the difficulties in the arts were due to a shortage of Government funds, whereas he very well knew that it was local authority support which had collapsed. Roy Shaw said he would seek an opportunity to correct the record. I said I might do something of the sort myself and went on to say that the 'response' theory of patronage enunciated by Hugh Willatt before his departure was as dead as the dodo and I suggested a new set of criteria should be

[17] *Hansard.* W. 317. 6.11.75.

evolved. Such criteria should place the Arts Council in the position of being able publicly to justify its methods, amounts and modes of patronage distribution. What was adequate for a topping-up operation of £2 million or so fifteen years ago was no longer appropriate for an organisation which was now a major source of revenue for the arts as a whole with a budget which would shortly exceed £30 million. The call for a more representative body, particularly for those working in the arts outside London, could not long be resisted. Meanwhile, the Council in its natural desire to satisfy its beneficiaries that it was doing its best for them, should avoid becoming a stick which could be used to beat the Government and the Minister for the Arts. I then allowed the atmosphere to mellow and poured a drink, saying that I had noticed that office-holding seemed to change people for the worse and hoped this was not happening to me.

'No,' said Shaw, 'Still the same attacking, abrasive man.' Lois, my Parliamentary Secretary could hardly believe this, for it seems I make no such impression on her.

Terminating the talk with Roy Shaw I remember sounding to myself just like any other Minister. I said I appreciated that in any complaints he had made about current financial difficulties he had exculpated me personally from blame, but I could not be separated from the Government. We should all try to make it clear that the real culprit was inflation. The Government's efforts to bring it under control deserved the support of all sections of the community, including artists and their supporters. Oh God, I said to myself as I walked back up the stairs, true, I suppose, but how platitudinous!

In answer to a question from George Strauss in the House I emphasised once more that the customer and the local authorities were not carrying their share of the inflationary burden in the arts, with the result that central Government funds were having to meet not only their own inflation but the total increased costs.

Gibson came to see me again. The atmosphere seemed to be thickening all the time. He appeared to be angry about something but unable or unwilling to say what was troubling him. I was happy to tell him of a substantial Supplementary Grant to come soon.

That evening I spoke to a very good meeting of the Paddington

Labour Party: 'The structure of state support for the Arts is
outdated and incapable of fulfilling the role it is being required to
play in the Seventies,' I said and added that with devolution
there might be more than one Arts Council but they should
always retain an appointed element. This should be sustained by
people responsible to local authorities and to art organisations.
'The Arts Council does a difficult job as well as it can be done but
this will not be generally accepted by the recipients of Arts
Council grants until they, themselves, have a representative
voice in the decision-making process.'

Enthusiastic applause, but no press.

The next day I saw Lord Redcliffe-Maude about his
Gulbenkian report on the arts. I liked him and talk was easy. We
thought devolution ought to bring an English Arts Council and a
super UK Council to co-ordinate. I said that if I had to, I would
settle for a basis of 51% appointees and 49% representative
members on all Councils.

By now the season of the pre-Christmas parties was on and at
one of them I encountered Fred Mulley who talked about
keeping the Arts Council under control and complained that
they were throwing money away on artists who painted turds.[18]

Lunching with Lord Goodman I began to understand that Pat
Gibson was presenting my ideas for mild reform of the Arts
Council as though they were revolutionary proposals for the
destruction of the arts. Although modest in demeanour, Gibson
was influential and carried weight among some Cabinet
Ministers. I told Goodman that Gibson had already won. I was
no longer a free agent and was only staying in office until fired. I
did not believe in resignation, and I also felt that all the arts
would suffer when I was replaced. Goodman agreed with this
conceited self-estimate wholeheartedly.

After this I wrote to Goodman, sending written evidence that if
Gibson was saying that I did not consult him on Arts Council
appointments, it was untrue.

In December I did a Party Political broadcast in which I
asserted that the arts *were* party political and instanced the Tory
decision to charge for entry into the national collections as

[18] This was a reference to Richard Hamilton's exhibition at the Serpentine
Gallery.

evidence. I said that the appointment of a Minister for the Arts heralded a change in the nature of British Society. That the post-war burgeoning of the arts in Britain was due to the establishment of a framework within which it was possible for artists to flourish. If the Tories got in, the entire structure of state support would be in danger. The civilised Conservatism of Macmillan and Heath was finished and if a Government led by Mrs. Thatcher came to power it would seek to put the clock back a generation or more.

Early in the New Year Harold Lever sent me a copy of a Minute to the Prime Minister. I wrote to him agreeing with it since it was based on material I had sent to Lever. There was, however, a major difference between us on the Wealth Tax. I suggested to Lever that he examine the consequences of devolution on the structure of arts organisations and recommended that the Regional Arts Associations should be financed directly by my Branch rather than through the Arts Council.

I had another go at the Treasury for more money and plagued the Chief Secretary, Joel Barnett. Rather to my surprise, I got valuable help from Fred Mulley.

At the end of January I received a delegation from the Association of Municipal Authorities who complained that I had not put any local authority representatives on the Arts Council. I agreed to consult them in future. I also saw David Crouch, the Conservative Member for Canterbury, and promised Government support to a Private Member's Bill he was introducing to set up a Theatre Trust to protect buildings.

Swansong

The fact that my views about the Arts Council were anything but revolutionary was sharply illustrated at this time by the circulation of draft proposals for changes in the arts intended for inclusion in the Labour Party's programme for 1976. These emanated from a Committee presided over by Renée Short. I had attended one or two meetings of this body but I strongly disagreed with their main proposal which, although a little vague in wording, appeared to me to involve the dismantling of the Arts Council and its substitution by a new body based on local authorities.

I wrote to Mrs. Short recommending the inclusion of a

H

paragraph summarising our achievements during the last two years. I went on to suggest that the central organisational proposal should be omitted. 'What you are proposing,' I said, 'is the transfer of power in patronage of the arts from organisations formed for the purpose and eager to fulfil it (the Arts Council and the Regional Arts Associations) to bodies not formed for the purpose and in some cases reluctant to carry it out – the local authorities.'

I went on to say that in making the Arts Council more democratic I should advocate local authority representation on it but I was not in favour of the dissolution of the Council and its replacement by a new structure. To do that would be to risk sending the arts into a period of decline. 'The importance of expert authority and integrity cannot be overestimated. I also take the view that local government as much as national government needs bodies like the Arts Council to prevent elected philistines from seeking to control art and artists by starving non-conformists into submission.' Finally, I said that local authorities should be given obligatory functions in the arts rather than compelled to levy a special rate which could be frittered away.

I reinforced this letter by going to the next meeting of the group where I was given a good hearing but thought that the issue would be fudged in the document in the end and this proved to be the case.

I asked for a paper to be prepared summarising what we had done in my two years.[19] Throughout the period I had been continually badgering the Treasury for more money for one reason or another. Almost every month I had secured sums ranging from a few hundred thousands to a couple of million with the result that the total annual cost of the arts to the Government would soon be not far short of a hundred million, with about half going to the Arts Council and the rest to Museums, Galleries, Libraries and other claimants. Before my time no one had dreamt of such figures. The Branch press people got us no publicity, as usual.

I was beginning to feel that if I did not get the bullet soon it would after all be best to resign. It was not so much the abuse, for

[19] See Appendix Three.

until I researched for this book I had forgotten its idiot virulence; my real complaint was against the Cabinet and especially against the system which rendered me helpless to do what I wanted to do and knew how to do. It was too frustrating to put up with for much longer.

It had been a wonderful thing to become a Member of Parliament at the age of 56. I still thought it a great honour and a privilege and I had never allowed my Ministerial work to interfere with my constituency duties. I had been happy and successful in that role, and although I had enjoyed the experience of being a Minister this was no longer enough. It would soon be time to return to the best place in Parliament, the back benches.

In March 1976 I visited Birmingham and while there talked to the local Fabian Society on 'A Socialist Policy for the Arts'. I said that achievement of socialism through peaceful evolution rather than violent revolution had great advantages but was emotionally unsatisfying.

'It demands a greater and more consistent effort of will than most of us are able to bring to it. It demands greater mental effort – the mental strife Blake spoke of – than any other form of government. It demands greater resistance to corruption of all kinds than most of us can muster, for we can be corrupted without knowing it. Indeed, the moment we place our hands upon those famous levers of power that Nye Bevan spoke of, they spring to life and as we clasp them so they clasp us and a struggle ensues. If we are not aware of that then we have lost the struggle before we start.

'So far from grasping power we have become its instrument and we are managed rather than managing. Ministers who are engaged in a constant battle in their area at the front, be it large or small, are acting as socialists should, and if they are derided in the press that should not make us doubt them but warm to them.

'Party aims and ambitions should always be well beyond those immediately attainable, but the path from the present to the future must be signposted. We have to insist; to reject advice to be passive; to explore the edges of what is possible even to the point of upsetting incumbents; to risk unpopularity even among colleagues who may have their own ideas of what is and what is not important. We have to be active; thinking all the time of ways in which we can forward party policy and avoid inertia.

'Senior Civil Servants are likely to be of a conservative turn of mind. So opposition must be expected. Generally civil servants have no loyalty to your party nor to your ideas but they will carry out your policy providing you know what you want and have Cabinet support. But instructions should only be given when necessary and officials must be allowed to do as they like on routine matters. Usually they will not offer you a choice of courses to follow; they will recommend a particular course and it is up to you to decide whether you will take their advice or not. Advice must not be rejected for the sake of it or simply to show who is Boss. If you have to do that you are not.

'Don't be frightened of criticism. If you are not being criticised you are no good. To be able to push a Branch of a Department of State in a direction it did not want to go and to see the results of that effort enacted is something worth striving for and worth tolerating the braying abuse of asses for.'

I then went on to criticise the proposals the Labour Party was considering which advocated the abolition of the Arts Council.

'These proposals are too complex; the balance is wrong and it is revolutionary rather than evolutionary. Now I think that the totality of evolution can be revolutionary, but under a Parliamentary democracy one has to proceed from a to b; one fashions a into b; one makes the Arts Council more responsive, more participatory, more democratic by changing its Charter in Parliament and while it is being changed it continues to fulfil its functions; one does not abolish it; to do that would be to risk the collapse of our entire artistic effort and we might finish up with a splendid organisational structure and no art and no artists. The changes which need to be made in the Arts Council are drastic but it does not need to be replaced. Its record is not one which suggests that it deserves to be abolished. On the contrary, it has a fine record and it stands as a barrier between us politicians and the artist. That is where it should stand. And this is where I have a fundamental difference of view from some of my colleagues. They do not like the independence of the Arts Council and the Regional Arts Associations. I do. I regard it as essential and the great British contribution to the organisation of the arts. It is why the arts in this country are thriving – precisely because the hand of Government is *not* closely upon them. I believe in accountability, I believe that all economic and commercial and industrial organisations should ultimately be directed by Ministers answerable to an electorate. I do not, however, believe in such accountability in the arts, in communications or in entertainment. In these areas of ideas, of thought, of taste and of opinion, it is vital for the Government to keep out and to be kept out.

'To my mind a socialist policy for the arts is not to be achieved by imposition. All that arises is such old-fashioned exercises in conformity as the so-called 'socialist realism' of Stalinist days; far better occasional absurdities from artists than any attempts to bring creative people within the control of the State whose duty it is to pay the piper while resolutely refusing to call the tune.

'It follows from this that the Arts Council must command the respect of artists and the confidence of the public. The two requirements are not easily achieved simultaneously and the balance has to be struck carefully. It is easy to underestimate the value of what we have – which is a form of public patronage generally accepted as incorruptible however wrong we may think the Arts Council to be from time to time. Public patronage now supports most of the country's artistic output and to dismantle the structure might be to see the precious fruits wither and die.

'There is powerful opposition to spreading and devolving control of public subsidy for the arts away from those now in charge and it is, of course, understandable that they should feel that way. They are the Lord's Anointed People, or at any rate the state's appointed people, chosen for their knowledge of the arts; for their probity and for their impartiality; they are excellent people. I know, for I was one of them for many years and when I suggested, as I did from time to time, that we ought to let in people who were not vetted and selected by our Chairman and Officers of the Council as being fit to associate with us and share our arduous and unpaid duties, the idea was always greeted with horror. It was always assumed that anything other than selection and appointment from above would result in the Arts Council being governed by a bunch of yahoos under whose fell command the prestige of the arts would collapse.

'Yet without protest from them or anyone else – several times the Royal Opera grant was and is being spent on military bands.

'This attitude of the Arts Council, recently repeated by its Chairman, is the essence of élitism. It is a total distrust of the capacity of any electorate to choose appropriate persons for particular purposes. Of course, the democratic process sometimes throws up stinkers but so does the process of appointment, as I know full well having occupied all four positions; elector, elected, appointer and appointed. I suggest a mixture of all the possible forms of choice. I suggest this because I think that there are virtues and dangers in all of them.

'Appointment tends to be élitist and ingrowing, but has the great advantage of being selective and capable of producing a balance of expertise; election brings freshness and keeps everyone on their toes but could produce an argumentative and disparate Council.'

I concluded by saying that we had to rediscover our nationhood.

'The concept of one world is too great for us to encompass at a stroke. We must think of ourselves as belonging to a smaller group, to a nation, for if we try to go beyond that, we may find our people are unwilling to come with us. The growth of Scottish and Welsh nationalism is, in part, a form of resistance to the diminution of the value of Britishness consequent upon entry into the Common Market. The health of our nation demands that we enjoy collective aims which we can recognise as uniting us; our 'King and Country' is not satisfying in a world where national military grandeur can no longer be expressed in toy soldier terms; in which struggle is to be seen as casual maiming by small bombs at one end and total incineration by nuclear war at the other. It no longer makes sense, if it ever did. Even God is not what He was. Increasingly people see religion in terms of what it is in Northern Ireland – an excuse for barbarism.

'So how can we see ourselves as the British? In our past, in our history, in our artistic achievements, in our literature, our music and our drama; in our contribution to the achievements of humanity. This is where we may legitimately take pride.

'Consciousness of this achievement is spreading– the practice and appreciation of the arts is growing all over the country and the difficulties from which we are suffering must not be allowed to blind us to the fact that, perhaps for the first time in our national life, interest in the arts is widespread and you will find it as much in Scunthorpe as in Sloane Square. Here is our real growth industry; the arts and skills associated with the arts are moving from the periphery of political interest into the centre of the stage and I expect in the next ten years that recognition of this fact will become widespread. Will it be socialist? Essentially, yes – the whole idea of state responsibility for the arts is socialist and the fact that, with some backsliding, the Tories maintained support when they were in office simply shows what we have always known, that when we create new instruments the Tories do not destroy them – they seek to take them over and use them in their own way. They have done this in the arts and we have the task of breaking sown élitism without losing excellence; of replacing the old slogan, 'Few but Roses' with a new one 'A Million Flowers Shall Bloom.' I seem to have heard something of the sort before.'

When I got back to London I found that Harold Wilson had resigned. Just at this point Milton Shulman called for my resignation in the Evening Standard. He was the only critic to be hostile to me throughout my entire period of office.

At the end of the month I noted in my diary that Jim Callaghan had been elected and that I should consequently be returning to the backbenches. 'There are attractions as well as losses in being a backbencher,' I wrote.

One of the few MPs consistently and constructively interested in the arts is Jim Callaghan. Not, alas, the PM, but the Labour Member for Middleton and Prestwich who used to teach art. Shulman's attack elicited a letter from Mr. Callaghan, printed in the Standard on April 1st in which he praised the record of my two years and said, 'All in all this makes a curious catalogue on which to call for the departure of Hugh Jenkins who has presided over the biggest ever increase in official support for the arts.'

I still hoped I might be given another six months to get PLR going but I did not even get the rest of that month. On the 20th April the guillotine fell and my Ministerial head rolled into the basket.

Postscript

'If you can meet with Triumph and Disaster
and treat those two impostors just the same.'

Rudyard Kipling

The Two Impostors.

In writing the last part of this book I decided on the device of two large chapters divided into subjects. The method has proved to have advantages and disadvantages. I grouped what might be called the triumphs under Chapter 7 and the disasters under Chapter 8. By this means I hoped to enable the reader to follow the means by which results were achieved and to experience, at one remove, the conditions which ensured failure. If I have attained that object to any extent I hope that the outcome will be to increase understanding of the difficulty of bringing about change our country and so to sharpen the weaponry of peaceful transition from the brutal and thrusting world in which we live towards a calmer and fairer state.

A disadvantage of my method is that in avoiding the confusion of a day-to-day diary presentation I have inevitably left out many matters which occupy the time of a Minister but do not lend themselves to description as continuing subjects. To that extent the picture is falsified and to demonstrate this, I am including as an appendix a sample daily diary. A progress chart covering two months is on page 98.

A Minister often spends a great deal of his time watching the product brought about by the money he distributes. That is why the Arts job is enviable. It is more enjoyable to listen to orchestras than to a sonic boom and pleasanter to watch ballet than to trudge round a hospital. The Arts Minister, like others, also makes speeches, accompanies Royalty on their visits, unveils plaques and opens events. Many of my speeches were impromptu, off-the-cuff affairs but I do recall deputising for the

Prime Minister at the Annual Royal Academy dinner on 1st May in 1974, and, a little to the astonishment of the assembled and decorated penguins, talking about Karl Marx and that other socialist, William Morris. On other occasions one was there to experience the work of creative artists and, to me, an omnivorous consumer of all art and entertainment forms, this made much of the job entirely delightful.

I have some outstanding recollections: Sutherland's Lucia at the Royal Opera House, the astounding work being done at a comprehensive school in Oldham, the new Library at Scunthorpe, the Eisteddfod at Criccieth, all the open-air museums, Gielgud at the Old Vic, Elizabeth Soederstrom and Kirsten Meyer in Edinburgh, Victoria de los Angeles in Ironbridge, and the opening of the Railway Museum at York by the Duke of Edinburgh after which everyone was soaked to the skin in a downpour of rain. There was the splendid work of the Mid-Pennine Arts Association under Jennifer Wilson and Ruari McNeill; Peter Cheeseman's Victoria Theatre Stoke-on-Trent, impressive craftsmanship at Lincoln and meeting Atarah Ben-Tovim. I could go on and on into tedium: but bless them all, they are the greatest.

The development of Community Theatre, of Arts Centres and of the crafts is of the utmost importance for the creative use of leisure. These developments can help to relieve the strains of dull and repetitive work, the stresses of caring every day for children, and the deep humiliation of unemployment. As machinery and amalgamation make millions redundant and reduce the work-load of others, a society without a common culture will be threatened with disintegration.

The relationship between the creative artist, the interpreter, the teacher, and the consumer is conditioned by the nature of the society in which they live but they, by their collective impact upon it, affect the world about them and so an interaction takes place which can make the texture of our lives more beautiful, or more bearable.

In this, the duty of Government is not fulfilled by making the best available to the few; a Government concerned with more than its own survival will seek to make the practice of the arts and crafts so widespread that rejection of the phoney and insistence upon the best in the arts becomes as common as the selection of a shirt or the choice of vegetables.

That will cost a great deal of money, for once people get the idea that they have skill and taste they will not be satisfied until the best is for the many.

A Government unleashing this force will make a new society and in that better world there will be no culture gap.

Appendices

APPENDIX ONE

A POLICY FOR
THE ARTS

THE FIRST STEPS

*Presented to Parliament by the Prime Minister
by Command of Her Majesty
February 1965*

LONDON
HER MAJESTY'S STATIONERY OFFICE
PRICE 1*s*. 6*d*. NET

Cmnd. 2601

A POLICY FOR THE ARTS

THE FIRST STEPS

CONTENTS

30091

1. The relationship between artist and State in a modern democratic community is not easily defined. No one would wish State patronage to dictate taste or in any way restrict the liberty of even the most unorthodox and experimental of artists.

2. But if a high level of artistic achievement is to be sustained and the best in the arts made more widely available, more generous and discriminating help is urgently needed, locally, regionally, and nationally.

3. In some parts of the country professional companies are non-existent. Even amateurs find it hard to keep going. And lack of suitable buildings makes it impossible to bring any of the leading national companies, orchestral, operatic, ballet or theatre, into those areas.

4. Fortunately, this state of affairs is coming increasingly under fire. So too are those of our museums, art galleries and concert halls that have failed to move with the times, retaining a cheerless unwelcoming air that alienates all but the specialist and the dedicated.

5. No greater disservice can be done to the serious artist than to present his work in an atmosphere of old-fashioned gloom and undue solemnity.

6. If we are concerned to win a wider and more appreciative public for the arts, all this must be changed. A new social as well as artistic climate is essential.

7. There is no easy or quick way of bringing this about, the more so as too many working people have been conditioned by their education and environment to consider the best in music, painting, sculpture and literature outside their reach. A younger generation, however, more self-confident than their elders, and beginning to be given some feeling for drama, music and the visual arts in their school years, are more hopeful material. They will want gaiety and colour, informality and experimentation. But there is no reason why attractive presentation should be left to those whose primary concern is with quantity and profitability.

8. Some of our new civic centres and art centres already demonstrate that an agreeable environment and a jealous regard for the maintenance of high standards are not incompatible. Centres that succeed in providing a friendly meeting ground where both light entertainment and cultural projects can be enjoyed help also to break down the isolation from which both artist and potential audience have suffered in the past.

9. Another encouraging trend is the growing recognition of the importance of strengthening contacts between regional and civic art associations in different parts of the country.

10. But we have a long way to go before effective associations of this kind become common form everywhere. If a sane balance of population between north and south, east and west, is to be achieved, this kind of development is just as essential as any movement of industry or provision of public utility service. If the eager and gifted, to whom we must look

5

for leadership in every field, are to feel as much at home in the north and west as in and near London, each region will require high points of artistic excellence. Of course no provincial centre can hope to rival the full wealth and diversity of London's art treasures, but each can have something of its own that is supreme in some particular field. This too must be the aim of the new towns, if they are to win and to hold the kind of residents they most need.

11. From the combined efforts of the Government and of regional associations that include representatives of industry, the trade unions and private donors as well as local authorities, the money must be found to provide the buildings needed to house the arts.

12. If we are prepared to accept this challenge, we must also be prepared within the limits of the resources that can be made available to give expenditure for these projects a higher priority than in the past.

13. The financial difficulties that so many of today's artists have to contend with must also be realistically examined.

14. In any civilised community the arts and associated amenities, serious or comic, light or demanding, must occupy a central place. Their enjoyment should not be regarded as something remote from everyday life. The promotion and appreciation of high standards in architecture, in industrial design, in town planning and the preservation of the beauty of the country side, are all part of it. Beginning in the schools, and reaching out into every corner of the nation's life, in city and village, at home, at work at play, there is an immense amount that could be done to improve the quality of contemporary life.

15. There is no short-term solution for what by its very nature is a long-term problem. This is a field in which, even in the most favourable circumstances, it will never be possible to do as much as we want to do as quickly as we want to do it. But that is no excuse for not doing as much as we can and more than has hitherto been attempted.

GOVERNMENT SUPPORT FOR THE ARTS

16. The support that the Government give to the arts can be grouped under three heads—education, preservation and patronage.

17. The main educational functions are carried out in England and Wales under the aegis of the Department of Education and Science, and in Scotland of the Scottish Education Department. In partnership with the local education authorities and voluntary bodies they are concerned with the arts in schools, colleges of further education, including colleges of art, adult education and community centres. To the responsibilities of the Department of Education and Science public libraries will soon be added. The Victoria and Albert Museum is the direct responsibility of the Department of Education and Science and the Royal Scottish Museum of the Scottish Education Department.

18. As for preservation, the Museums and Galleries, largely financed directly by the Treasury, and the Historic Buildings and Ancient Monuments looked after by the Ministry of Public Building and Works, are the most important. The National Trust, and the National Trust for Scotland

private bodies with great houses and collections under their wing, receive on occasion substantial grants towards repair and maintenance from the Ministry of Public Building and Works. There are also other bodies receiving financial support from the Government, such as the British Institute of Recorded Sound.

19. The patronage given by the State to music, drama, painting, sculpture and poetry is largely channelled through the Arts Council and their Scottish and Welsh Committees. The Council thus cover most of the fields not provided for by other agencies.

National Museums and Galleries

20. There are seventeen main national museums and galleries, two of which are scientific. Government Departments are directly responsible for three of them: the Victoria and Albert, the Science and the Royal Scottish Museums. The rest are administered by Trustees appointed in most instances by the Prime Minister.

21. The management of their affairs is in their own hands and they can spend their purchase grants as they like. Special grants can also be made towards the cost of exceptional purchases.

22. Building for these museums in London and Edinburgh is arranged by the Ministry of Public Building and Works, which in turn looks for advice on priorities to the Standing Commission on Museums and Galleries, a body of twelve appointed by the Prime Minister. A twelve-year programme covering England and Scotland has been drawn up costing in all £5m. starting in 1964–65. In addition there are several large special projects outside the twelve-year programme, notably the British Museum Library, estimated at £15m., and the National Science Reference Library £1½m.); a bill now before Parliament provides for an Exchequer contribution to a new Museum of London. A separate programme of £700,000 over twelve years has been agreed for the Welsh Institutions.

Provincial Museums and Galleries

23. There are some 900 of these supported or administered mainly by local authorities whose expenditure on them does not rank for calculating general grant. They vary greatly in size and scope. The Standing Commission surveyed these museums in 1960 and, commented unfavourably on the small amounts of money spent on many of them.

24. A fund (£50,000 in 1964–65) for local purchases comes from the Victoria and Albert Museum which also provides loans of travelling exhibitions culled from the museum's material. The Royal Scottish Museum operates a similar fund. Regional schemes of co-operation through Area Councils are beginning to get under way. These will enable the smaller museums in an area to call on the larger for advice and help. Exchequer grants are made to the Area Councils, but until the schemes are in full working order this expenditure will not be large.

The Arts Council

25. Support for the living arts is mainly channelled through the Arts Council whose task was set out in their Royal Charter of 1946 as the development of " a greater knowledge, understanding and practice of the fine arts

exclusively and in particular to increase the accessibility of the fine arts to the public throughout Our Realm, to improve the standard of execution of the fine arts and to advise and co-operate with Our Government Departments, local authorities and other bodies on any matters concerned directly or indirectly with those objects."

26. Sixteen persons appointed by the Chancellor of the Exchequer after consultation with the Education Ministers are chosen for their knowledge of, or concern with, one or more of the fine arts. They are responsible for the allocation of the grant-in-aid given them through the Treasury Vote for Grants for the Arts. In 1963–64 a triennial basis was adopted with an annual 10 per cent. increase. The Charter provides for the appointment of committees for Scotland and Wales to which the Council entrust the discharge of their functions in these countries.

27. With these funds the Council organise exhibitions, some of them the most important held in this country, or indeed anywhere, since the war. They send groups performing " Opera for All " widely through the country, and organise some concerts. But for the most part the Council give grants or guarantees to activities for which other sources contribute equal or greater support.

28. The following are the main objects which the Council support :—

Opera and Ballet :
  Covent Garden and Royal Ballet.
  Sadler's Wells.
  Welsh National Opera Company.
  Scottish Opera Society.
  London Opera Centre.
  Ballet Rambert.
  Western Theatre Ballet and some small companies.

Music :
  Orchestras.
    By an arrangement with the London County Council, orchestral concerts in the Royal Festival Hall are subsidised. Outside London orchestras which obtain help from the Arts Council include :
      Scottish National Orchestra.
      Hallé.
      Liverpool Philharmonic.
      City of Birmingham.
      Western Orchestral Society.
      Northern Sinfonia.
  Also through the National Federation of Music Societies small grants are made to a large number of musical bodies with the aim of improving performance by guaranteeing concerts and enabling amateurs to improve their quality and engage professional conductors, singers and players.

Theatre :
  The National Theatre.
  Royal Shakespeare Company.
  English Stage Society.

Some 45 other repertory companies.

Training schemes for writers, producers, designers and administrators.

Other grants by Scottish Committee (e.g. Glasgow Citizens' Theatre) and Welsh Committee.

Art :

Mainly through exhibitions, grants and guarantees to local arts societies, and occasional purchases.

Poetry :

Grants, guarantees and direct promotion.

The Edinburgh Festival.

Arts Festivals.

Arts Associations and Clubs.

British Film Institute

29. This body receives direct grants from the Treasury and the Department of Education and Science. Its main objects are to run the National Film Archive, the National Film Theatre and a Film Distribution Library. It issues several publications, including Sight and Sound, and generally concerns itself with " the development of the film as a means of entertainment and instruction ", as does the Scottish Film Council which is also grant-aided.

Other bodies

30. Grants are also made to the following: The British Academy, which finances schools of archaeology overseas, the British Institute of Recorded Sound, the Royal Academy of Dramatic Art, the Royal Academy of Music, the Royal College of Music, the Royal Scottish Academy of Music, and the Royal Manchester College of Music.

Historic houses and Ancient Monuments

31. The Ministry of Public Building and Works is responsible for the administration of the Ancient Monuments and Historic Buildings Acts that give it the power to make grants towards the repair of buildings of outstanding historic or architectural interest, acting on the advice of the three Historic Buildings Councils for England, Wales and Scotland. A grant is normally made only on condition that the house is opened to the public.

32. The Ministry is also responsible for the upkeep of a number of buildings of special historic interest, such as Burlington House, Lancaster House, Marlborough House, the Tower of London, the Banqueting House, the Royal Naval College Greenwich, and Royal Palaces not occupied by the Sovereign such as Hampton Court, parts of Holyroodhouse and Osborne House.

33. *Statues.* A good many of the London statues are in the charge of the Ministry. When Parliament approves a statue the Ministry normally commissions and erects it.

34. *Sculpture and pictures.* Sometimes a new public building calls for sculpture or other special type of decoration and the Ministry thus exercises a limited amount of patronage. It also purchases a number of pictures

9

every year, for diplomatic buildings overseas, official residences and Government offices. It also has a team of artists skilled in picture conservation and the restoration of works of art.

35. *The Ministry of Housing and Local Government* also has responsibilities for buildings of special architectural or historic interest. The Ministry issues lists of such buildings for the guidance of local plannning authorities, in order to ensure that the special interest of the buildings is taken into account when proposals affecting their future are put forward. In addition to their normal powers of development control, the local authorities may make building preservation orders (subject to confirmation by the Minister) where necessary.

36. Local authorities are also authorised, in England and Wales by the Local Authorities (Historic Buildings) Act 1962 and in Scotland by the Local Government (Scotland) Act 1947, to contribute towards the repair and maintenance of buildings of architectural or historic interest. The consent of the Minister of Housing and Local Government is required only if the building is not a listed building.

37. *The British Council* is responsible for displaying overseas the best of British drama, music, and the visual arts. In co-operation with local museums and art galleries abroad, paintings and sculpture by British artists are sent for exhibition at international art festivals, and on extended tours through a number of countries. Photographic displays dealing with such subjects as architecture or social services are also supplied. The Council organises tours overseas by British theatre, ballet and opera companies and by orchestras and individual musicians, enabling them to perform not only in Europe but sometimes in countries farther afield where opportunities of seeing or hearing British actors or musicians are rare. It maintains an information and reference service for specialists in the arts and sends copies of plays, gramophone records (including recorded speech and literature), and music to its libraries overseas.

LOCAL AND REGIONAL EFFORT

38. Local authorities depend, for authority to incur expenditure, mainly but not entirely on Section 132 of the Local Government Act 1948. This permits them to spend the product of a 6d. rate on entertainment in all its forms. They can also spend whatever income they receive from entertainment. There is similar provision for Scotland. It may well be worth considering whether these powers should not be extended to the county councils in England and Wales. The Greater London Council will have them from next April and the L.C.C. obtained similar powers some years ago.

39. Some of the most progressive local authorities already show what can be done. Birmingham, for example, besides having one of the finest museums in the country, in part finances its orchestra, plans to build a new Repertory Theatre and has made an interest-free loan to the amateur Crescent Theatre. It is also contributing to an adventurous scheme for an arts centre for youth at Cannon Hill. Manchester at the Library Theatre runs one of the few civic theatres that is completely financed from local funds. Sunderland has added an arts centre to its museum and generously supports its theatre. The London County Council has a proud record of support for the arts. It has

built the Royal Festival Hall and is building an arts centre on the South Bank, contributes half the pool which guarantees the concerts of three great orchestras, supports several museums, took the initiative over the National Theatre and commissions a wide variety of sculpture for its schools. The City, too, plans to build an arts centre in the new Barbican development and will contribute one third of the cost of the new Museum of London.

40. In Scotland, Glasgow has now embarked on a scheme for a cultural centre which will include two theatres and a concert hall.

41. The New Towns in England, Wales and Scotland are also showing enterprise. They have powers to make contributions to the cost of providing amenities and to appoint Social Development Officers who make the needs of voluntary organisations known to the Corporations. Harlow, for instance, has appointed its own arts council which receives financial help from the local authority and is preparing a scheme for a theatre and arts centre. It has also introduced and supports a professional string quartet for whose members the Corporation has made houses available. Welwyn Garden City provides in Digswell House living accommodation for sixteen artists and students. An example from Scotland is the help given to the Glenrothes Arts Club which has premises in an adapted farmhouse. Others have formed arts trusts which serve as intermediary between the local authority and the cultural organisations.

42. An enterprise that grows steadily in popularity and enjoys Arts Council support is the Arts Festival. This brings cultural opportunities to the residents and also brings visitors to the town. In addition to the International Festival at Edinburgh there are festivals among other places at Aldeburgh, Bath, Cambridge, Cheltenham, Little Missenden, Haslemere, Ludlow and York ; also the Three Choirs Festival. In Wales, there is the national Eisteddfod. In Scotland, Stirling has led the way in local festivals. But too many centres, especially in the drabber industrial areas, do not as yet share in these activities.

43. Go-ahead local enterprises need more than encouragement and advice. They also need more financial help, and this is where regional associations for the arts can perform an important function, for regional planning is as valuable in this as in the economic sphere. At this level a small staff with a few keen local enthusiasts backing them can stimulate the co-operation of other authorities, and by calling on each for a fairly small levy provide funds with which to finance a variety of projects—concerts, exhibitions, film shows and lectures—which few authorities by themselves could afford. By invoking the help of the local education authorities they can also bring the schools into the picture. It is important to win the goodwill and co-operation of employers and trade unions. Universities too have an important part to play. A network of this kind should be developed to cover the whole country. Once an association has been formed it can act with and for the Arts Council in a mutually beneficial relationship.

44. At present the biggest association of this kind is in the North-East. It received £30,000 from the Arts Council in 1964–65 and helps to support among other things the Northern Sinfonia Orchestra, the Sunderland ventures already mentioned, an arts centre at Billingham and the People's Theatre Arts Centre in Newcastle upon Tyne.

45. The most recent of the regional bodies is the Eastern Authorities Orchestral Association formed at the instance of the Arts Council and the London Philharmonic Orchestra. Some 93 local authorities from the Humber to the Thames will contribute £2 per thousand head of population to be matched £ for £ by the Arts Council, so that all members can benefit from the visit of an orchestra, even if the concert is given in surroundings not devised for orchestral work and at somewhat irregular intervals.

46. Another advantage of the regional association is that it calls forth from a larger area the able individuals who are the key to success. It gives them wider scope and puts their special gifts at the disposal of many local authorities besides their own.

47. This paper has laid emphasis on the fact that the municipalities are the corner stone without which effective local and regional art associations cannot be started or kept going. But ample scope remains for private donors and trusts such as the Carnegie U.K. Trust, the Pilgrim and Foyle Trusts, the Gulbenkian and Rayne Foundations. One of their most valuable contributions is to assist projects during their early stages, as the Carnegie U.K. Trust has done in its support of local museums.

48. There is also the considerable contribution made by private collectors and a welcome beginning to patronage of the arts by progressive industrialists and trade unions.

HOUSING THE ARTS

49. There is a dearth of good local buildings for showing and practising the arts. Part of the reason is that after the war there was such urgent need for houses and factories that little provision could be made for the civilising influences of concert halls, theatres or art centres. Money, labour and materials were not available. Habits of neighbourliness and co-operation in community projects were not developed. The damage then unavoidably done is only now being remedied. People who had never known what they were missing did not press for galleries, theatres and concert halls. Certain sections of the press, by constantly sniping at cultural expenditure, made philistinism appear patriotic.

50. Another reason was that the Arts Council were not able to provide significant capital sums for building.

51. In meeting contemporary trends the concept of the arts centre is most valuable since such a centre can be of almost any size and cover any range of activities. A single hall can provide a place where local people can meet, perform an amateur play, hold an exhibition of their own or of professional work, put on a film show, lecture or recital and generally act as focal point for cultural activities and amenities. It may be run solely by amateurs or by a mixture of amateurs and professionals. At the other end of the scale the arts centre may cover a long stretch of the South Bank, with Festival Hall, Recital Room, National Theatre, Art Galleries, restaurant and Film Theatre. In between there are for instance the Little Theatre Guild of Great Britain whose twenty-six members, in towns as far apart as Salisbury and Llangefni or Newcastle upon Tyne, have built or adapted their own theatres and support them with other activities concerned with the arts—films, collections of costumes,

and art exhibitions. Another notable example is the Cannon Hill Trust, where the plans include a library, three theatres (one open-air), swimming pool and multi-purpose studio, and where the emphasis is educational aiming at winning and holding the interest of the young. In Scotland, Greenock has provided an enterprising arts centre consisting of a theatre, gallery for small exhibitions, lecture room and small restaurant.

52. Demand is increasing and far more money could be spent on housing the arts than is likely to be immediately available. As a first step the Arts Council will be authorised to enter into commitments up to £250,000 in 1965–66, in order to encourage regional and local authorities to develop their plans in this field. If this has the desired effect, the Government will be ready, when the time comes, to consider authorising the Arts Council to enter into substantially higher levels of commitment in future years.

53. There is no reason other than lack of energy and interest why every community, large and small, should not form its own arts centre, aiming at growth and improvement of quality. The Regional Arts Association should be there to help ; and one of the purposes of Centre 42, which has recently acquired a lease of the Round House in Camden Town, is to have groups of fully professional artists ready to respond to calls on their services from other parts of the country. Sometimes a historic building can be adapted at comparatively little cost—certainly less than the cost of a new centre—and used as an arts centre. When this happens two objects are achieved in one. Examples are, on a large scale, Temple Newsam outside Leeds and Corsham Court in Wiltshire, and on a smaller scale the adaptation of Canonbury Tower for a theatre and arts centre in Islington.

54. It is to be hoped that one day fine permanent buildings for housing the arts will be universally available. But in the meantime enterprising localities might well investigate the possibility of mobile art centres and travelling theatres. This means growing accustomed to some of the latest developments in building techniques. Temporary inflatable structures are already in use in industry. All that is needed is to find models that can be given the gay " Come to the Fair " atmosphere essential for recreational purposes. Besides providing much needed colour in the immediate future, these temporary theatres could help to create the climate of opinion needed to encourage expenditure from the rates on permanent buildings.

55. The recent actions of the Arts Council in launching an enquiry into the future needs of the provincial theatre and a second enquiry into ways of bringing the theatre to children are welcome and point the way to future developments.

56. As new theatres come to be built, there is a strong case for standardising backstage fitments and equipment. In some countries, notably West Germany, this is already done. It makes the work of touring companies very much easier.

57. Under the present town planning law a building which is in use as a theatre may be put to a variety of other uses without the need for prior planning permission. This has resulted in the loss of existing theatres. The Government regard this as unsatisfactory and they have therefore amended the relevant statutory instrument—the Town and Country Planning (Use Classes) Order, 1963 (in Scotland, the Town and Country Planning

(Use Classes) (Scotland) Order, 1950). This will limit to use as a music hall, or as a cinema, the changes of use from a theatre which, under the terms of the Order, can be carried out without involving the need for planning permission.

THE INFLUENCE OF EDUCATION

58. Almost all the activities described in this White Paper are linked directly or indirectly with education. If children at an early age become accustomed to the idea of the arts as a part of everyday life, they are more likely in maturity first to accept and then to demand them. The links are not limited to the primary and secondary schools : they extend to the art schools, the colleges of further education, the colleges of education for teachers, the universities and the classes for adults. The place that the arts occupy in the life of the nation is largely a reflection of the time and effort devoted to them in schools and colleges.

59. Nearly all children enjoy singing and dancing and most of them delight in poetry and in mime or dramatic exercises. There is no more excited audience at the right play. Many of them have a natural talent for painting and drawing, and for making things, that surprises their parents.

60. Many schools, particularly perhaps primary schools, have successfully fostered these abilities, and in some of the arts the schools have had notable help from radio and television. But too often, as boys and girls grow up, the impetus seems to weaken, so that as adults we are more vulnerable than we should be to criticisms of our inadequate uses of literacy, of our failure to appreciate poetry, of our limited tastes in music and drama, of our ignorance of the visual arts and of our blindness to good design.

61. Here is a challenge to the schools, and many of them are already showing that it can be met. The imagination and free flow of some of the writing in prose and poetry, the quality of some of the painting and pottery, and the high standard of some of the choral singing and of the orchestral playing, culminating in the National Youth Orchestra, outshine the achievements of any previous generation. But the base is still too narrow.

62. In these efforts the schools need the support both of their communities and of the expert practitioners in the various arts. This begins with the quality of the school buildings themselves. There are schools built since 1945 where children have shown how they appreciate and respect well-designed buildings, enlivened by the occasional mural or piece of sculpture, stimulating colours, well-chosen furniture and fittings, and skilful landscaping. Many schools, too, have shown the benefits that can be derived from arranging close links with local museums, theatres and arts centres, from encouraging performances by school children to wider audiences, from inviting experts in the various arts to talk about their activities and demonstrate them, and from arranging visits by school children to exhibitions and performances.

63. As such activities become more widespread, more and more people will be inclined as they grow up to practise and appreciate the arts. The professionals of the future will require more and better facilities for their training, the amateurs will swell the growing ranks of those who attend the already remarkable variety of part-time classes or occasional lectures, and the arts as a whole will reach wider and better informed audiences.

64. Success will depend to a great extent on what is done in the places where research is undertaken, where standards are set and where expert practitioners are educated. A major responsibility therefore lies with the universities, with the colleges of education for teachers, and with the schools and colleges specialising in art, ballet, drama, music and opera. For example, the work of the National Advisory Council for Diplomas in Art and Design should lead to a marked improvement in higher education in art, and the Royal College of Art has shown how immediate an influence a leading educational institution can have not only on the standards of individual artistic achievement but on the quality of design in commerce, fashion and industry.

65. But ample scope remains for further effort. Not all universities and colleges can claim that they have yet done their utmost to foster knowledge and appreciation of the arts, either within or outside their own boundaries.

66. The role of education should not be interpreted too narrowly. It is true that much will have been achieved when many more people have become acquainted with the arts and have come to realise the interest and enjoyment that can lie in well-written books, good plays, more demanding programmes on radio and television, concerts of serious music and exhibitions of great pictures. But surroundings are important as well, and here too the arts can make an invaluable contribution. In this connection the Government will continue to support the Council of Industrial Design. They welcome the encouragement that the Council are giving to good industrial design in a wide range of products in everyday use at home and at work.

67. The crafts also have an important contribution to make in the field of education and leisure pursuits as well as in their influence on good design. In an age of progress the traditional crafts must move with the times and the Government will encourage them to take their place in future developments.

68. The quality of buildings and of the setting in which they stand also exerts an important influence on our lives. This brings into the picture not only the aesthetic merit of the buildings themselves but the contribution that sculpture, other works of art and landscaping can make to the environment—a contribution that also helps the arts by providing opportunities for sculptors, artists and landscape architects.

69. In the buildings for which they are themselves directly responsible the Government will continue to pay regard in all appropriate cases to the importance of this kind of contribution ; and whenever practicable they will make a suitable provision. They hope that local authorities, New Town Corporations and other public bodies, some of whom have already done much in this way, will follow the same policy. They hope, also, that private donors will support these efforts.

70. In existing buildings too the Government would like to see more and better pictures displayed. They intend to arrange for this in those of their own buildings that are suitable, either by buying the work of living artists or by loans from local sources.

71. Appreciation of this kind of good design is not the end of the matter. Indeed, diffusion of culture is now so much a part of life that there is no precise point at which it stops. Advertisements, buildings, books, motor cars, radio and television, magazines, records, all can carry a cultural aspect and

15

affect our lives for good or ill as a species of "amenity". No democratic government would seek to impose controls on all the things that contribute to our environment and affect our senses. But abuses can be spotted and tackled, high standards encouraged, and opportunities given for wider enjoyment. It is partly a question of bridging the gap between what have come to be called the "higher" forms of entertainment and the traditional sources—the brass band, the amateur concert party, the entertainer, the music hall and pop group—and to challenge the fact that a gap exists. In the world of jazz the process has already happened ; highbrow and lowbrow have met.

72. Radio and television have much to contribute to the encouragement of artistic activity and appreciation. If little is said about them in this White Paper it is largely because in this field the Government have no direct responsibility. These media are managed by public corporations whose relationship with the Government is defined by statute. How the corporations use broadcasting time and deploy their resources is for them to decide.

73. But it is clear that radio and television have enormous opportunities in the sphere of the arts, and their responsibilities to the nation are correspondingly great. Radio has done much for drama, music and poetry. The use of television for similar purposes is still at a relatively early stage, but it is to be hoped that the introduction of additional channels for television will encourage further experiment and development. If in time a greater number of local stations is set up, these will have an important part to play in the encouragement of local artistic activity and the enrichment and diversification of regional cultures. THE GOVERNMENT'S PROPOSALS

74. Government aid to the arts has hitherto been on a relatively modest scale, and has grown up in response to spasmodic pressures rather than as a result of a coherent plan.

75. The same picture emerges locally. There is no common pattern among local authorities when it comes to support for the arts. Some are generous, some have no regard for art at all, and sometimes such facilities as there are, for instance a library or museum, are not used to the best advantage.

76. There is ample evidence of the need for a more coherent, generous and imaginative approach to the whole problem. It will take time to work out such a policy in full detail. In the meantime the need for further progress is urgent. The Government have decided therefore to advance by stages, at each stage making the necessary assistance available in support of the following objectives:

(i) Today's artists need more financial help, particularly in the early years before they have become established. Their ability to develop and sustain a high level of artistic achievement lies at the centre of any national policy for the arts.

(ii) The Government hope to see a great increase in local and regional activity, while maintaining the development of the national institutions. They are convinced that the interests of the whole country will be best served in this way.

(iii) The Government appreciate the need to sustain and strengthen all that is best in the arts, and the best must be made more widely available.

(iv) There is need for more systematic planning and a better co-ordination of resources.

77. With these objectives in mind the Government have reviewed their own administrative arrangements. They have reached the conclusion that the time has come for the Government's responsibility for the arts to be centred in a Department other than the Treasury, since public expenditure on the arts has developed to a stage when it has already become anomalous for the Treasury to remain the sponsoring Department. These functions are accordingly being transferred to the Secretary of State for Education and Science, who will delegate responsibility to one of the Joint Parliamentary Under-Secretaries of State in his Department. Appropriate arrangements will be made to meet the special interests of Scotland and Wales. The necessary administrative changes are being put in hand immediately.

78. The greater part of Exchequer aid is channelled through the Arts Council. This arrangement will be maintained within the broader context now set by the Government's policy and with due regard to the pattern of developments described in this White Paper. The Council will continue to enjoy the same powers as they have exercised hitherto and will in particular retain their full freedom to allocate the grant in aid made available to them. Similarly bodies such as the Historic Buildings Councils, the British Council and the Council of Industrial Design will continue to play an invaluable part in their respective fields.

79. Notwithstanding the difficulties of the present situation the Government propose to increase substantially their grant to the Arts Council. In 1964–65 the Council received from the Exchequer £2,150,000 (excluding the grant in respect of Covent Garden). The figure for 1965–66 (again excluding Covent Garden but including the new expenditure incurred as a result of commitments on housing the arts and the extra subsidies for young artists) will be £2,815,000.

80. Among other things this will enable the Arts Council to make a larger contribution to regional associations, to increase their assistance to the leading artistic enterprises in Scotland and Wales, to ease the financial burdens of provincial repertory theatres, to give a much needed impetus to the development of arts centres and to provide additional assistance for first-class orchestras. The position of the London orchestras is now under consideration by a committee under the chairmanship of Mr. Arnold Goodman. It is recognised that action to implement the recommendations of the Goodman Committee may require a further subvention of the major symphony orchestras and other musical groups. In addition the Arts Council have been asked to review requirements for this year and to submit revised proposals for certain specialised projects which can reasonably be advanced during the coming year. On receipt of these additional estimates the Government will, in the light of the prevailing economic situation, give sympathetic consideration to asking Parliament for additional funds during the financial year 1965–66.

81. In order to bring the best of the arts within reach of a wider public, greater use might be made of the subsidised travel for special occasions which the Arts Council already operate and the practice of giving specially reduced theatre prices to students and to special groups should be more widely adopted. Looking further ahead, as development becomes possible, it will be desirable to provide more generally attractive restaurants, lecture rooms and other amenities for visitors who may travel long distances

to the national institutions. The question of adjusting opening hours of museums and galleries to enable visits to be made out of school and working hours will need to be considered. In these ways our most precious national treasures, usually housed in the capital cities, and often difficult or impossible to transport without undue cost and risk, could be more widely enjoyed.

82. In addition to Arts Council expenditure, the purchase grants to local museums made through the Victoria and Albert and Royal Scottish Museums will be increased from £54,000 in 1964–65 to £108,000 in 1965–66. In consultation with the Standing Commission the present basis of Exchequer grants to the Area Councils will be reviewed to see whether a more flexible arrangement can be made.

83. As has been said, one of the main objectives of the Government's policy is to encourage the living artist. At present the young artist, having finished his schooling, has still to gain experience and has difficulty in obtaining employment. Many turn aside to other types of employment because the life of the artist is too precarious, and their talents are not used to the best advantage. Painters, poets, sculptors, writers, and musicians are sometimes lost to art for lack of a comparatively small sum of money which would support their start in life. The increase in the Government's grant to the Arts Council will enable them to raise from about £10,000 to £50,000 the sum allocated for awards and assistance to young artists in all fields. Awards can be used for travelling abroad and study if so desired.

84. In the field of literature several schemes for providing financial assistance to authors have been put forward. Proposals have been made to the Government by the Society of Authors and others on behalf, for example, of young authors of special promise before they have been able to establish themselves, of authors in mid-career who are prevented by lack of funds from undertaking prolonged research required for some work of particular academic value, and of older authors who are suffering hardship.

85. Various sources have been suggested from which the necessary funds might be drawn. One possible source is private contributions, which in the past have provided useful assistance on a modest scale. As another possibility the Government's attention has been drawn to developments overseas, notably in Sweden where the necessary finance is provided by the State, and in France where it is supplied from a variety of sources including a small levy on the turnover of publishing firms. Another suggestion received by the Government is that the law of copyright might be amended so as to extend the period during which royalties are payable to, say, 60 years (instead of 50 years) after the author's death, but to provide that for the last ten years the royalties would be payable not to the author's estate but to a fund administered by a statutory body for the benefit of living authors.

86. Some of those who have made representations to the Government have suggested that any scheme should be limited to literature and, so far as benefits are concerned, to authors. Others would prefer to extend the scope.

87. The Government propose to examine these matters further in consultation with the interested parties.

88. By far the most valuable help that can be given to the living artist is to provide him with a larger and more appreciative public. Everything

possible must be done to enlarge the area of appreciation of the arts while at the same time guarding against any lowering of standards.

89. Concern has been expressed in the press and elsewhere that the independent film producer should not be crowded out because the distribution of films to exhibitors is in the hands of two main companies, and the question of supply of films to exhibitors has been referred by the Board of Trade to the Monopolies Commission. Further developments must now await the Commission's report.

90. The success of such television talks as have already been given is one among several heartening examples both of the willingness of men and women of outstanding talent to co-operate in mass education and of the response that is there to be awakened, given the right kind of approach.

91. In an age of increasing automation bringing more leisure to more people than ever before, both young and old will increasingly need the stimulus and refreshment that the arts can bring. If one side of life is highly mechanised, another side must provide for diversity, adventure, opportunities both to appreciate and to participate in a wide range of individual pursuits. An enlightened Government has a duty to respond to these needs.

92. But there can be no compulsion of any kind in this most sensitive field of human endeavour. Nor must Government support be given only to established institutions. New ideas, new values, the involvement of large sections of the community hitherto given little or no opportunity to appreciate the best in the arts, all have their place. It will take time for the Arts Council and other organisations working in this field to adjust their plans to the wider opportunities now offered to them.

93. Compared with many other civilised countries we have been in the habit of financing some fields of the arts on no more than a poor law relief basis. However, as a first step towards a new policy, the Arts Council grant (excluding Covent Garden) in 1965–66 will be higher by £665,000 (30 per cent.) than in 1964–65, or nearly £500,000 higher than the 1965–66 figure agreed two years ago under the triennial plan.

94. Even more important are the three new points of departure that underline the seriousness of the Government's intention to follow up these first steps as rapidly as possible with further aid where the need for aid is proved.

95. For the first time a building fund has been established to encourage local authorities and regional associations to come forward with building plans. The sum allocated, a quarter of a million, is modest compared with expenditure in some other fields, but because of the delays, inevitable and otherwise, in starting new projects, its provision represents a challenge as well as welcome material encouragement. It is now up to the local authorities and the other agencies concerned to prove by their response that the Government would be justified in the following financial years in entering into substantially higher levels of commitment.

96. The Goodman Committee has been asked to provide precise authoritative information on the proper cost of maintaining our great London orchestras, and the Government have made plain their recognition that additional funds may be required for this purpose.

97. The Arts Council are being invited to review requirements for the coming year and to submit revised proposals for certain specialised projects.

98. Some local authorities will need a good deal of persuading before they are convinced that the money it is in their power to spend on art and amenities is money well spent and deserving a much higher priority than hitherto. But it can be done. All new social services have to fight long and hard before they establish themselves. Only yesterday it was the fight for a free health service. The day before it was the struggle to win education for all.

99. Today a searching reappraisal of the whole situation in relation to cultural standards and opportunities is in progress. More and more people begin to appreciate that the exclusion of so many for so long from the best of our cultural heritage can become as damaging to the privileged minority as to the under-privileged majority. We walk the same streets, breathe the same air, are exposed to the same sights and sounds.

100. Nor can we ignore the growing revolt, especially among the young, against the drabness, uniformity and joylessness of much of the social furniture we have inherited from the industrial revolution. This can be directed, if we so wish, into making Britain a gayer and more cultivated country.

101. It is fitting that the present Government should seek to encourage all who are furthering these aims. The proposals outlined in this White Paper, though no more than the first steps in the direction of a fully comprehensive policy for the arts, demonstrate the Government's concern that immediate progress should be made.

APPENDIX TWO

ENGAGEMENT DIARY OF MINISTER FOR THE ARTS, MR. HUGH JENKINS MP
22 MARCH – 26 MARCH 1976

Monday 22 March

11.00 a.m.	Progress Meeting, 38 Belgrave Square, (Messrs. Wright, Spence, Graham, Rackham, Mrs. Taylor MP, Lord Strabolgi
11.45 a.m.	Mr. D. O'Reilly joins the meeting
4.15 p.m.	Political Engagement, House of Commons
5.00 p.m.	Ministerial Group on the Film Industry (Misc 123 (76) 2nd), 10 Downing Street
6.00 p.m.	three line whip ≡ Impact of Personal Taxation
9.00 p.m.	three line whip ≡ Defence cuts in their application to Northern Ireland ˉ
	two line whip = Prevention of Terrorism (Temporary Provisions) Bill

Tuesday 23 March

10.00 a.m.	Meeting with Library Advisers, 38 Belgrave Square
12.00 noon	Tour of the House of Commons, Mrs. Richardson and Civil Service Retirement Fellowship
6.30 p.m. to 8.30	Reception hosted by Robin Thompson and Partners and Brian Thompson, Waldorf Hotel, Aldwych, WC2 (Mrs. Jenkins)
9.00 p.m.	three line whip ≡ continued New Towns (Amendment Bill: 2nd reading
	two line whip = Motion on the Property Services Agency Order and Water Charges Bill

Wednesday 24 March

10.30 a.m.	Meeting on Finance (Wright, Spence)
12.30 p.m.	Showing of the films 'Building the Industrial Revolution' and 'Lautrec' at the Arts Council, 105 Piccadilly (Miss Giles)
1.00 p.m. for 1.15	Lunch with the Arts Council, 6th Floor dining room (Miss Giles)
6.00 p.m.	three line whip ≡ Debate of International Trade
8.00 p.m.	Speech on Devolution. Putney Labour Party Headquarters, 168 Upper Richmond Road
9.30 p.m.	three line whip ≡ (continued) Motion on Financial Assistance to Industry

Thursday 25 March

10.30 a.m.	Meeting on PLR (Spence, Rackham)
11.30 a.m.	Meeting with Mrs. Greenall to discuss Public Expenditure Survey '76, 38 Belgrave Square
1.30 p.m.	Political engagement, House of Commons
6.00 p.m.	Party Meeting, Committee Room 10, House of Commons
9.00 p.m.	three line whip ≡ Weights and Measures Bill

Friday 26 March

10.00 a.m.	Briefing Meeting on PLR, Lord Strabolgi
11.00 a.m.	Meeting with Lord Perth, 38 Belgrave Square
1.15 p.m.	Commonwealth Parliamentary Association, Lunch to meet members of Commonwealth Legislatures attending the Parliamentary Seminar
6.30 p.m.	Putney Surgery

APPENDIX THREE

Department of Education and Science

ARTS PRESS NOTICE

38 Belgrave Square   London SW1X 8NR   Telephone: 01-235-4801

Press Office extn 32

2 April 1976

ACHIEVEMENTS IN THE ARTS

A list of the Government's main achievements in the arts field was given in the House of Commons yesterday (April 1) by Mr. Hugh Jenkins, Minister for the Arts. Answering a question from Mr. Jim Callaghan, MP for Middleton and Prestwich, who asked if he will publish his official list of the major achievements in the arts in the last two years, Mr. Jenkins said:

'Among the Government's achievements in the arts during the last two difficult years, the following are noteworthy.

'Government expenditure on the arts (excluding libraries and local museums and galleries) increased from £42.5 million in 1973/74 to £52.9 million in 1974/75 and to an estimated £67.6 million in 1975/76. The grant to the Arts Council alone was over £28 million in 1975/76 compared with £17.4 million in 1973/74. The grant for the Crafts was raised from £336,700 in 1973/74 to £589,300 in 1975/76, and expenditure on Area Museums Councils was increased from £120,500 to £550,000 in the same period. The British Library grant-in-aid rose from £12.2 million in 1974/75 to £16.7 million in 1975/76. The level of annual purchase grants for the national collections was increased to £3.44 million from 1975/76, compared with £1.5 million in the previous five-year period.

'Charges for entry to the national museums and galleries were removed in March 1974 and attendances, which had dropped to 14.8 million in 1974 from 16 million in 1973 when charges were introduced, increased to 17.6 million in 1975.

'A major extension to the National Gallery was opened on 6 June 1975, and the National Railway Museum, York, opened on 27 September 1975. The Western Extension of the Tate Gallery and the new Museum of London are nearing completion. A start has been possible for the Amenities Block at the British Museum. The site for any future development of the Royal Opera House was safeguarded by the Arts Council's purchase in March 1975 of land at a cost of over £3.1 million. Negotiations for the purchase of the British Library Somers Town site are well advanced, and outline plans for the new building are under consideration by the local planning authority.

'The National Theatre opened on 16 March 1976, following arrangements made for financing the completion of the building.

'Discussions were held with the Arts Council and steps taken towards a greater degree of democratisation of the membership of the Council.

'In February 1976 there was agreement in principle with the CBI to the setting up of an independent organisation to bring together potential business sponsors and arts clients and to publicise the benefits of such collaboration.

'A Bill on the Public Lending Right for authors was introduced in the House of Lords on 18 March 1976.

'From the financial year 1975/76, new grant arrangements have applied to five major trustee museums (British Museum, Imperial War Museum, National Gallery, National Maritime Museum and the Tate Gallery) giving the Trustees greater responsibility and freedom to manage their own institutions within an approved overall net vote. Extension of the arrangements to certain other national museums and galleries is now under consideration.'

Among items not included in this answer were the following:

Approval of a national museum and gallery building programme with all major projects planned to start by 1979.
Purchase of land for future extension of the Royal Opera House. Seven special purchase grants to enable public collections to buy important items. Sixteen works of art accepted in lieu of estate duty.

The following details of Arts Council grants were also omitted:

3% increase over and above inflation in the Arts Council grant for 1974/75. (This compares with only a 1% increase in the Science Budget).
Supplementaries 1974/75 —

include:	reimbursement of VAT to ACGB clients for 1973/74	£750,000	June 1974
	increased costs of clients of ACGB	£1,750,000	Jan. 1975
	increased costs of build-ing National Theatre	£1,025,000	

29.11.74 Passing of the National Theatre Act. Removed the ceiling on government contributions to the project and effectively assured in its completion. At that time, over £1 m. more was expected to be necessary from Government sources; this, largely because of inflation, will be in the region of £3 m.
3.3.75 Annual recurrent grant to Arts Council of £25m., the figure which the ACGB had advertised as being needed. Total grant, incl. capital, was £26.15 m.
Supplementaries 1975/76 —

include:	towards 'get in' costs of National Theatre	£300,000 (so far)	Dec. 1975
	deficits of clients of ACGB	£2,000,000	
	increased costs of build-ing National Theatre	£750,000	

APPENDIX FOUR

GOVERNMENT SPENDING ON THE ARTS 1964/5 – 1974/5

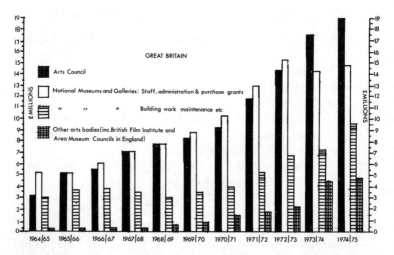

Spending on the British Museum library is included above for the years up to 1972/73 when it totalled about £2 m. After that year the library became part of the British Library The 1972/73 figure also includes £4000,000 as a special purchase grant and another £450,000 as an advance of annual purchase grant, repayable over the following 3 years, towards the purchase of Titian's "Death of Actaeon" by the National Gallery.

Arts Council Expenditure 1974/75

ARTS COUNCIL EXPENDITURE
1974-75[†]

NATIONAL (G.B.)

- Drama
- Music, opera and ballet
- Art
- Housing the Arts
- Literature
- Other inc. festivals
- + English Regions
- SCOTLAND
- WALES

[†] Proportions, relate to the estimated expenditure for the finacial year 1974/75. Grants for operations based in Scotland and Wales are included in proportions for Scotland Wales. These grants are the responsibility of the Scottish and Welsh Arts Council.

+ The item "English Regions" is only for grants to Regional Arts Associations and for direct grants specific projects in the regions, and does not include regional aspects of other artistic activities supported e.g. touring by national companies.

APPENDIX SIX

PROVINCIAL MINISTERIAL VISITS BY THE MINISTER FOR THE ARTS

7 March 1974 — Mr. Hugh Jenkins MP appointed Minister for the Arts

7 June 1974 — *Chichester*
West Dean College
Opening of Hambrook Barn
Open Air Museum
Festival Theatre

21 June 1974 — *Bath*
Holburne Museum
Linley House – Festival Gallery
Opening Concert of Festival 1974 in Bath Abbey

28 June 1974 — *Brighton*
University of Sussex, to address the Regional Studies Association Conference

12 July 1974 — *Cambridge*
Kings College to address the Standing Conference of Regional Arts Association

20 July 1974 — *Kendal*
Abbot Hall Art Gallery
(Unveiling of the Romney Painting)
Museum of Lakeland Life and Industry
Brewery Arts and Community Centre

26 July 1974 — *Preston*
Harris Art Gallery and Museum
Charter Theatre – Youth Theatre
Art Faculty of Polytechnic

9 August 1974 — *Stoke on Trent*
City Museum and Art Gallery
Victoria Theatre

21 August 1974	*Billingham* Forum Theatre Opening the CIOFF Conference Forum
30 August – 4 September 1974	*Scotland* Scottish Arts Council Edinburgh Festival etc. Visits accompanied by Mr. Robert Hughes, MP, PUSS, Scottish Office, to Edinburgh, Glasgow, Livingston, Dunbartonshire, Stirling
10 September 1974	*Lincoln* Open new Regional Crafts Centre Usher Art Gallery Concert in Lincoln Cathedral Visit to Lincoln Theatre
31 January 1975	*Plymouth* Open new extension of City Museum and Art Gallery Royal William Victualling Yard Plymouth Theatre Company headquarters
28 February 1975	*Leeds* Kirkstall Abbey and Abbey Folk Museum Leeds Playhouse, Lotherton Hall, Temple Newsam House
28/29 April 1975	*Boston Spa and York* Opening of the New Lending Division building of the British Library Visit to the National Railway Museum, York
9 May 1975	*Northampton* Opening of the Weston Favell Library Tour of Lings Forum
20 May 1975	*Telford* Wrekin and Telford Festival Telford Leisure Centre
6 June 1975	*Welwyn* Old Welwyn Library Roman Bath House, Welwyn
20 June 1975	*Manchester* Opening of the Precinct Centre Library City Art Gallery

27 June 1975   *Stratford upon Avon*
                             Centenary of the Royal Shakespeare Theatre

13/14 July 1975   *Blyth and Durham*
                             Blyth Arts Centre
                             Address the Annual Conference of the Museums
                             Association

7 August 1975 to
18 August 1975   *Wales*
                             National Eisteddfod of Wales, Criccieth –
                             Segontium Roman Fort – Caernarvon Castle –
                             North Wales Quarrying Museum, Llanberis –
                             Mold Arts Centre – Welsh National Opera and
                             Drama Company – National Museum of Wales –
                             Welsh Folk Museum, St. Fagans – National
                             Library of Wales, Aberystwyth

20 August 1975/
21 August 1975   *Southport and Merseyside*
                             Southport Arts Centre
                             Walker Art Gallery
                             Playhouse Theatre
                             Croxeth Hall and Park
                             Maritime Museum site

20 September 1975   *Cambridge*
                             Address the Royal Television Society Conference at
                             Kings College

27 September 1975   *York*
                             Speaking at the Opening of the National Railway
                             Museum

3 October 1975   *Chester*
                             Opening of the John Hutton Glass Exhibition at
                             the Chester Arts and Recreation Trust Centre

7 October 1975   *Leicester and Hinckley*
                             Opening of Hinckley Library
                             Visit to Leicester Museum and Art Gallery
                             Costume Museum and Haymarket Theatre

22 October 1975   *Bristol*
                             Visit to St. Nicholas Church Museum
                             Press Conference on Industrial Sponsorship

25 October 1975   *Sheppey*
                             Opening of the Sheppey Little Theatre

30 October 1975   *Deal*
                             Royal Marines School of Music

14 November 1975   *Oldham*
Opening of the Grange Arts Centre
Visit to Grange Comprehensive School

15 November 1975   *Burnley, Blackburn and Area*
Visit to Whitworth High School to see Theatre
Mobile Co. in rehearsal
Mid Pennine Arts Association and Artshop
Visit to Rhyddings School, Oswaldtwistle to see
Theatre 69

21 November 1975   *Hull*
Opening of the Town Docks Museum
Ceremony of the Freedom of the City to HMS
Galatea
Visit to the Humberside Theatre

26 November 1975   *Berkhamstead and Aston Clinton*
Visit to the National Film Archive

17 January 1976   *Gt. Yarmouth, Norwich and Hadleigh*
Address a Public Meeting at Gt. Yarmouth
Visit to the Theatre Royal, Norwich
Concert by the City of London

23 January 1976   *Rochester*
Medway Little Theatre

13 February 1976   *Cambridge*
Debate at the Cambridge Union
'British Art is too Middle Class'

21 February 1976   *Scunthorpe*
Visit to Scunthorpe Library, Civic Theatre and
Borough Museum
Opening of the Foxhills Arts Festival, Foxhills
School

12 March 1976   *Birmingham*
Birmingham Arts Shop
National Exhibition Centre
Museum of Science and Industry
Midlands Art Centre for Young People

7 March 1976   *Duxford*
Imperial War Museum – aircraft

Programme of Mr. Hugh Jenkins, Minister for the Arts, visit to Birmingham on Friday 12 March

9.40 a.m.	The Minister, and Mr. D. O'Reilly depart from Euston Station for Birmingham New Street
9.56 a.m.	Miss Giles joins the train at Watford
11.15 a.m.	Arrive at Birmingham New Street Station to be met by Government car
11.20 a.m.	Courtesy call on the Lord Mayor, Councillor Albert Jackson in his Parlour at the Council House with Councillor Clive Wilkinson, Leader of the Birmingham District Council and Mr. Francis J. C. Amos, Chief Executive
11.35 a.m. approx	depart with the Lord Mayor for the Birmingham Artshop, City Arcade
11.45 a.m.	Visit to the Birmingham Artshop, City Arcade, to be met by John Murphy, Director of West Midlands Arts and for coffee and informal discussions with officials of the West Midlands Arts

Manageress – Gill Powderhill

John Murphy – director, West Midlands Arts. A director of Birmingham Artshop Information Limited. Joined West Midlands Arts in 1974 just as the first part of the Marketing Project was completed. Accepted recommendations to move West Midlands Arts press and information staff to new premises over Artshop

Lisa Henderson – Visual Arts Officer with responsibility for fine art, craft, film and photography

John de la Cour – Music Officer with responsibility for local arts associations, arts centres and festivals

Elizabeth de Mestre – Press and Publicity Officer

Frank Challenger – Area Officer for Stoke and Newcastle under Lyme

1.00 p.m.	Visit National Exhibition Centre

meet Manager of Tourism and Entertainments Centre, Denis Broach

1.30 p.m.	lunch at Centre with Chairman of West Midlands Arts, Councillor Ashley Neale

Councillor Neale is a member of West Midlands
Metropolitan County Council and also Dudley
Metropolitan District Council. He is Labour Party Whip
at the County and the Chairman of the Metropolitan
Leisure and Recreation Committee. Councillor Neale also
serves as a member of the Birmingham Repertory Theatre
Trust

Ken Rose – Honorary Treasurer of West Midlands Arts.
Mr. Rose is a Treasurer of the West Midlands
Metropolitan County Council and Treasurer of
Birmingham Artshop Information Limited

John Greenwood – Mr. Greenwood is the General
Manager of the Birmingham Repertory Theatre and also
Chairman of BAS Information Limited, the parent
company administrating the Birmingham Artshop and
the Tourism and Entertainment Centre at the National
Exhibition Centre

and Director of West Midlands Arts, John Murphy

2.45 p.m.	depart from the National Exhibition Centre for the Museum of Science and Industry, Newhall Street
3.15 p.m.	arrive at the Museum of Science and Industry to be met by Dennis Farr, Director
	Proceed through the Engineering Hall, past the lighthouse, through the Engineering Hall Extension into the Machine Tool Section
3.30 p.m.	Turn right into the Transport Section, perhaps pausing briefly to see the Musical Boxes if time permits
	short rest for tea then:-
3.45 p.m.	Up the stairs to the Science Section
3.55 p.m.	From the Science Section over the bridge to Aeroplane Section, round the aeroplanes and out into the yard by the Ocker Hill Engine entering the Locomotive Hall by the small door at the canal side and proceed through, past the City of Birmingham Locomotive, back to the entrance where the Blackpool Organ could be rendering suitable music
4.30 p.m.	depart Museum of Science and Industry for the Midland Hotel
	Tea at the Midland Hotel
5.45 p.m. to arrive at 6.00 p.m.	depart from the Midland Hotel for the Midlands Art Centre for Young People, Cannon Hill Park to be met by John English, Director of City Museums and Art Gallery

	and Dr. N. W. Bertenshaw, Director of Science and Industry Museum
	Buffet supper party
7.30 p.m. approx	Miss Giles and Mr. O'Reilly depart for New Street Station
7.30 p.m.	Address the Birmingham Fabian Society on 'A Socialist Policy for the Arts' at the Midland Art Centre for Young People
9.30 p.m.	Depart from the Midlands Centre for Young People for Birmingham New Street Station
9.51 p.m.	Depart from New Street Station on the *last train* for Euston
11.28 p.m.	Arrive at Euston Station to be met by Tony

APPENDIX SEVEN

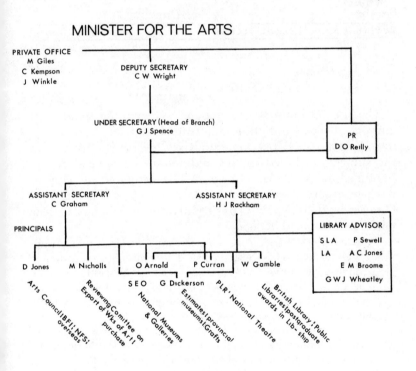

MINISTER FOR THE ARTS

PRIVATE OFFICE
M Giles
C Kempson
J Winkle

DEPUTY SECRETARY
C W Wright

UNDER SECRETARY (Head of Branch)
G J Spence

PR
D O Reilly

ASSISTANT SECRETARY
C Graham

ASSISTANT SECRETARY
H J Rackham

PRINCIPALS

LIBRARY ADVISOR

SLA   P Sewell
LA   A C Jones
       E M Broome
G W J Wheatley

D Jones   M Nicholls   O Arnold   P Curran   W Gamble

SEO   G Dickerson

Arts Council/BFI/NFS/overseas

Reviewing Comittee on Export of Wks of Art/purchase

National Museums & Galleries

Estimates/provincial museums/Grants

PLR/National Theatre

British Library/Public Libraries/postgraduate awards in Lib. ship

257

Department of Education and Science

ARTS PRESS NOTICE

38 Belgrave Square London SW1X 8NR	Telephone: 01·235·4801

Press Office extn 32

26 March 1975

PUBLIC LENDING RIGHT

The use by libraries of computer systems, the number of authors affected and time and cost factors involved in the introduction of a Public Lending Right for authors are among the subjects included in the findings of a technical report published today (26 March 1975)* The technique and costs of paying authors in proportion to the loans of their books from libraries or, alternatively, of paying them for the purchase of their books are examined in detail.

> In a foreword to the Report, the Arts Minister, Mr. Hugh Jenkins, says: 'This Report, which I commissioned immediately following my appointment as Minister for the Arts, is the outcome of a year's effort by members of the Technical Investigation Group and those who worked on the provision of the material leading to their conclusions.
>
> The Report demonstrates that the implementation of any form of public lending right is no simple and easy task. Furthermore the Report presents much hitherto unknown material, for example, about authors and the library use of books.
>
> I have there decided that it is right that the Report should be published.'

Membership of the Technical Investigation Group which produced the report included representatives of authors, pub-

---

* *'Public Lending Right: an account of an investigation of technical and cost aspects.'*

lishers, librarians and public library authorities, the Department of Education and Science and the Central Statistical Office. In forwarding the Report, the Group, whose work is continuing, say that:

'It is concerned with technical matters only, and participation in the work embodied in it carries no implication that all the members of the Group, or the organisations they represent, agree to the principle that a Public Lending Right should be established or that if a Public Lending Right is established they endorse any one method rather than another of assessing authors' entitlement under the right.'

The main findings of the investigation which incorporate studies by a firm of independent consultants, Logica Limited, were that under the purchase-based scheme 87,000 authors could be eligible for payment and under the loans-sampling scheme 113,000. These figures include some but not all foreign authors who may be eligible. The two main schemes examined, one based on counting books written by sole authors and bought after the inception of the scheme by library authorities, the other on recording loans of books by sole authors in a sample of libraries, would cost about the same to work (£300,000 per annum on average at September 1974 prices). Either could take about 2 years to bring into full operation.

The Report discusses in detail the procedures which might be adopted for registration and payment. Authors' entitlements, calculated on the basis of one or other of these schemes, or possibly on a combination of the two, would be distributed, noted the Report, by a Registrar of Public Lending Right. Funds would be provided by Central Government. The cost of operating PLR will depend, say the Group, on the efficiency with which data can be processed. Estimates of the cost of PLR in the Report are based on the use of electronic data equipment of a kind already used in some libraries. Advances in technology may lead to less expensive equipment. Moreover, if the use by libraries of computer based systems is extended and if the future design of these systems takes PLR into account, data required to operate either scheme could be obtained as a by-product of the libraries' normal operations.

The Group were asked to assume that the costs to libraries in operating a PLR scheme would be reimbursed from a PLR fund.

The likely costs to libraries under the two main schemes are set out with the recommendation that a unit cost formula for paying library expenses should be looked at in further discussion with the authorities concerned.

The Group reported that one of the most difficult issues they had encountered was providing, in a loans based scheme, for books in reference libraries and sections because of the impracticability of counting consultations of these books. Two methods, one based on annual sample of reference books in stock, the other on annual purchases, have been considered; investigation is continuing.

The most efficient method of operating both main schemes would be to include machine readable codes in books printed, if practicable, during the course of production. There are several machines made by different manufacturers capable of creating or reading machine readable codes, and some libraries already use these. The Technical Investigation Group recommended that books should be identified for PLR purposes by their unique International Standard Book Numbers (ISBNs) set out in machine readable code form. Practically all books published in this country since 1968, and some foreign-published books, are automatically assigned unique ISBNs at the time of publication and in 1970 all books then still in print were similarly numbered. The precise means by which ISBNs should be represented in code form is the subject of further research commissioned by the Department of Education and Science and the Technical Group.

The Report says that research is also continuing into several further topics: the probable pattern of payments to authors; problems of relocating stock in a loan based scheme; other methods of producing library records under a purchase-based scheme; and practical experiments to assess the effects on libraries of both schemes.

Finally, the report contains basic statistics on libraries, authors and books assembled in the course of the study. In 1974 there were an estimated 113m books in the stocks of UK public libraries, of which 14m are in reference stock and 99m in lending stock; 13m books, of which 5% were for reference use, were purchased and there were 603m annual loans of books with an average number of loans per book on library shelves of 7.

APPENDIX NINE

To: Fred Mulley

From: Hugh Jenkins

28 July 1975

PUBLIC LENDING RIGHT

I am sending you this personal note as an addition to the material on this subject.

When I became Minister for the Arts last year the hostility between the Branch and the representatives of the authors' organisations was immediately apparent. At that time there was no one in the Branch in favour of a loan-based PLR. This is hardly surprising as it is, of course, the Arts and Libraries Branch and librarians whose views are much more influential in the Branch than those of authors, have nothing to gain from PLR and feel that they may well have something to lose. The widespread fear has always been that, in one way or another, the costs of running PLR will be taken from the libraries and, in any event, it will be a nuisance.

I got all concerned together in a meeting at Belgrave Square and from that time on real progress began to be made but distrust and hostility were too ingrained to disappear overnight. The leaders of the Writers' Action Guild were always referred to pejoratively by both Willie Wright and John Spence, reflecting the attitude of St. John-Stevas which they shared. It was not until I got Brophy and Duffy into the office, put Duffy on to the Technical Investigation Group and made it clear that in my view there was no point in introducing any form of PLR which was unacceptable to the authors' organisations that, as good civil servants will the officials began to modify their attitude.

One reason why I put my head on the block and said I would introduce a PLR bill by last December was to persuade the Branch that they must drop their ideological opposition and get down to work. This was successful and the Chairing of the TIG by Harvey particularly successful. Harvey is now totally committed to a loan-based PLR system but, of course, we could not meet the December deadline and when I eventually produced a bill which was acceptable to the H. Committee it was scuppered by Legislation and I withdrew it rather than have it defeated. It seemed to Legislation that the fact that we were providing in the bill for either a loan or purchase based scheme was undesirable and that we should make up our minds prior to legislating.

By this time I was entirely convinced that only a loan-based scheme was desirable and practical, and as the tests have shown such a scheme can now be introduced providing we either leave reference books out of it, or put them on a purchase basis. So, in fact, the Bill Legislation turned down would have suited the actual situation very well.

However, we can now proceed to re-brief Counsel. The Bill will not vary too much from the one we presented earlier in the year and I propose to instruct that the brief be prepared and that we go both to the H. Committee and to Legislation as soon as possible with a view to having a bill ready to introduce before the end of the present session.

In all this the plight of the author has been lost sight of. If we start now there will be no money for writers for two years if we leave it, some amelioration of their condition will be further deferred. We are committed, we can do it and we should get on with it without further delay.

Index